# THE ONE-MINUTE BIBLE™

John R. Kohlenberger III, EDITOR

Benjamin Unseth, ASSOCIATE EDITOR

Bloomington, MN 55420

# TABLE OF CONTENTS

# A General Introduction to *The One-Minute Bible*™

The Bible is the greatest of all books. More than a book, it is in fact a collection of sixty-six books written over the span of sixteen centuries by kings and peasants, poets and prophets.

The books of the Law, Genesis through Deuteronomy, recount the early history of humanity and the great covenant at Sinai by which the living God of the universe bound himself to the nation of Israel. The historical books of Joshua through Esther highlight the covenant history of Israel, noting both Israel's successes and failures in keeping the covenant and God's patience and grace in enforcing its terms.

The books of poetry and wisdom, Job through Song of Songs, celebrate the God of Israel for his goodness, his holiness, and his accessibility to all who approach him on his terms. Wisdom offers timeless principles for a successful life in relation to God and his creation.

The prophets, Isaiah through Malachi, were the preachers of old. They proclaimed to the Israelites their failure to honor covenant obligations to their God, warned them of his impending righteous judgment, and offered hope to all nations of his coming salvation.

The Gospels, Matthew through John, tell of the life and teaching of Jesus the Messiah, the promised Savior of Israel and the nations. The book of Acts recounts the early history of the Christian church as the followers of Jesus take his message to the farthest corners of the globe.

The letters or epistles, Romans through Jude, were written by the first leaders of the church to Christian congregations and their leadership, offering encouragement, discipline, teaching, and hope. The book of Revelation tells of the end of this present world and of the establishment of the new heavens and new earth in which God will live with his people forever.

We hope *The One-Minute Bible*™ offers you a taste of God's Word that will not be fully satisfied by our bite-sized sampling. We encourage you to read daily from a full-text Bible, perhaps following one of the two annual reading schedules offered in the back of this book.

— THE EDITOR

# A Special Introduction to *The One-Minute Bible*™

*The One-Minute Bible*™ draws on the timeless truths of God's Word from all eras of its history and from all forms of its literature. Always sensitive to context and historical application, the texts reproduced in these daily readings communicate in isolation the same message they present in their original location.

*The One-Minute Bible*™ offers 366 daily one-minute readings from the world's greatest literary treasure: the Holy Bible. Each day of the year, from January 1 through December 31, is indicated at the top of each page. Although this calendar can guide you through a one-year reading plan, please do not limit yourself to starting in January or limit your reading to one page a day!

One minute a day will allow you to survey the heart of the Bible in one year. If you want more, the related texts at the bottom of each page direct you to nearly 1,800 passages of Scripture that will further your understanding of the topics covered in that day's reading. Many of these texts are in *The One-Minute Bible*™—and you can find them by means of the Scripture Index on pages 403-410. However, we recommend that you look up these verses in a full-text Bible in case you want to read even more of the context than we suggest.

If you fall behind in the suggested daily reading program, don't worry! You can make up one week in seven minutes, half a month in fifteen. But again, don't be discouraged by failing to follow our schedule. If you get behind, simply jump back in where you left off and "Just Read It!"

## Topical Headings and Organization

*The One-Minute Bible*™ begins with the first verse of Genesis and ends with the last verse of Revelation. Readings follow the general flow of biblical history, interlaced with several topical series, such as two weeks for Easter in April and a week for mothers in May. (A two-page table of contents precedes this introduction.) Some readings reproduce an entire passage of Scripture, such as Psalm 2 on December 22. Often, several passages are combined to show the whole spectrum of biblical teaching on an important topic.

For example, in January 1, Genesis 1:1-2 introduces you to the Bible itself and to Creation in particular. John 1:1-5 introduces you to Jesus—the Word—through whom all things were created. Psalm 148:1-6 invites you to praise the Lord as the Creator. January 2 continues the Creation account, with five texts enlarging on the theme of light.

vi

Blocks of text from different passages of Scripture are separated by a full space; their references are listed at the end of each reading. Half spaces indicate section breaks in poetry, such as after "Praise the LORD" on page 1. The text follows the wording of the King James Version of the Bible; the paragraphing and poetic formatting follows *The One-Minute Bible*™: New International Version. On occasion, we have substituted proper nouns for pronouns to make our selection more clear. We want you to know when Jesus is speaking, so we inserted [Jesus said,] into such readings as Matthew 11:28-30 on March 24.

The 700 selected scriptures and 1,800 related texts were chosen to present the key themes of the Bible from each of its sixty-six books. Great care was taken to ensure that each text has the same meaning in *The One-Minute Bible*™ that it has in its larger context in the Holy Bible.

Each month is introduced by a selection of quotations on the importance of the Bible—thirty-four quotations from international leaders in politics and religion, key figures in the arts, sciences, and humanities.

## Indexes and Maps

*The One-Minute Bible*™ guides you through an overview of the Bible in daily one-minute readings. Immediately following the last reading are two daily reading schedules that will guide you through the entire Bible in a year. The morning and evening schedule outlines readings from both Old and New Testaments for each day of the year. The chronological schedule works through the Bible in historical order.

More than 450 key topics and personalities are indexed in the Topical Index found on pages 411-416. With this index you can find every reference to comfort, salvation, or the names of God found in *The One-Minute Bible*™. If you want to study any word or topic more thoroughly, we recommend *The NIV Exhaustive Concordance* (Zondervan, 1990) and *The NIV Nave's Topical Bible* (Zondervan, 1992), both edited by John R. Kohlenberger III. The Scripture Index, mentioned above, locates every text printed in *The One-Minute Bible.*™

Six maps show the land of Israel in Old and New Testament times and the world of the Bible in antiquity and today. Most of the countries, regions, and major cities mentioned in *The One-Minute Bible*™ can be located on these maps. For more thorough study of biblical geography and history, we recommend *The New Bible Dictionary* (Tyndale, 1982) and *The NIV Atlas of the Bible* (Zondervan, 1989).

— THE PUBLISHER

*"Blessed Lord,
who hast caused
all Holy Scriptures
to be written for
our learning;*

*Grant that we may...
hear them, read, mark,
learn and inwardly
digest them."*

**Book of Common Prayer**

# Creation: *In the Beginning*

In the beginning God created the heaven and the earth. And the earth was without form, and void; and darkness *was* upon the face of the deep. And the Spirit of God moved upon the face of the waters.

In the beginning was the Word, and the Word was with God, and the Word was God. The same was in the beginning with God.

All things were made by him; and without him was not any thing made that was made. In him was life; and the life was the light of men. And the light shineth in darkness; and the darkness comprehended it not.

Praise ye the LORD.

Praise ye the LORD from the heavens:
  praise him in the heights.
Praise ye him, all his angels:
  praise ye him, all his hosts.
Praise ye him, sun and moon:
  praise him, all ye stars of light.
Praise him, ye heavens of heavens,
  and ye waters that *be* above the heavens.
Let them praise the name of the LORD:
  for he commanded, and they were created.
He hath also stablished them for ever and ever:
  he hath made a decree which shall not pass.

GENESIS 1:1-2; JOHN 1:1-5; PSALM 148:1-6

*Related texts:* PSALMS 102:25-28; 139:13-18; PROVERBS 8; ISAIAH 40:12-31; 45:18-25; HEBREWS 11:1-3

## Creation: *Let There Be Light*

**THE ONE MINUTE BIBLE**

And God said, Let there be light: and there was light. And God saw the light, that *it was* good: and God divided the light from the darkness. And God called the light Day, and the darkness he called Night. And the evening and the morning were the first day.

For thou *art* my lamp, O LORD:
    and the LORD will lighten my darkness.

The LORD *is* my light and my salvation;
    whom shall I fear?
The LORD *is* the strength of my life;
    of whom shall I be afraid?

Then spake Jesus again unto them, saying, I am the light of the world: he that followeth me shall not walk in darkness, but shall have the light of life.

And there shall be no more curse: but the throne of God and of the Lamb shall be in it; and his servants shall serve him: and they shall see his face; and his name *shall be* in their foreheads. And there shall be no night there; and they need no candle, neither light of the sun; for the Lord God giveth them light: and they shall reign for ever and ever.

GENESIS 1:3-5; 2 SAMUEL 22:29; PSALM 27:1; JOHN 8:12; REVELATION 22:3-5

*Related texts:* LEVITICUS 24:1-4; JOB 24:13-17; 38:8-20; JOHN 3:19-21; 1 JOHN 1:5-8

## Creation: *The Sky Above*

And God said, Let there be a firmament in the midst of the waters, and let it divide the waters from the waters. And God made the firmament, and divided the waters which *were* under the firmament from the waters which *were* above the firmament: and it was so. And God called the firmament Heaven. And the evening and the morning were the second day.

The heavens declare the glory of God;
 and the firmament showeth his handiwork.
Day unto day uttereth speech,
 and night unto night showeth knowledge.
*There is* no speech nor language,
 *where* their voice is not heard.

I will praise thee, O Lord, among the people:
 I will sing unto thee among the nations.
For thy mercy *is* great unto the heavens,
 and thy truth unto the clouds.
Be thou exalted, O God, above the heavens:
 *let* thy glory *be* above all the earth.

He hath made the earth by his power,
 he hath established the world by his wisdom,
 and hath stretched out the heavens by his discretion.
When he uttereth his voice, *there is* a multitude of
 waters in the heavens,
 and he causeth the vapours to ascend from the
 ends of the earth;
he maketh lightnings with rain,
 and bringeth forth the wind out of his treasures.

GENESIS 1:6-8; PSALMS 19:1-3; 57:9-11; JEREMIAH 10:12-13

*Related texts:* 1 CHRONICLES 16:23-31; JOB 38:22-38; PSALM 102:25-28; ACTS 1:1-12

## Creation: *Land and Seas, Plants and Trees*

**THE ONE**

**MINUTE**

**BIBLE**

And God said, Let the waters under the heaven be gathered together unto one place, and let the dry *land* appear: and it was so. And God called the dry *land* Earth; and the gathering together of the waters called he Seas: and God saw that *it was* good.

And God said, Let the earth bring forth grass, the herb yielding seed, *and* the fruit tree yielding fruit after his kind, whose seed *is* in itself, upon the earth: and it was so. And the earth brought forth grass, *and* herb yielding seed after his kind, and the tree yielding fruit, whose seed *was* in itself, after his kind: and God saw that *it was* good. And the evening and the morning were the third day.

Fear ye not me? saith the LORD:
    will ye not tremble at my presence,
which have placed the sand *for* the bound of the sea
    by a perpetual decree, that it cannot pass it:
and though the waves thereof toss themselves,
        yet can they not prevail;
    though they roar, yet can they not pass over it?

He causeth the grass to grow for the cattle,
    and herb for the service of man:
    that he may bring forth food out of the earth;
and wine *that* maketh glad the heart of man,
    *and* oil to make *his* face to shine,
    and bread *which* strengtheneth man's heart.

GENESIS 1:9-13; JEREMIAH 5:22; PSALM 104:14-15

---

***Related texts:*** JOB 12:7-12; 38:8-11; PSALM 104; REVELATION 20:11–21:4; 22:1-3

# Creation: *Sun, Moon and Stars*

And God said, Let there be lights in the firmament of the heaven to divide the day from the night; and let them be for signs, and for seasons, and for days, and years: and let them be for lights in the firmament of the heaven to give light upon the earth: and it was so.

And God made two great lights; the greater light to rule the day, and the lesser light to rule the night: *he made* the stars also. And God set them in the firmament of the heaven to give light upon the earth, and to rule over the day and over the night, and to divide the light from the darkness: and God saw that *it was* good. And the evening and the morning were the fourth day.

And I saw no temple therein: for the Lord God Almighty and the Lamb are the temple of it. And the city had no need of the sun, neither of the moon, to shine in it: for the glory of God did lighten it, and the Lamb *is* the light thereof. And the nations of them which are saved shall walk in the light of it: and the kings of the earth do bring their glory and honour into it.

And the gates of it shall not be shut at all by day: for there shall be no night there. And they shall bring the glory and honour of the nations into it. And there shall in no wise enter into it any thing that defileth, neither *whatsoever* worketh abomination, or *maketh* a lie: but they which are written in the Lamb's book of life.

GENESIS 1:14-19; REVELATION 21:22-27

---

*Related texts:* NEHEMIAH 9:5-6; JOB 9:1-9; PSALMS 19:1-6; 104:19-23; PROVERBS 4:18-19; EPHESIANS 5:8-16

# Creation: *All Creatures Great and Small*

**THE ONE**
**MINUTE**
**BIBLE**

And God said, Let the waters bring forth abundantly the moving creature that hath life, and fowl *that* may fly above the earth in the open firmament of heaven. And God created great whales, and every living creature that moveth, which the waters brought forth abundantly, after their kind, and every winged fowl after his kind: and God saw that *it was* good. And God blessed them, saying, Be fruitful, and multiply, and fill the waters in the seas, and let fowl multiply in the earth. And the evening and the morning were the fifth day.

O Lord, how manifold are thy works!
    In wisdom hast thou made them all:
    the earth is full of thy riches.
*So is* this great and wide sea,
    wherein *are* things creeping innumerable,
    both small and great beasts.
There go the ships:
    *there is* that leviathan, *whom* thou hast made
        to play therein.

These wait all upon thee;
    that thou mayest give *them* their meat in due season.
*That* thou givest them
    they gather:
thou openest thine hand,
    they are filled with good.

GENESIS 1:20-23; PSALM 104:24-28

*Related texts:* PSALMS 104:11-18; 148:7-12; MATTHEW 6:25-33; 10:29-31; REVELATION 5:11-13

# Creation: *The Cattle on a Thousand Hills*

And God said, Let the earth bring forth the living creature after his kind, cattle, and creeping thing, and beast of the earth after his kind: and it was so. And God made the beast of the earth after his kind, and cattle after their kind, and every thing that creepeth upon the earth after his kind: and God saw that *it was* good.

**THE ONE MINUTE BIBLE**

I will not reprove thee for thy sacrifices
    or thy burnt offerings, *to* have been continually
      before me.
I will take no bullock out of thy house,
    *nor* he goats out of thy folds.
For every beast of the forest *is* mine,
    *and* the cattle upon a thousand hills.
I know all the fowls of the mountains:
    and the wild beasts of the field *are* mine.
If I were hungry, I would not tell thee:
    for the world *is* mine, and the fulness thereof.
Will I eat the flesh of bulls,
    or drink the blood of goats?
Offer unto God thanksgiving;
    and pay thy vows unto the most High:
And call upon me in the day of trouble:
    I will deliver thee, and thou shalt glorify me.

GENESIS 1:24-25; PSALM 50:8-15

*Related texts:* GENESIS 9:1-3; PSALM 8; PROVERBS 12:10;
ISAIAH 11:1-10; 65:17-25

# Creation: *Mankind—The Image of God*

**THE ONE
MINUTE
BIBLE**

And God said, Let us make man in our image, after our likeness: and let them have dominion over the fish of the sea, and over the fowl of the air, and over the cattle, and over all the earth, and over every creeping thing that creepeth upon the earth.

So God created man in his *own* image,
in the image of God created he him;
male and female created he them.

And God blessed them, and God said unto them, Be fruitful, and multiply, and replenish the earth, and subdue it: and have dominion over the fish of the sea, and over the fowl of the air, and over every living thing that moveth upon the earth.

And God said, Behold, I have given you every herb bearing seed, which *is* upon the face of all the earth, and every tree, in the which *is* the fruit of a tree yielding seed; to you it shall be for meat. And to every beast of the earth, and to every fowl of the air, and to every thing that creepeth upon the earth, wherein *there is* life, *I have given* every green herb for meat: and it was so.

And God saw every thing that he had made, and, behold, *it was* very good. And the evening and the morning were the sixth day.

Genesis 1:26-31

---

*Related texts:* Genesis 2:4-25; 9:6-7; Psalm 8; 1 Corinthians 6:1-4;
2 Corinthians 4:4-6; Colossians 1:9-20; 3:5-10

# Creation: *God Rests*

THE ONE
MINUTE
BIBLE

Thus the heavens and the earth were finished, and all the host of them.

And on the seventh day God ended his work which he had made; and he rested on the seventh day from all his work which he had made. And God blessed the seventh day, and sanctified it: because that in it he had rested from all his work which God created and made.

Remember the sabbath day, to keep it holy. For *in* six days the LORD made heaven and earth, the sea, and all that in them *is*, and rested the seventh day: wherefore the LORD blessed the sabbath day, and hallowed it.

And it came to pass, that Jesus went through the corn fields on the sabbath day; and his disciples began, as they went, to pluck the ears of corn. And the Pharisees said unto him, Behold, why do they on the sabbath day that which is not lawful?

And he said unto them, Have ye never read what David did, when he had need, and was an hungred, he, and they that were with him? How he went into the house of God in the days of Abiathar the high priest, and did eat the showbread, which is not lawful to eat but for the priests, and gave also to them which were with him?

And he said unto them, The sabbath was made for man, and not man for the sabbath: therefore the Son of man is Lord also of the sabbath.

GENESIS 2:1-3; EXODUS 20:8, 11; MARK 2:23-28

*Related texts:* EXODUS 16:11-30; PSALM 62:1-5; MATTHEW 11:25-30; MARK 6:30-32; HEBREWS 4:1-4

## Adam and Eve: The First Man and Woman

**THE ONE**
**MINUTE**
**BIBLE**

And the LORD God formed man *of* the dust of the ground, and breathed into his nostrils the breath of life; and man became a living soul.

And the LORD God took the man, and put him into the garden of Eden to dress it and to keep it. And the LORD God commanded the man, saying, Of every tree of the garden thou mayest freely eat: but of the tree of the knowledge of good and evil, thou shalt not eat of it: for in the day that thou eatest thereof thou shalt surely die.

And the LORD God said, *It is* not good that the man should be alone; I will make him an help meet for him.

But for Adam there was not found an help meet for him. And the LORD God caused a deep sleep to fall upon Adam, and he slept: and he took one of his ribs, and closed up the flesh instead thereof; and the rib, which the LORD God had taken from man, made he a woman, and brought her unto the man.

And Adam said,

> This *is* now bone of my bones,
>     and flesh of my flesh:
> she shall be called Woman,
>     because she was taken out of Man.

Therefore shall a man leave his father and his mother, and shall cleave unto his wife: and they shall be one flesh.

And they were both naked, the man and his wife, and were not ashamed.

GENESIS 2:7, 15-18, 20b-25

*Related texts:* GENESIS 1:26-29; MATTHEW 19:1-12; MARK 10:1-12; 1 CORINTHIANS 6:15–7:40

## *Rulers of God's Creation*

**THE ONE
MINUTE
BIBLE**

O LORD our Lord,
    how excellent *is* thy name in all the earth!

Who hast set thy glory
    above the heavens.
Out of the mouth of babes and sucklings
    hast thou ordained strength
because of thine enemies,
    that thou mightest still the enemy and the avenger.

When I consider thy heavens,
    the work of thy fingers,
the moon and the stars,
    which thou hast ordained;
what is man, that thou art mindful of him?
    And the son of man, that thou visitest him?
For thou hast made him a little lower than the angels,
    and hast crowned him with glory and honour.

Thou madest him to have dominion
    over the works of thy hands;
    thou hast put all *things* under his feet:
all sheep and oxen,
    yea, and the beasts of the field;
the fowl of the air,
    and the fish of the sea,
    *and whatsoever* passeth through the paths
        of the seas.

O LORD our Lord,
    how excellent *is* thy name in all the earth!

PSALM 8

---

***Related texts:*** GENESIS 1–2; MATTHEW 21:16; HEBREWS 2:5-9

## *The Fall of Mankind*

**THE ONE
MINUTE
BIBLE**

Now the serpent was more subtle than any beast of the field which the LORD God had made. And he said unto the woman, Yea, hath God said, Ye shall not eat of every tree of the garden?

And the woman said unto the serpent, We may eat of the fruit of the trees of the garden: but of the fruit of the tree which *is* in the midst of the garden, God hath said, Ye shall not eat of it, neither shall ye touch it, lest ye die.

And the serpent said unto the woman, Ye shall not surely die: for God doth know that in the day ye eat thereof, then your eyes shall be opened, and ye shall be as gods, knowing good and evil.

And when the woman saw that the tree *was* good for food, and that it *was* pleasant to the eyes, and a tree to be desired to make *one* wise, she took of the fruit thereof, and did eat, and gave also unto her husband with her; and he did eat. And the eyes of them both were opened, and they knew that they *were* naked; and they sewed fig leaves together, and made themselves aprons.

And they heard the voice of the LORD God walking in the garden in the cool of the day: and Adam and his wife hid themselves from the presence of the LORD God amongst the trees of the garden.

GENESIS 3:1-8

*Related texts:* EZEKIEL 28:13-19; ROMANS 5:12-19; 1 TIMOTHY 2:11-15; JAMES 1:12-15

## *God Judges the First Sin*

**THE ONE
MINUTE
BIBLE**

And the L ORD God called unto Adam, and said unto him, Where *art* thou?

And he said, I heard thy voice in the garden, and I was afraid, because I *was* naked; and I hid myself.

And he said, Who told thee that thou *wast* naked? Hast thou eaten of the tree, whereof I commanded thee that thou shouldest not eat?

And the man said, The woman whom thou gavest *to be* with me, she gave me of the tree, and I did eat.

And the L ORD God said unto the woman, What *is* this *that* thou hast done?

And the woman said, The serpent beguiled me, and I did eat.

And the L ORD God said unto the serpent, Because thou hast done this,

Thou *art* cursed above all cattle,
and above every beast of the field;
upon thy belly shalt thou go,
and dust shalt thou eat all the days of thy life:
and I will put enmity between thee and the woman,
and between thy seed and her seed;
it shall bruise thy head,
and thou shalt bruise his heel.

Unto the woman he said,
I will greatly multiply thy sorrow and thy conception;
in sorrow thou shalt bring forth children;
and thy desire *shall be* to thy husband,
and he shall rule over thee.

*There is* therefore now no condemnation to them which are in Christ Jesus, who walk not after the flesh, but after the Spirit.

GENESIS 3:9-16; ROMANS 8:1

*Related texts:* DEUTERONOMY 32:1-6; ROMANS 3:9-18;
REVELATION 12:9; 20:1-3, 7-15; 22:1-3

## God Exiles Adam and Eve from the Garden

**THE ONE
MINUTE
BIBLE**

And unto Adam the LORD God said, Because thou hast hearkened unto the voice of thy wife, and hast eaten of the tree, of which I commanded thee, saying, Thou shalt not eat of it:

Cursed *is* the ground for thy sake;
  in sorrow shalt thou eat *of* it
  all the days of thy life;
thorns also and thistles shall it bring forth to thee;
  and thou shalt eat the herb of the field;
in the sweat of thy face
  shalt thou eat bread,
till thou return unto the ground;
  for out of it wast thou taken:
for dust thou *art*,
  and unto dust shalt thou return.

And Adam called his wife's name Eve; because she was the mother of all living.

Unto Adam also and to his wife did the LORD God make coats of skins, and clothed them. And the LORD God said, Behold, the man is become as one of us, to know good and evil: and now, lest he put forth his hand, and take also of the tree of life, and eat, and live for ever: therefore the LORD God sent him forth from the garden of Eden, to till the ground from whence he was taken. So he drove out the man; and he placed at the east of the garden of Eden Cherubims, and a flaming sword which turned every way, to keep the way of the tree of life.

For as in Adam all die, even so in Christ shall all be made alive.

GENESIS 3:17-24; 1 CORINTHIANS 15:22

*Related texts:* GENESIS 18:16-33; PSALM 50; ROMANS 8:18-25; REVELATION 22

# Death in Adam, Life in Christ

Wherefore, as by one man sin entered into the world, and death by sin; and so death passed upon all men, for that all have sinned: (for until the law sin was in the world: but sin is not imputed when there is no law. Nevertheless death reigned from Adam to Moses, even over them that had not sinned after the similitude of Adam's transgression, who is the figure of him that was to come.

But not as the offence, so also *is* the free gift. For if through the offence of one many be dead, much more the grace of God, and the gift by grace, *which is* by one man, Jesus Christ, hath abounded unto many.

And not as *it was* by one that sinned, *so is* the gift: for the judgment *was* by one to condemnation, but the free gift *is* of many offences unto justification. For if by one man's offence death reigned by one; much more they which receive abundance of grace and of the gift of righteousness shall reign in life by one, Jesus Christ.)

For the wages of sin *is* death; but the gift of God *is* eternal life through Jesus Christ our Lord.

ROMANS 5:12-17; 6:23

***Related texts:*** GENESIS 3; ROMANS 5:18–6:23; EPHESIANS 2:1-10; COLOSSIANS 3:1-17

## Cain and Abel: The First Murder

**THE ONE
MINUTE
BIBLE**

And Adam knew Eve his wife; and she conceived, and bare Cain, and said, I have gotten a man from the LORD. And she again bare his brother Abel.

And Abel was a keeper of sheep, but Cain was a tiller of the ground. And in process of time it came to pass, that Cain brought of the fruit of the ground an offering unto the LORD. And Abel, he also brought of the firstlings of his flock and of the fat thereof. And the LORD had respect unto Abel and to his offering: but unto Cain and to his offering he had not respect. And Cain was very wroth, and his countenance fell.

And the LORD said unto Cain, Why art thou wroth? And why is thy countenance fallen? If thou doest well, shalt thou not be accepted? And if thou doest not well, sin lieth at the door. And unto thee *shall be* his desire, and thou shalt rule over him.

And Cain talked with Abel his brother: and it came to pass, when they were in the field, that Cain rose up against Abel his brother, and slew him.

And the LORD said unto Cain, Where *is* Abel thy brother?

And he said, I know not: *am* I my brother's keeper?

And he said, What hast thou done? The voice of thy brother's blood crieth unto me from the ground. And now *art* thou cursed from the earth, which hath opened her mouth to receive thy brother's blood from thy hand; when thou tillest the ground, it shall not henceforth yield unto thee her strength; a fugitive and a vagabond shalt thou be in the earth.

GENESIS 4:1-12

*Related texts:* EXODUS 20:13; MATTHEW 5:21-26; HEBREWS 11:4; 1 JOHN 3:11-12

## *Noah: The Just Man*

These *are* the generations of Noah:

Noah was a just man *and* perfect in his generations, *and* Noah walked with God. And Noah begat three sons, Shem, Ham, and Japheth.

The earth also was corrupt before God, and the earth was filled with violence. And God looked upon the earth, and, behold, it was corrupt; for all flesh had corrupted his way upon the earth. And God said unto Noah, The end of all flesh is come before me; for the earth is filled with violence through them; and, behold, I will destroy them with the earth. Make thee an ark of gopher wood; rooms shalt thou make in the ark, and shalt pitch it within and without with pitch.

And, behold, I, even I, do bring a flood of waters upon the earth, to destroy all flesh, wherein *is* the breath of life, from under heaven; *and* every thing that *is* in the earth shall die. But with thee will I establish my covenant; and thou shalt come into the ark, thou, and thy sons, and thy wife, and thy sons' wives with thee. And of every living thing of all flesh, two of every *sort* shalt thou bring into the ark, to keep *them* alive with thee; they shall be male and female. And take thou unto thee of all food that is eaten, and thou shalt gather *it* to thee; and it shall be for food for thee, and for them.

Thus did Noah; according to all that God commanded him, so did he.

GENESIS 6:9-14, 17-19, 21-22

**THE ONE MINUTE BIBLE**

---

*Related texts:* PSALMS 29; 36; HEBREWS 11:1-7; 1 PETER 3:18-22

**THE ONE**
**MINUTE**
**BIBLE**

## The Great Flood

And Noah *was* six hundred years old when the flood of waters was upon the earth. And Noah went in, and his sons, and his wife, and his sons' wives with him, into the ark, because of the waters of the flood. Of clean beasts, and of beasts that *are* not clean, and of fowls, and of every thing that creepeth upon the earth, there went in two and two unto Noah into the ark, the male and the female, as God had commanded Noah. And it came to pass after seven days, that the waters of the flood were upon the earth.

In the six hundredth year of Noah's life, in the second month, the seventeenth day of the month, the same day were all the fountains of the great deep broken up, and the windows of heaven were opened.

And the flood was forty days upon the earth; and the waters increased, and bare up the ark, and it was lift up above the earth. And the waters prevailed, and were increased greatly upon the earth; and the ark went upon the face of the waters. And the waters prevailed exceedingly upon the earth; and all the high hills, that *were* under the whole heaven, were covered. And every living substance was destroyed which was upon the face of the ground, both man, and cattle, and the creeping things, and the fowl of the heaven; and they were destroyed from the earth: and Noah only remained *alive*, and they that *were* with him in the ark.

By faith Noah, being warned of God of things not seen as yet, moved with fear, prepared an ark to the saving of his house; by the which he condemned the world, and became heir of the righteousness which is by faith.

GENESIS 7:6-11, 17-19, 23; HEBREWS 11:7

*Related texts:* PSALM 93; NAHUM 1:1-8; MATTHEW 24:36-42; LUKE 17:26-36; 2 PETER 2:4-9

## *After the Flood*

**THE ONE MINUTE BIBLE**

And God remembered Noah, and every living thing, and all the cattle that *was* with him in the ark: and God made a wind to pass over the earth, and the waters asswaged.

And it came to pass at the end of forty days, that Noah opened the window of the ark which he had made: and he sent forth a raven, which went forth to and fro, until the waters were dried up from off the earth. Also he sent forth a dove from him, to see if the waters were abated from off the face of the ground.

But the dove found no rest for the sole of her foot, and she returned unto him into the ark, for the waters *were* on the face of the whole earth: then he put forth his hand, and took her, and pulled her in unto him into the ark. And he stayed yet other seven days; and again he sent forth the dove out of the ark; and the dove came in to him in the evening; and, lo, in her mouth *was* an olive leaf plucked off: so Noah knew that the waters were abated from off the earth.

And Noah went forth, and his sons, and his wife, and his sons' wives with him.

And Noah builded an altar unto the LORD; and took of every clean beast, and of every clean fowl, and offered burnt offerings on the altar. And the LORD smelled a sweet savour; and the LORD said in his heart, I will not again curse the ground any more for man's sake; for the imagination of man's heart *is* evil from his youth; neither will I again smite any more every thing living, as I have done.

GENESIS 8:1, 6-11, 18, 20-21

*Related texts:* GENESIS 9; 2 PETER 3:1-14; REVELATION 21:1-4

## *God Calls Abraham*

**THE ONE
MINUTE
BIBLE**

Now the LORD had said unto Abraham, Get thee out of thy country, and from thy kindred, and from thy father's house, unto a land that I will show thee:

And I will make of thee a great nation,
    and I will bless thee,
and make thy name great;
    and thou shalt be a blessing:
and I will bless them that bless thee,
    and curse him that curseth thee:
and in thee shall all families of the earth be blessed.

So Abraham departed, as the LORD had spoken unto him; and Lot went with him: and Abraham *was* seventy and five years old when he departed out of Haran. And Abraham took Sarah his wife, and Lot his brother's son, and all their substance that they had gathered, and the souls that they had gotten in Haran; and they went forth to go into the land of Canaan; and into the land of Canaan they came.

And Abraham passed through the land unto the place of Sichem, unto the plain of Moreh. And the Canaanite *was* then in the land. And the LORD appeared unto Abraham, and said, Unto thy seed will I give this land: and there builded he an altar unto the LORD, who appeared unto him.

GENESIS 12:1-7

*Related texts:* PSALM 67; ACTS 7:2-5; HEBREWS 6:13-16; 11:8-10

## *God Promises Abraham a Son*

After these things the word of the Lord came unto Abraham in a vision, saying,

Fear not, Abraham:
  I *am* thy shield,
  *and* thy exceeding great reward.

And Abraham said, Lord God, what wilt thou give me, seeing I go childless, and the steward of my house *is* this Eliezer of Damascus? And Abraham said, Behold, to me thou hast given no seed: and, lo, one born in my house is mine heir.

And, behold, the word of the Lord *came* unto him, saying, This shall not be thine heir; but he that shall come forth out of thine own bowels shall be thine heir. And he brought him forth abroad, and said, Look now toward heaven, and tell the stars, if thou be able to number them: and he said unto him, So shall thy seed be.

And he believed in the Lord; and he counted it to him for righteousness.

Now it was not written for his sake alone, that it was imputed to him; but for us also, to whom it shall be imputed, if we believe on him that raised up Jesus our Lord from the dead; who was delivered for our offences, and was raised again for our justification.

GENESIS 15:1-6; ROMANS 4:23-25

---

*Related texts:* GENESIS 21:1-5; ROMANS 4; GALATIANS 3:1-9

## Ishmael and Isaac: Abraham's Sons

**THE ONE
MINUTE
BIBLE**

Now Sarah Abraham's wife bare him no children: and she had an handmaid, an Egyptian, whose name *was* Hagar. And Sarah said unto Abraham, Behold now, the LORD hath restrained me from bearing: I pray thee, go in unto my maid; it may be that I may obtain children by her.

And Abraham hearkened to the voice of Sarah. And Sarah Abraham's wife took Hagar her maid the Egyptian, after Abraham had dwelt ten years in the land of Canaan, and gave her to her husband Abraham to be his wife. And he went in unto Hagar, and she conceived.

And Hagar bare Abraham a son: and Abraham called his son's name, which Hagar bare, Ishmael. And Abraham *was* fourscore and six years old, when Hagar bare Ishmael to Abraham.

And the LORD visited Sarah as he had said, and the LORD did unto Sarah as he had spoken. For Sarah conceived, and bare Abraham a son in his old age, at the set time of which God had spoken to him. And Abraham called the name of his son that was born unto him, whom Sarah bare to him, Isaac. And Abraham circumcised his son Isaac being eight days old, as God had commanded him. And Abraham was an hundred years old, when his son Isaac was born unto him.

Through faith also Sarah herself received strength to conceive seed, and was delivered of a child when she was past age, because she judged him faithful who had promised.

GENESIS 16:1-4a, 15-16; 21:1-5; HEBREWS 11:11

---

*Related texts:* GENESIS 21:6-21; ACTS 7:1-8; ROMANS 4; GALATIANS 4:22-31

## *Abraham Offers Isaac As a Sacrifice*

THE ONE
MINUTE
BIBLE

And it came to pass after these things, that God did tempt Abraham, and said unto him, Abraham.

And he said, Behold, *here* I *am*.

And God said, Take now thy son, thine only *son* Isaac, whom thou lovest, and get thee into the land of Moriah; and offer him there for a burnt offering upon one of the mountains which I will tell thee of.

And they came to the place which God had told him of; and Abraham built an altar there, and laid the wood in order, and bound Isaac his son, and laid him on the altar upon the wood. And Abraham stretched forth his hand, and took the knife to slay his son. And the angel of the LORD called unto him out of heaven, and said, Abraham, Abraham.

And he said, Here *am* I.

And he said, Lay not thine hand upon the lad, neither do thou any thing unto him: for now I know that thou fearest God, seeing thou hast not withheld thy son, thine only *son* from me.

And Abraham lifted up his eyes, and looked, and behold behind *him* a ram caught in a thicket by his horns: and Abraham went and took the ram, and offered him up for a burnt offering in the stead of his son. And Abraham called the name of that place Jehovah-jireh: as it is said *to* this day, In the mount of the LORD it shall be seen.

Herein is love, not that we loved God, but that he loved us, and sent his Son *to be* the propitiation for our sins.

GENESIS 22:1-2, 9-14; 1 JOHN 4:10

*Related texts:* GENESIS 22:15-19; JOHN 3:16; ROMANS 8:31-39; HEBREWS 11:17-19

## Esau and Jacob: Isaac's Sons

**THE ONE
MINUTE
BIBLE**

And these *are* the generations of Isaac, Abraham's son:

Abraham begat Isaac: and Isaac was forty years old when he took Rebekah to wife, the daughter of Bethuel the Syrian of Padan-aram, the sister to Laban the Syrian.

And Isaac entreated the LORD for his wife, because she *was* barren: and the LORD was entreated of him, and Rebekah his wife conceived. And the children struggled together within her; and she said, If *it be* so, why *am* I thus? And she went to inquire of the LORD.

And the LORD said unto her,

Two nations *are* in thy womb,
   and two manner of people shall be separated
      from thy bowels;
and *the one* people shall be stronger than
     *the other* people;
   and the elder shall serve the younger.

And when her days to be delivered were fulfilled, behold, *there were* twins in her womb. And the first came out red, all over like an hairy garment; and they called his name Esau. And after that came his brother out, and his hand took hold on Esau's heel; and his name was called Jacob: and Isaac *was* threescore years old when she bare them.

And the boys grew: and Esau was a cunning hunter, a man of the field; and Jacob *was* a plain man, dwelling in tents. And Isaac loved Esau, because he did eat of *his* venison: but Rebekah loved Jacob.

GENESIS 25:19-28

*Related texts:* 1 SAMUEL 1; MALACHI 1:1-5; ROMANS 9

## *Esau Sells His Inheritance to Jacob*

THE ONE
MINUTE
BIBLE

And Jacob sod pottage: and Esau came from the field, and he *was* faint: and Esau said to Jacob, Feed me, I pray thee, with that same red *pottage*; for I *am* faint: therefore was his name called Edom.

And Jacob said, Sell me this day thy birthright.

And Esau said, Behold, I *am* at the point to die: and what profit shall this birthright do to me?

And Jacob said, Swear to me this day; and he sware unto him: and he sold his birthright unto Jacob.

Then Jacob gave Esau bread and pottage of lentiles; and he did eat and drink, and rose up, and went his way: thus Esau despised *his* birthright.

I have loved you, saith the LORD.

Yet ye say, Wherein hast thou loved us?

*Was* not Esau Jacob's brother? saith the LORD: yet I loved Jacob, *and* I hated Esau, and laid his mountains and his heritage waste for the dragons of the wilderness.

Lest there *be* any fornicator, or profane person, as Esau, who for one morsel of meat sold his birthright. For ye know how that afterward, when he would have inherited the blessing, he was rejected: for he found no place of repentance, though he sought it carefully with tears.

GENESIS 25:29-34; MALACHI 1:2-3; HEBREWS 12:16-17

*Related texts:* GENESIS 27–36; PSALM 60; OBADIAH

## Joseph the Dreamer: Jacob's Favorite Son

**THE ONE
MINUTE
BIBLE**

Joseph, *being* seventeen years old, was feeding the flock with his brethren; and the lad *was* with the sons of Bilhah, and with the sons of Zilpah, his father's wives: and Joseph brought unto his father their evil report.

Now Jacob loved Joseph more than all his children, because he was the son of his old age: and he made him a coat of *many* colours. And when his brethren saw that their father loved him more than all his brethren, they hated him, and could not speak peaceably unto him.

And Joseph dreamed a dream, and he told *it* his brethren: and they hated him yet the more. And he said unto them, Hear, I pray you, this dream which I have dreamed: For, behold, we *were* binding sheaves in the field, and, lo, my sheaf arose, and also stood upright; and, behold, your sheaves stood round about, and made obeisance to my sheaf.

And he dreamed yet another dream, and told it his brethren, and said, Behold, I have dreamed a dream more; and, behold, the sun and the moon and the eleven stars made obeisance to me.

And he told *it* to his father, and to his brethren: and his father rebuked him, and said unto him, What *is* this dream that thou hast dreamed? Shall I and thy mother and thy brethren indeed come to bow down ourselves to thee to the earth? And his brethren envied him; but his father observed the saying.

GENESIS 37:2b-7, 9-11

***Related texts:*** GENESIS 28:10-19; 41:1-45; JOEL 2:28-32; MATTHEW 1:18–2:22

## Jacob Moves His Family to Egypt

**THE ONE
MINUTE
BIBLE**

And God gave Abraham the covenant of circumcision: and so *Abraham* begat Isaac, and circumcised him the eighth day; and Isaac *begat* Jacob; and Jacob *begat* the twelve patriarchs.

And the patriarchs, moved with envy, sold Joseph into Egypt: but God was with him, and delivered him out of all his afflictions, and gave him favour and wisdom in the sight of Pharaoh king of Egypt; and he made him governor over Egypt and all his house.

Now there came a dearth over all the land of Egypt and Chanaan, and great affliction: and our fathers found no sustenance. But when Jacob heard that there was corn in Egypt, he sent out our fathers first. And at the second *time* Joseph was made known to his brethren; and Joseph's kindred was made known unto Pharaoh. Then sent Joseph, and called his father Jacob to *him*, and all his kindred, threescore and fifteen souls. So Jacob went down into Egypt, and died, he, and our fathers.

And Jacob lived in the land of Egypt seventeen years: so the whole age of Jacob was an hundred forty and seven years.

ACTS 7:8-15; GENESIS 47:28

***Related texts:*** GENESIS 37–50; PSALM 46; MATTHEW 8:5-13; MARK 12:24-27

## *Joseph: God Intended it for Good*

**THE ONE**
**MINUTE**
**BIBLE**

And when Joseph's brethren saw that their father was dead, they said, Joseph will peradventure hate us, and will certainly requite us all the evil which we did unto him. And they sent a messenger unto Joseph, saying, Thy father did command before he died, saying, So shall ye say unto Joseph, Forgive, I pray thee now, the trespass of thy brethren, and their sin; for they did unto thee evil: and now, we pray thee, forgive the trespass of the servants of the God of thy father. And Joseph wept when they spake unto him.

And his brethren also went and fell down before his face; and they said, Behold, we *be* thy servants.

And Joseph said unto them, Fear not: for *am* I in the place of God? But as for you, ye thought evil against me; *but* God meant it unto good, to bring to pass, as *it is* this day, to save much people alive. Now therefore fear ye not: I will nourish you, and your little ones. And he comforted them, and spake kindly unto them.

And Joseph said unto his brethren, I die: and God will surely visit you, and bring you out of this land unto the land which he sware to Abraham, to Isaac, and to Jacob.

And we know that all things work together for good to them that love God, to them who are the called according to *his* purpose.

Genesis 50:15-21, 24; Romans 8:28

---

***Related texts:*** Genesis 37–50; Exodus 1; 13:17-19; Joshua 24:32; Psalm 105:7-25; Hebrews 11:21-22

## *Job: Blameless and Blessed*

There was a man in the land of Uz, whose name *was* Job; and that man was perfect and upright, and one that feared God, and eschewed evil. This man was the greatest of all the men of the east.

Now there was a day when the sons of God came to present themselves before the LORD, and Satan came also among them. And the LORD said unto Satan, Whence comest thou?

Then Satan answered the LORD, and said, From going to and fro in the earth, and from walking up and down in it.

And the LORD said unto Satan, Hast thou considered my servant Job, that *there is* none like him in the earth, a perfect and an upright man, one that feareth God, and escheweth evil?

Then Satan answered the LORD, and said, Doth Job fear God for nought? Hast not thou made an hedge about him, and about his house, and about all that he hath on every side? Thou hast blessed the work of his hands, and his substance is increased in the land. But put forth thine hand now, and touch all that he hath, and he will curse thee to thy face.

And the LORD said unto Satan, Behold, all that he hath *is* in thy power; only upon himself put not forth thine hand.

So Satan went forth from the presence of the LORD.

JOB 1:1, 3b, 6-12

THE ONE
MINUTE
BIBLE

---

*Related texts:* JOB 28; PROVERBS 1:7; 8:13; 9:10; PHILIPPIANS 2:14-15; 1 PETER 5:8-11

# Job Loses His Wealth and His Children

**THE ONE
MINUTE
BIBLE**

And there was a day when his sons and his daughters *were* eating and drinking wine in their eldest brother's house: and there came a messenger unto Job, and said, The oxen were plowing, and the asses feeding beside them: and the Sabeans fell *upon them*, and took them away; yea, they have slain the servants with the edge of the sword; and I only am escaped alone to tell thee.

While he *was* yet speaking, there came also another, and said, The fire of God is fallen from heaven, and hath burned up the sheep, and the servants, and consumed them; and I only am escaped alone to tell thee.

While he *was* yet speaking, there came also another, and said, The Chaldeans made out three bands, and fell upon the camels, and have carried them away, yea, and slain the servants with the edge of the sword; and I only am escaped alone to tell thee.

While he *was* yet speaking, there came also another, and said, Thy sons and thy daughters *were* eating and drinking wine in their eldest brother's house: and, behold, there came a great wind from the wilderness, and smote the four corners of the house, and it fell upon the young men, and they are dead; and I only am escaped alone to tell thee.

Then Job arose, and rent his mantle, and shaved his head, and fell down upon the ground, and worshipped, and said,

Naked came I out of my mother's womb,
   and naked shall I return thither:
the LORD gave, and the LORD hath taken away;
   blessed be the name of the LORD.
In all this Job sinned not, nor charged God foolishly.

JOB 1:13-22

*Related texts:* HABAKKUK 3:17-19; 1 THESSALONIANS 5:16-18;
REVELATION 7:13-17

## *Job Loses His Health*

Again there was a day when the sons of God came to present themselves before the LORD, and Satan came also among them to present himself before the LORD. And the LORD said unto Satan, From whence comest thou?

And Satan answered the LORD, and said, From going to and fro in the earth, and from walking up and down in it.

And the LORD said unto Satan, Hast thou considered my servant Job, that *there is* none like him in the earth, a perfect and an upright man, one that feareth God, and escheweth evil? And still he holdeth fast his integrity, although thou movedst me against him, to destroy him without cause.

And Satan answered the LORD, and said, Skin for skin, yea, all that a man hath will he give for his life. But put forth thine hand now, and touch his bone and his flesh, and he will curse thee to thy face.

And the LORD said unto Satan, Behold, he *is* in thine hand; but save his life.

So went Satan forth from the presence of the LORD, and smote Job with sore boils from the sole of his foot unto his crown. And he took him a potsherd to scrape himself withal; and he sat down among the ashes.

Then said his wife unto him, Dost thou still retain thine integrity? Curse God, and die.

But he said unto her, Thou speakest as one of the foolish women speaketh. What? Shall we receive good at the hand of God, and shall we not receive evil?

In all this did not Job sin with his lips.

JOB 2:1-10

*Related texts:* JOB 19:25-27; PROVERBS 11:2-6; PHILIPPIANS 3:7-11

*A thorough knowledge of the Bible is worth more than a college education.*

**Theodore Roosevelt (1858-1919)**
UNITED STATES PRESIDENT

*I am a man of one book.*

**St. Thomas Aquinas (1227-1274)**
ITALIAN THEOLOGIAN/PHILOSOPHER

*The man of one book is always formidable; but when that book is the Bible he is irresistible.*

**William Mackergo Taylor (1829-1895)**
SCOTTISH CLERGYMAN

# *Is Suffering Always Punishment?*

Now when Job's three friends heard of all this evil that was come upon him, they came every one from his own place; Eliphaz the Temanite, and Bildad the Shuhite, and Zophar the Naamathite: for they had made an appointment together to come to mourn with him and to comfort him. And when they lifted up their eyes afar off, and knew him not, they lifted up their voice, and wept; and they rent every one his mantle, and sprinkled dust upon their heads toward heaven. So they sat down with him upon the ground seven days and seven nights, and none spake a word unto him: for they saw that *his* grief was very great.

**THE ONE MINUTE BIBLE**

Then Eliphaz the Temanite answered and said,

Remember, I pray thee, who *ever* perished,
> being innocent?
*or* where were the righteous cut off?
Even as I have seen, they that plow iniquity,
> and sow wickedness, reap the same.
By the blast of God they perish,
> and by the breath of his nostrils are they consumed.

I would seek unto God,
> and unto God would I commit my cause.

Behold, happy *is* the man whom God correcteth:
> therefore despise not thou the chastening
> > of the Almighty:
for he maketh sore, and bindeth up:
> he woundeth, and his hands make whole.

Lo this, we have searched it, so it *is*;
> hear it, and know thou *it* for thy good.

JOB 2:11-13; 4:1, 7-9; 5:8, 17-18, 27

*Related texts:* JOB 4–5; 8; 11; 15; 18; 20; 22; 25; 32–37;
HEBREWS 12:5-11

## Job Protests His Innocence

**THE ONE
MINUTE
BIBLE**

Then Job answered and said,

How long will ye vex my soul,
   and break me in pieces with words?
These ten times have ye reproached me:
   ye are not ashamed *that* ye make yourselves
      strange to me.
And be it indeed *that* I have erred,
   mine error remaineth with myself.
If indeed ye will magnify *yourselves* against me,
   and plead against me my reproach:
know now that God hath overthrown me,
   and hath compassed me with his net.

Behold, I cry out of wrong, but I am not heard:
   I cry aloud, but *there is* no judgment.

Moreover Job continued his parable, and said,

*As* God liveth, *who* hath taken away my judgment;
   and the Almighty, *who* hath vexed my soul;
all the while my breath *is* in me,
   and the spirit of God *is* in my nostrils;
my lips shall not speak wickedness,
   nor my tongue utter deceit.
God forbid that I should justify you:
   till I die I will not remove mine integrity from me.
My righteousness I hold fast, and will not let it go:
   my heart shall not reproach *me* so long as I live.

JOB 19:1-7; 27:1-6

---

***Related texts:*** JOB 3; 6–7; 9–10; 12–14; 16–17; 19; 21; 23–24; 26–31;
PSALM 7; LUKE 18:1-8

## *God Answers Job*

Then the LORD answered Job out of the whirlwind, and
said,
   Who *is* this that darkeneth counsel
     by words without knowledge?
   Gird up now thy loins like a man;
     for I will demand of thee, and answer thou me.
   Where wast thou when I laid the foundations
      of the earth?
     Declare, if thou hast understanding.
   Who hath laid the measures thereof, if thou knowest?
     Or who hath stretched the line upon it?
   Whereupon are the foundations thereof fastened?
     Or who laid the corner stone thereof;
   when the morning stars sang together,
     and all the sons of God shouted for joy?

Moreover the LORD answered Job, and said,
   Shall he that contendeth with the Almighty
      instruct *him*?
   He that reproveth God, let him answer it.

Then Job answered the LORD, and said,
   Behold, I am vile; what shall I answer thee?
     I will lay mine hand upon my mouth.
   Once have I spoken; but I will not answer:
     yea, twice; but I will proceed no further.

Then answered the LORD unto Job out of the whirlwind,
and said,
   Gird up thy loins now like a man:
     I will demand of thee, and declare thou unto me.
   Wilt thou also disannul my judgment?
     Wilt thou condemn me,
      that thou mayest be righteous?

JOB 38:1-7; 40:1-8

**THE ONE
MINUTE
BIBLE**

*Related texts:* PSALM 30; JOB 38–41; HABAKKUK 1:1–2:1; ROMANS 9–10

## God Vindicates and Restores Job

**THE ONE
MINUTE
BIBLE**

Then Job answered the Lord, and said,

> I know that thou canst do every *thing*,
>> and *that* no thought can be withholden from thee.
> Who *is* he that hideth counsel without knowledge?
>> Therefore have I uttered that I understood not;
>> things too wonderful for me, which I knew not.

> Hear, I beseech thee, and I will speak:
>> I will demand of thee, and declare thou unto me.
> I have heard of thee by the hearing of the ear:
>> but now mine eye seeth thee.
> Wherefore I abhor *myself*,
>> and repent in dust and ashes.

And it was *so*, that after the Lord had spoken these words unto Job, the Lord said to Eliphaz the Temanite, My wrath is kindled against thee, and against thy two friends: for ye have not spoken of me *the thing that is* right, as my servant Job *hath*. Therefore take unto you now seven bullocks and seven rams, and go to my servant Job, and offer up for yourselves a burnt offering; and my servant Job shall pray for you: for him will I accept: lest I deal with you *after your* folly, in that ye have not spoken of me *the thing which is* right, like my servant Job. So Eliphaz the Temanite and Bildad the Shuhite *and* Zophar the Naamathite went, and did according as the Lord commanded them: the Lord also accepted Job.

And the Lord turned the captivity of Job, when he prayed for his friends: also the Lord gave Job twice as much as he had before.

Job 42:1-10

---

***Related texts:*** Psalms 17; 37; Matthew 5:1-6; James 5:11

# The Beatitudes: *Poor in Spirit*

And seeing the multitudes, Jesus went up into a mountain: and when he was set, his disciples came unto him: and he opened his mouth, and taught them, saying,

Blessed *are* the poor in spirit:
for theirs is the kingdom of heaven.

The sacrifices of God *are* a broken spirit:
a broken and a contrite heart,
O God, thou wilt not despise.

For thus saith the high and lofty One
that inhabiteth eternity, whose name *is* Holy;
I dwell in the high and holy *place*,
with him also *that is* of a contrite and humble spirit,
to revive the spirit of the humble,
and to revive the heart of the contrite ones.

My brethren, have not the faith of our Lord Jesus Christ, *the Lord* of glory, with respect of persons. For if there come unto your assembly a man with a gold ring, in goodly apparel, and there come in also a poor man in vile raiment; and ye have respect to him that weareth the gay clothing, and say unto him, Sit thou here in a good place; and say to the poor, Stand thou there, or sit here under my footstool: are ye not then partial in yourselves, and are become judges of evil thoughts?

Hearken, my beloved brethren, Hath not God chosen the poor of this world rich in faith, and heirs of the kingdom which he hath promised to them that love him?

MATTHEW 5:1-3; PSALM 51:17; ISAIAH 57:15; JAMES 2:1-5

*Related texts:* JOB 34:17-19; ISAIAH 57:15-19; 66:2; LUKE 6:20; ACTS 10:34-35; EPHESIANS 6:5-9

# The Beatitudes: *Those Who Mourn*

**THE ONE**
**MINUTE**
**BIBLE**

Blessed *are* they that mourn:
>    for they shall be comforted.

The Spirit of the Lord God *is* upon me;
>    because the Lord hath anointed me
>    to preach good tidings unto the meek;
he hath sent me to bind up the brokenhearted,
>    to proclaim liberty to the captives,
>    and the opening of the prison to *them that are* bound;
to proclaim the acceptable year of the Lord,
>    and the day of vengeance of our God;
to comfort all that mourn;
>    to appoint unto them that mourn in Zion,
to give unto them beauty
>    for ashes,
the oil of joy
>    for mourning,
the garment of praise
>    for the spirit of heaviness;
that they might be called trees of righteousness,
>    the planting of the Lord,
>    that he might be glorified.

And I heard a great voice out of heaven saying, Behold, the tabernacle of God *is* with men, and he will dwell with them, and they shall be his people, and God himself shall be with them, *and be* their God. And God shall wipe away all tears from their eyes; and there shall be no more death, neither sorrow, nor crying, neither shall there be any more pain: for the former things are passed away.

Matthew 5:4; Isaiah 61:1-3; Revelation 21:3-4

---

*Related texts:* Nehemiah 8:1-12; Ecclesiastes 3:1-8; Psalm 119:49-50; Luke 6:21; 2 Corinthians 1:3-7; 7:8-11

# The Beatitudes: *The Meek*

THE ONE
MINUTE
BIBLE

Blessed *are* the meek:
for they shall inherit the earth.

Fret not thyself because of evildoers,
neither be thou envious against the workers of iniquity.
For they shall soon be cut down like the grass,
and wither as the green herb.
Trust in the LORD, and do good;
*so* shalt thou dwell in the land, and verily thou
shalt be fed.
Delight thyself also in the LORD;
and he shall give thee the desires of thine heart.
Commit thy way unto the LORD;
trust also in him; and he shall bring *it* to pass.
And he shall bring forth thy righteousness as the light,
and thy judgment as the noonday.
Rest in the LORD, and wait patiently for him:
fret not thyself because of him who prospereth
in his way,
because of the man who bringeth wicked devices
to pass.
Cease from anger, and forsake wrath:
fret not thyself in any wise to do evil.
For evildoers shall be cut off:
but those that wait upon the LORD,
they shall inherit the earth.
For yet a little while, and the wicked *shall* not *be*:
yea, thou shalt diligently consider his place,
and it *shall* not *be*.
But the meek shall inherit the earth;
and shall delight themselves in the abundance of peace.

MATTHEW 5:5; PSALM 37:1-11

---

*Related texts:* PSALMS 25:12-13; 37:12-40; MATTHEW 11:25-30;
GALATIANS 5:19-23; 2 CORINTHIANS 10:1-5; 1 PETER 3:8-9

# The Beatitudes: *Hungry for Righteousness*

**THE ONE
MINUTE
BIBLE**

Blessed *are* they which do hunger and thirst
    after righteousness:
for they shall be filled.

As the hart panteth after the water brooks,
    so panteth my soul after thee, O God.
My soul thirsteth for God, for the living God:
    when shall I come and appear before God?

Jesus answered and said unto her, Whosoever
drinketh of this water shall thirst again: but whosoever
drinketh of the water that I shall give him shall never
thirst; but the water that I shall give him shall be in him
a well of water springing up into everlasting life.

And Jesus said unto them, I am the bread of life: he
that cometh to me shall never hunger; and he that
believeth on me shall never thirst.

In the last day, that great *day* of the feast, Jesus stood
and cried, saying, If any man thirst, let him come unto
me, and drink. He that believeth on me, as the scripture
hath said, out of his belly shall flow rivers of living
water. (But this spake he of the Spirit, which they that
believe on him should receive: for the Holy Ghost was
not yet *given*; because that Jesus was not yet glorified.)

And the Spirit and the bride say, Come. And let him
that heareth say, Come. And let him that is athirst come.
And whosoever will, let him take the water of life freely.

MATTHEW 5:6; PSALM 42:1-2; JOHN 4:13-14; 6:35; 7:37-39;
REVELATION 22:17

*Related texts:* PSALMS 107:1-9; 146; ISAIAH 55:1-2; LUKE 6:21;
REVELATION 7:16-17

# The Beatitudes: *The Merciful*

Blessed *are* the merciful:
for they shall obtain mercy.

(For the Lord thy God *is* a merciful God;) he will not forsake thee, neither destroy thee, nor forget the covenant of thy fathers which he sware unto them.

Unto thee lift I up mine eyes,
O thou that dwellest in the heavens.
Behold, as the eyes of servants *look* unto the hand
of their masters,
*and* as the eyes of a maiden unto the hand
of her mistress;
so our eyes *wait* upon the Lord our God,
until that he have mercy upon us.
Have mercy upon us, O Lord, have mercy upon us:
for we are exceedingly filled with contempt.
Our soul is exceedingly filled with the scorning
of those that are at ease,
*and* with the contempt of the proud.

For I desired mercy, and not sacrifice;
and the knowledge of God more than burnt offerings.

He hath showed thee, O man, what *is* good;
and what doth the Lord require of thee,
but to do justly, and to love mercy,
and to walk humbly with thy God?

So speak ye, and so do, as they that shall be judged by the law of liberty. For he shall have judgment without mercy, that hath showed no mercy; and mercy rejoiceth against judgment.

Matthew 5:7; Deuteronomy 4:31; Psalm 123:1-4; Hosea 6:6;
Micah 6:8; James 2:12-13

*Related texts:* Psalm 6; Micah 7:18-19; Zechariah 7:9-10;
Luke 6:27-38; 10:25-37; Jude 1:20-23

# The Beatitudes: *The Pure in Heart*

**THE ONE
MINUTE
BIBLE**

Blessed *are* the pure in heart:
    for they shall see God.

Who shall ascend into the hill of the LORD?
    Or who shall stand in his holy place?
He that hath clean hands, and a pure heart;
    who hath not lifted up his soul unto vanity,
    nor sworn deceitfully.
He shall receive the blessing from the LORD,
    and righteousness from the God of his salvation.

Create in me a clean heart, O God;
    and renew a right spirit within me.

    Flee also youthful lusts: but follow righteousness, faith, charity, peace, with them that call on the Lord out of a pure heart.

    Having therefore, brethren, boldness to enter into the holiest by the blood of Jesus, by a new and living way, which he hath consecrated for us, through the veil, that is to say, his flesh; and *having* an high priest over the house of God; let us draw near with a true heart in full assurance of faith, having our hearts sprinkled from an evil conscience, and our bodies washed with pure water.

MATTHEW 5:8; PSALMS 24:3-5; 51:10; 2 TIMOTHY 2:22;
HEBREWS 10:19-22

*Related texts:* 2 CHRONICLES 30:13-20; PROVERBS 20:5-11; MARK 7:1-23; HEBREWS 3; 12:14-29

# The Beatitudes: *The Peacemakers*

THE ONE
MINUTE
BIBLE

Blessed *are* the peacemakers:
    for they shall be called the children of God.

Come, ye children, hearken unto me:
    I will teach you the fear of the LORD.
What man *is he that* desireth life,
    *and* loveth *many* days, that he may see good?
Keep thy tongue from evil,
    and thy lips from speaking guile.
Depart from evil, and do good;
    seek peace, and pursue it.

Mark the perfect *man*, and behold the upright:
    for the end of *that* man *is* peace.
But the transgressors shall be destroyed together:
    the end of the wicked shall be cut off.

*There is* no peace, saith the LORD, unto the wicked.

If it be possible, as much as lieth in you, live
peaceably with all men.

But the wisdom that is from above is first pure, then
peaceable, gentle, *and* easy to be entreated, full of
mercy and good fruits, without partiality, and without
hypocrisy.

MATTHEW 5:9; PSALMS 34:11-14; 37:37-38; ISAIAH 48:22;
ROMANS 12:18; JAMES 3:17

*Related texts:* ISAIAH 9:6-7; JOHN 1:1-13; ROMANS 8:9-23;
GALATIANS 3:26–4:7; 1 JOHN 3:1-11

# The Beatitudes: *The Persecuted Righteous*

**THE ONE**
**M I N U T E**
**B I B L E**

Blessed *are* they which are persecuted
    for righteousness' sake:
    for theirs is the kingdom of heaven.

    Blessed are ye, when *men* shall revile you, and
persecute *you*, and shall say all manner of evil against
you falsely, for my sake. Rejoice, and be exceeding glad:
for great *is* your reward in heaven: for so persecuted
they the prophets which were before you.

But the LORD *is* with me as a mighty terrible one:
    therefore my persecutors shall stumble,
    and they shall not prevail:
they shall be greatly ashamed; for they shall not prosper:
    *their* everlasting confusion shall never be forgotten.

    For this *is* thankworthy, if a man for conscience
toward God endure grief, suffering wrongfully. For what
glory *is it*, if, when ye be buffeted for your faults, ye
shall take it patiently? But if, when ye do well, and
suffer *for it*, ye take it patiently, this *is* acceptable with
God. For even hereunto were ye called: because Christ
also suffered for us, leaving us an example, that ye
should follow his steps.

    Therefore I take pleasure in infirmities, in
reproaches, in necessities, in persecutions, in distresses
for Christ's sake: for when I am weak, then am I strong.

MATTHEW 5:10-12; JEREMIAH 20:11; 1 PETER 2:19-21;
2 CORINTHIANS 12:10

*Related texts:* JOB 36:15-17; ISAIAH 53; 1 PETER 1:3-9; 4:12-19

## *Unconditional Love*

Who shall separate us from the love of Christ? *Shall* tribulation, or distress, or persecution, or famine, or nakedness, or peril, or sword? As it is written,

For thy sake we are killed all the day long;
we are accounted as sheep for the slaughter.

Nay, in all these things we are more than conquerors through him that loved us. For I am persuaded, that neither death, nor life, nor angels, nor principalities, nor powers, nor things present, nor things to come, nor height, nor depth, nor any other creature, shall be able to separate us from the love of God, which is in Christ Jesus our Lord.

And we have known and believed the love that God hath to us.

God is love; and he that dwelleth in love dwelleth in God, and God in him. Herein is our love made perfect, that we may have boldness in the day of judgment: because as he is, so are we in this world. There is no fear in love; but perfect love casteth out fear: because fear hath torment. He that feareth is not made perfect in love.

We love him, because he first loved us.

Romans 8:35-39; 1 John 4:16-19

**THE ONE
MINUTE
BIBLE**

---

*Related texts:* Deuteronomy 7:7-11; 10:14-15; John 3:16-19; Romans 5:8-11; Ephesians 2:4-10

## *The Greatest Is Love*

**THE ONE
MINUTE
BIBLE**

Though I speak with the tongues of men and of angels, and have not charity, I am become *as* sounding brass, or a tinkling cymbal. And though I have *the gift of* prophecy, and understand all mysteries, and all knowledge; and though I have all faith, so that I could remove mountains, and have not charity, I am nothing. And though I bestow all my goods to feed *the poor*, and though I give my body to be burned, and have not charity, it profiteth me nothing.

Charity suffereth long, *and* is kind; charity envieth not; charity vaunteth not itself, is not puffed up, doth not behave itself unseemly, seeketh not her own, is not easily provoked, thinketh no evil; rejoiceth not in iniquity, but rejoiceth in the truth; beareth all things, believeth all things, hopeth all things, endureth all things.

Charity never faileth.

And now abideth faith, hope, charity, these three; but the greatest of these *is* charity.

Set me as a seal upon thine heart,
    as a seal upon thine arm:
for love *is* strong as death;
    jealousy *is* cruel as the grave:
the coals thereof *are* coals of fire,
    *which hath* a most vehement flame.
Many waters cannot quench love,
    neither can the floods drown it:
if a man would give all the substance of his house
      for love,
    it would utterly be contemned.

Husbands, love your wives, even as Christ also loved the church, and gave himself for it.

1 Corinthians 13:1-8a, 13; Song of Songs 8:6-7; Ephesians 5:25

*Related texts:* Deuteronomy 6:1-5; Psalm 136; John 15:9-17; 1 John 3

48

## Israelites Oppressed in Egypt

THE ONE
MINUTE
BIBLE

Now these *are* the names of the children of Israel, which came into Egypt; every man and his household came with Jacob. Reuben, Simeon, Levi, and Judah, Issachar, Zebulun, and Benjamin, Dan, and Naphtali, Gad, and Asher. And all the souls that came out of the loins of Jacob were seventy souls: for Joseph was in Egypt *already*.

And Joseph died, and all his brethren, and all that generation. And the children of Israel were fruitful, and increased abundantly, and multiplied, and waxed exceeding mighty; and the land was filled with them.

Now there arose up a new king over Egypt, which knew not Joseph. And he said unto his people, Behold, the people of the children of Israel *are* more and mightier than we: come on, let us deal wisely with them; lest they multiply, and it come to pass, that, when there falleth out any war, they join also unto our enemies, and fight against us, and *so* get them up out of the land.

Therefore they did set over them taskmasters to afflict them with their burdens. And they built for Pharaoh treasure cities, Pithom and Raamses. But the more they afflicted them, the more they multiplied and grew. And they were grieved because of the children of Israel. And the Egyptians made the children of Israel to serve with rigour.

And Pharaoh charged all his people, saying, Every son that is born ye shall cast into the river, and every daughter ye shall save alive.

EXODUS 1:1-13, 22

---

*Related texts:* PSALM 105:23-25; ACTS 7:9-34; 1 CORINTHIANS 7:21-23; GALATIANS 3:26-28

## The Birth of Moses

**THE ONE
MINUTE
BIBLE**

And there went a man of the house of Levi, and took *to wife* a daughter of Levi. And the woman conceived, and bare a son: and when she saw him that he *was a* goodly *child*, she hid him three months. And when she could not longer hide him, she took for him an ark of bulrushes, and daubed it with slime and with pitch, and put the child therein; and she laid *it* in the flags by the river's brink. And his sister stood afar off, to wit what would be done to him.

And the daughter of Pharaoh came down to wash *herself* at the river; and her maidens walked along by the river's side; and when she saw the ark among the flags, she sent her maid to fetch it. And when she had opened *it*, she saw the child: and, behold, the babe wept. And she had compassion on him, and said, This *is one* of the Hebrews' children.

Then said his sister to Pharaoh's daughter, Shall I go and call to thee a nurse of the Hebrew women, that she may nurse the child for thee?

And Pharaoh's daughter said to her, Go. And the maid went and called the child's mother. And Pharaoh's daughter said unto her, Take this child away, and nurse it for me, and I will give *thee* thy wages. And the woman took the child, and nursed it. And the child grew, and she brought him unto Pharaoh's daughter, and he became her son. And she called his name Moses: and she said, Because I drew him out of the water.

Exodus 2:1-10

***Related texts:*** Isaiah 49:13-19; Acts 7:20-22; Hebrews 11:23

## Moses Flees from Egypt

And it came to pass in those days, when Moses was grown, that he went out unto his brethren, and looked on their burdens: and he spied an Egyptian smiting an Hebrew, one of his brethren. And he looked this way and that way, and when he saw that *there was* no man, he slew the Egyptian, and hid him in the sand. And when he went out the second day, behold, two men of the Hebrews strove together: and he said to him that did the wrong, Wherefore smitest thou thy fellow?

And he said, Who made thee a prince and a judge over us? Intendest thou to kill me, as thou killedst the Egyptian? And Moses feared, and said, Surely this thing is known.

Now when Pharaoh heard this thing, he sought to slay Moses. But Moses fled from the face of Pharaoh, and dwelt in the land of Midian.

And it came to pass in process of time, that the king of Egypt died: and the children of Israel sighed by reason of the bondage, and they cried, and their cry came up unto God by reason of the bondage. And God heard their groaning, and God remembered his covenant with Abraham, with Isaac, and with Jacob. And God looked upon the children of Israel, and God had respect unto *them*.

The LORD sent redemption unto his people:
  he hath commanded his covenant for ever:
  holy and reverend *is* his name.

EXODUS 2:11-15a, 23-25; PSALM 111:9

---

*Related texts:* NUMBERS 32:23; ACTS 7:23-29; HEBREWS 11:24-27

# The LORD Appears to Moses

**THE ONE
MINUTE
BIBLE**

Now Moses kept the flock of Jethro his father in law, the priest of Midian: and he led the flock to the backside of the desert, and came to the mountain of God, *even* to Horeb. And the angel of the LORD appeared unto him in a flame of fire out of the midst of a bush: and he looked, and, behold, the bush burned with fire, and the bush *was* not consumed. And Moses said, I will now turn aside, and see this great sight, why the bush is not burnt.

And when the LORD saw that he turned aside to see, God called unto him out of the midst of the bush, and said, Moses, Moses.

And he said, Here *am* I.

And he said, Draw not nigh hither: put off thy shoes from off thy feet, for the place whereon thou standest *is* holy ground. Moreover he said, I *am* the God of thy father, the God of Abraham, the God of Isaac, and the God of Jacob. And Moses hid his face; for he was afraid to look upon God.

And the LORD said, I have surely seen the affliction of my people which *are* in Egypt, and have heard their cry by reason of their taskmasters; for I know their sorrows; and I am come down to deliver them out of the hand of the Egyptians, and to bring them up out of that land unto a good land and a large, unto a land flowing with milk and honey.

Come now therefore, and I will send thee unto Pharaoh, that thou mayest bring forth my people the children of Israel out of Egypt.

EXODUS 3:1-8a, 10

***Related texts:*** ISAIAH 6; ACTS 7:30-35; REVELATION 15:2-4

## *The LORD Reveals His Name to Moses*

THE ONE
MINUTE
BIBLE

And Moses said unto God, Who *am* I, that I should go unto Pharaoh, and that I should bring forth the children of Israel out of Egypt?

And he said, Certainly I will be with thee; and this *shall be* a token unto thee, that I have sent thee: when thou hast brought forth the people out of Egypt, ye shall serve God upon this mountain.

And Moses said unto God, Behold, *when* I come unto the children of Israel, and shall say unto them, The God of your fathers hath sent me unto you; and they shall say to me, What *is* his name? What shall I say unto them?

And God said unto Moses, I AM THAT I AM: and he said, Thus shalt thou say unto the children of Israel, I AM hath sent me unto you.

And God said moreover unto Moses, Thus shalt thou say unto the children of Israel, The LORD God of your fathers, the God of Abraham, the God of Isaac, and the God of Jacob, hath sent me unto you: this *is* my name for ever, and this *is* my memorial unto all generations.

And God spake unto Moses, and said unto him, I *am* the LORD: and I appeared unto Abraham, unto Isaac, and unto Jacob, by *the name of* God Almighty, but by my name JEHOVAH was I not known to them.

EXODUS 3:11-15; 6:2-3

*Related texts:* EXODUS 20:7: JOHN 6:35; 8:12, 58; 10:7, 11; 11:25; 14:6; 15:1; REVELATION 1:8

# Names of God: *The* LORD

**THE ONE**
**MINUTE**
**BIBLE**

The LORD also will be a refuge for the oppressed,
    a refuge in times of trouble.
And they that know thy name will put their trust in thee:
    for thou, LORD, hast not forsaken them that seek thee.

Thou shalt not take the name of the LORD thy God in vain; for the LORD will not hold him guiltless that taketh his name in vain.

Because I will publish the name of the LORD:
    ascribe ye greatness unto our God.
*He is* the Rock, his work *is* perfect:
    for all his ways *are* judgment:
a God of truth and without iniquity,
    just and right *is* he.

Give thanks unto the LORD, call upon his name,
    make known his deeds among the people.
Sing unto him, sing psalms unto him,
    talk ye of all his wondrous works.
Glory ye in his holy name:
    let the heart of them rejoice that seek the LORD.

The name of the LORD *is* a strong tower:
    the righteous runneth into it, and is safe.

Forasmuch as *there is* none like unto thee, O LORD;
    thou *art* great,
    and thy name *is* great in might.

PSALM 9:9-10; EXODUS 20:7; DEUTERONOMY 32:3-4;
1 CHRONICLES 16:8-10; PROVERBS 18:10; JEREMIAH 10:6

---

***Related texts:*** EXODUS 15:1-3; ISAIAH 42:5-9; COLOSSIANS 3:16-17;
HEBREWS 13:15

# Names of God: *The Lord GOD*

For thou *art* my hope, O Lord GOD:
   *thou art* my trust from my youth.

For, lo, they that are far from thee shall perish:
   thou hast destroyed all them that go a whoring
      from thee.
But *it is* good for me to draw near to God:
   I have put my trust in the Lord GOD,
   that I may declare all thy works.

**THE ONE
MINUTE
BIBLE**

For thus saith the Lord GOD; Behold, I, *even* I, will both search my sheep, and seek them out. As a shepherd seeketh out his flock in the day that he is among his sheep *that are* scattered; so will I seek out my sheep, and will deliver them out of all places where they have been scattered in the cloudy and dark day. And I will bring them out from the people, and gather them from the countries, and will bring them to their own land, and feed them upon the mountains of Israel by the rivers, and in all the inhabited places of the country. I will feed them in a good pasture, and upon the high mountains of Israel shall their fold be: there shall they lie in a good fold, and *in* a fat pasture shall they feed upon the mountains of Israel. I will feed my flock, and I will cause them to lie down, saith the Lord GOD. I will seek that which was lost, and bring again that which was driven away, and will bind up *that which was* broken, and will strengthen that which was sick: but I will destroy the fat and the strong; I will feed them with judgment.

PSALMS 71:5; 73:27-28; EZEKIEL 34:11-16

*Related texts:* ISAIAH 50:4-11; EZEKIEL 36; ACTS 4:23-35;
EPHESIANS 5:19-20

# Names of God: *The LORD of Hosts*

**THE ONE
MINUTE
BIBLE**

Lift up your heads, O ye gates;
    and be ye lift up, ye everlasting doors;
    and the King of glory shall come in.
Who *is* this King of glory?
    The LORD strong and mighty,
    the LORD mighty in battle.
Lift up your heads, O ye gates;
    even lift *them* up, ye everlasting doors;
    and the King of glory shall come in.
Who is this King of glory?
    The LORD of hosts,
    he *is* the King of glory.


Thus saith the LORD,
which giveth the sun
    for a light by day,
*and* the ordinances of the moon and of the stars
    for a light by night,
which divideth the sea
    when the waves thereof roar;
    The LORD of hosts *is* his name:
If those ordinances depart from before me,
    saith the LORD,
*then* the seed of Israel also shall cease
    from being a nation before me for ever.
Thus saith the LORD;
If heaven above can be measured,
    and the foundations of the earth searched out beneath,
I will also cast off all the seed of Israel
    for all that they have done,
                            saith the LORD.

PSALM 24:7-10; JEREMIAH 31:35-37

*Related texts:* 1 SAMUEL 17:39-51; PSALM 46; ISAIAH 54:5

# Names of God: *The Almighty*

Therefore hearken unto me, ye men of understanding:
    far be it from God, *that he should do* wickedness;
    and *from* the Almighty, *that he should* commit iniquity.
For the work of a man shall he render unto him,
    and cause every man to find according to *his* ways.
Yea, surely God will not do wickedly,
    neither will the Almighty pervert judgment.

**THE ONE**
**MINUTE**
**BIBLE**

*Touching* the Almighty, we cannot find him out:
    *he is* excellent in power,
  and in judgment, and in plenty of justice:
    he will not afflict.
Men do therefore fear him:
    he respecteth not any *that are* wise of heart.

He that dwelleth in the secret place of the most High
    shall abide under the shadow of the Almighty.
I will say of the LORD, *He is* my refuge and my fortress:
    my God; in him will I trust.
Surely he shall deliver thee from the snare of the fowler,
    *and* from the noisome pestilence.
He shall cover thee with his feathers,
    and under his wings shalt thou trust:
    his truth *shall be thy* shield and buckler.

I am Alpha and Omega, the beginning and the
ending, saith the Lord, which is, and which was, and
which is to come, the Almighty.

JOB 34:10-12; 37:23-24; PSALM 91:1-4; REVELATION 1:8

*Related texts:* GENESIS 17:1; 28:3; 35:11; 43:14; 48:3; 49:25;
EXODUS 6:2-4; REVELATION 4:1-8; 15:2-4; 21:22-27

**THE ONE
MINUTE
BIBLE**

# Names of God: *The Lord*

For the LORD your God *is* God of gods, and Lord of lords, a great God, a mighty, and a terrible, which regardeth not persons, nor taketh reward: he doth execute the judgment of the fatherless and widow, and loveth the stranger, in giving him food and raiment.

O LORD our Lord,
  how excellent *is* thy name in all the earth!

Lord, thou hast been our dwelling place
  in all generations.
Before the mountains were brought forth,
  or ever thou hadst formed the earth and the world,
even from everlasting to everlasting, thou *art* God.

That if thou shalt confess with thy mouth the Lord Jesus, and shalt believe in thine heart that God hath raised him from the dead, thou shalt be saved. For with the heart man believeth unto righteousness; and with the mouth confession is made unto salvation. For the scripture saith, Whosoever believeth on him shall not be ashamed. For there is no difference between the Jew and the Greek: for the same Lord over all is rich unto all that call upon him. For whosoever shall call upon the name of the Lord shall be saved.

As ye have therefore received Christ Jesus the Lord, *so* walk ye in him: rooted and built up in him, and stablished in the faith, as ye have been taught, abounding therein with thanksgiving.

DEUTERONOMY 10:17-18; PSALMS 8:9; 90:1-2; ROMANS 10:9-13;
COLOSSIANS 2:6-7

***Related texts:*** JOB 28; PSALMS 8; 86; 110; DANIEL 9:1-19;
PHILIPPIANS 2:5-11

# Names of God: *The Most High*

THE ONE
MINUTE
BIBLE

God *is* our refuge and strength,
a very present help in trouble.
Therefore will not we fear, though the earth be removed,
and though the mountains be carried into the midst
of the sea;
*though* the waters thereof roar *and* be troubled,
*though* the mountains shake with the swelling thereof.
*There is* a river, the streams whereof shall make glad
the city of God,
the holy *place* of the tabernacles of the most High.
God *is* in the midst of her; she shall not be moved:
God shall help her, *and that* right early.
The heathen raged, the kingdoms were moved:
he uttered his voice, the earth melted.
The LORD of hosts *is* with us;
the God of Jacob *is* our refuge.

O clap your hands, all ye people;
shout unto God with the voice of triumph.
For the LORD most high *is* terrible;
*he is* a great King over all the earth.

*It is a* good *thing* to give thanks unto the LORD,
and to sing praises unto thy name, O most High:
to show forth thy lovingkindness in the morning,
and thy faithfulness every night,
upon an instrument of ten strings, and upon the psaltery;
upon the harp with a solemn sound.
For thou, LORD, hast made me glad through thy work:
I will triumph in the works of thy hands.
O LORD, how great are thy works!
*And* thy thoughts are very deep.

PSALMS 46:1-7; 47:1-2; 92:1-5

*Related texts:* GENESIS 14:18-24; PSALMS 7; 9:1-2; 91; LUKE 1:26-38

# Names of God: *The Creator*

**THE ONE
MINUTE
BIBLE**

Remember now thy Creator
  in the days of thy youth,
while the evil days come not,
  nor the years draw nigh, when thou shalt say,
  I have no pleasure in them;
while the sun, or the light,
  or the moon, or the stars, be not darkened,
  nor the clouds return after the rain:
in the day when the keepers of the house shall tremble,
  and the strong men shall bow themselves,
and the grinders cease because they are few,
  and those that look out of the windows be darkened,
and the doors shall be shut in the streets,
  when the sound of the grinding is low,
and he shall rise up at the voice of the bird,
  and all the daughters of music shall be brought low;
also *when* they shall be afraid of *that which is* high,
  and fears *shall be* in the way,
and the almond tree shall flourish,
  and the grasshopper shall be a burden,
  and desire shall fail:
because man goeth to his long home,
  and the mourners go about the streets:
or ever the silver cord be loosed,
  or the golden bowl be broken,
or the pitcher be broken at the fountain,
  or the wheel broken at the cistern.
Then shall the dust return to the earth as it was:
  and the spirit shall return unto God who gave it.

ECCLESIASTES 12:1-7

---

***Related texts:*** GENESIS 1; 14:18-24; ECCLESIASTES 12:9-14;
ISAIAH 40:27-31; REVELATION 4:11

# Names of God: *Everlasting God, King Eternal*

Why sayest thou, O Jacob,
and speakest, O Israel,
My way is hid from the LORD,
and my judgment is passed over from my God?
Hast thou not known?
Hast thou not heard,
*that* the everlasting God, the LORD,
the Creator of the ends of the earth,
fainteth not, neither is weary?
*There is* no searching of his understanding.
He giveth power to the faint;
and to *them that have* no might he increaseth
strength.
Even the youths shall faint and be weary,
and the young men shall utterly fall:
but they that wait upon the LORD
shall renew *their* strength;
they shall mount up with wings as eagles;
they shall run, and not be weary;
*and* they shall walk, and not faint.


This *is* a faithful saying, and worthy of all
acceptation, that Christ Jesus came into the world to
save sinners; of whom I am chief. Howbeit for this
cause I obtained mercy, that in me first Jesus Christ
might show forth all longsuffering, for a pattern to them
which should hereafter believe on him to life
everlasting. Now unto the King eternal, immortal,
invisible, the only wise God, *be* honour and glory for
ever and ever. Amen.

ISAIAH 40:27-31; 1 TIMOTHY 1:15-17

---

*Related texts:* DEUTERONOMY 33:27; PSALM 90:1-2; ROMANS 16:25-27;
HEBREWS 9:14

# Names of God: *The Holy One*

**THE ONE
MINUTE
BIBLE**

But thou *art* holy,
    O *thou* that inhabitest the praises of Israel.
Our fathers trusted in thee:
    they trusted, and thou didst deliver them.
They cried unto thee, and were delivered:
    they trusted in thee, and were not confounded.

The fear of the LORD *is* the beginning of wisdom:
    and the knowledge of the holy *is* understanding.
For by me thy days shall be multiplied,
    and the years of thy life shall be increased.
If thou be wise, thou shalt be wise for thyself:
    but *if* thou scornest, thou alone shalt bear *it*.

*As for* our redeemer, the LORD of hosts *is* his name,
    the Holy One of Israel.

And in the synagogue there was a man, which had a
spirit of an unclean devil, and cried out with a loud
voice, saying, Let *us* alone; what have we to do with
thee, *thou* Jesus of Nazareth? Art thou come to destroy
us? I know thee who thou art; the Holy One of God.
    And Jesus rebuked him, saying, Hold thy peace, and
come out of him. And when the devil had thrown him in
the midst, he came out of him, and hurt him not.
    And they were all amazed, and spake among
themselves, saying, What a word *is* this! For with
authority and power he commandeth the unclean
spirits, and they come out.

PSALM 22:3-5; PROVERBS 9:10-12; ISAIAH 47:4; LUKE 4:33-36

*Related texts:* PSALM 16; ISAIAH 40:25-31; 54:5; ACTS 2:22-39

# Names of God: *Judge*

But the Lord shall endure for ever:
  he hath prepared his throne for judgment.
And he shall judge the world in righteousness,
  he shall minister judgment to the people
    in uprightness.

O Lord God, to whom vengeance belongeth;
  O God, to whom vengeance belongeth, show thyself.
Lift up thyself, thou judge of the earth:
  render a reward to the proud.

And there shall come forth a rod out of the stem of Jesse,
  and a Branch shall grow out of his roots:
and the spirit of the Lord shall rest upon him,
  the spirit of wisdom and understanding,
  the spirit of counsel and might,
  the spirit of knowledge and of the fear of the Lord;
  and shall make him of quick understanding in the
    fear of the Lord:
and he shall not judge after the sight of his eyes,
  neither reprove after the hearing of his ears:
but with righteousness shall he judge the poor,
  and reprove with equity for the meek of the earth:
and he shall smite the earth with the rod of his mouth,
  and with the breath of his lips shall he slay the wicked.
And righteousness shall be the girdle of his loins,
  and faithfulness the girdle of his reins.

For the Lord *is* our judge,
  the Lord *is* our lawgiver,
the Lord *is* our king;
  he will save us.

PSALMS 9:7-8; 94:1-2; ISAIAH 11:1-5; 33:22

**THE ONE
MINUTE
BIBLE**

---

***Related texts:*** JUDGES 11:27; PSALMS 7; 82; 96; JOHN 5:25-30;
ACTS 10:34-43; JAMES 4:11-12; REVELATION 19:11-16

*All human history as described in
the Bible, may be summarized in one phrase,
God in Search of Man. There are no words in
the world more knowing, more disclosing and
more indispensable, words both stern and
graceful, heart-rending and healing.*

**Abraham Joshua Heschel (1907-   )**
AMERICAN THEOLOGIAN

*I was dazzled by the revelation of the truth
and obtained complete answers to the
questions: What is the meaning of my life?
And the meaning of other people's lives?*

**Leo Tolstoy (1828-1910)**
RUSSIAN NOVELIST
*(On studying the Gospels)*

*Prayer, in its turn, needs to be sustained
by reading the Holy Scripture.*

**Francois Fenelon (1651-1715)**
FRENCH ROMAN CATHOLIC BISHOP

# Names of God: *King*

The LORD sitteth upon the flood;
  yea, the LORD sitteth King for ever.
The LORD will give strength unto his people;
  the LORD will bless his people with peace.

I *am* the LORD, your Holy One,
  the creator of Israel, your King.

  And Pilate asked Jesus, saying, Art thou the King of
the Jews?
  And Jesus answered him and said, Thou sayest *it.*

  And I saw heaven opened, and behold a white horse;
and he that sat upon him *was* called Faithful and True,
and in righteousness he doth judge and make war. His
eyes *were* as a flame of fire, and on his head *were* many
crowns; and he had a name written, that no man knew,
but he himself. And he *was* clothed with a vesture
dipped in blood: and his name is called The Word of
God. And the armies *which were* in heaven followed him
upon white horses, clothed in fine linen, white and
clean. And out of his mouth goeth a sharp sword, that
with it he should smite the nations: and he shall rule
them with a rod of iron: and he treadeth the winepress
of the fierceness and wrath of Almighty God. And he
hath on *his* vesture and on his thigh a name written,
KING OF KINGS, AND LORD OF LORDS.

PSALM 29:10-11; ISAIAH 43:15; LUKE 23:3; REVELATION 19:11-16

*Related texts:* PSALMS 47; 95:1-7; ISAIAH 44:6-8; JEREMIAH 10:6-10;
MATTHEW 21:1-5; 1 TIMOTHY 1:17; 6:15

**THE ONE**
**MINUTE**
**BIBLE**

# Names of God: *The Mighty One*

Whereas thou hast been forsaken and hated,
    so that no man went through *thee*,
I will make thee an eternal excellency,
    a joy of many generations.
Thou shalt also suck the milk of the Gentiles,
    and shalt suck the breast of kings:
and thou shalt know that I the LORD *am* thy Saviour
    and thy Redeemer, the mighty One of Jacob.

And Mary said,

My soul doth magnify the Lord,
    and my spirit hath rejoiced in God my Saviour.
For he hath regarded
    the low estate of his handmaiden:
for, behold, from henceforth all generations
      shall call me blessed.
    For he that is mighty hath done to me great things;
    and holy *is* his name.
And his mercy *is* on them that fear him
    from generation to generation.
He hath showed strength with his arm;
    he hath scattered the proud in the imagination of
      their hearts.
He hath put down the mighty from *their* seats,
    and exalted them of low degree.
He hath filled the hungry with good things;
    and the rich he hath sent empty away.
He hath holpen his servant Israel,
    in remembrance of *his* mercy;
as he spake to our fathers, to Abraham,
    and to his seed for ever.

ISAIAH 60:15-16; LUKE 1:46-55

---

*Related texts:* JOSHUA 22:22; PSALMS 50; 132; ISAIAH 49:24-26;
MARK 14:60-62

# Names of God: *Redeemer*

For I know *that* my redeemer liveth,
    and *that* he shall stand at the latter *day* upon the earth:
and *though* after my skin *worms* destroy this *body*,
    yet in my flesh shall I see God:
whom I shall see for myself,
    and mine eyes shall behold, and not another;
    *though* my reins be consumed within me.

Who can understand *his* errors?
    Cleanse thou me from secret *faults*.
Keep back thy servant also from presumptuous *sins*;
    let them not have dominion over me:
then shall I be upright,
    and I shall be innocent from the great transgression.
Let the words of my mouth, and the meditation
      of my heart,
    be acceptable in thy sight,
    O LORD, my strength, and my redeemer.

Thus saith the LORD
    the King of Israel, and his redeemer the LORD of hosts;
I *am* the first, and I *am* the last;
    and beside me *there is* no God.
And who, as I, shall call, and shall declare it,
    and set it in order for me,
since I appointed the ancient people?
    And the things that are coming,
    and shall come, let them show unto them.
Fear ye not, neither be afraid:
    have not I told thee from that time, and have declared *it*?
Ye *are* even my witnesses. Is there a God beside me?
    Yea, *there is* no God; I know not *any*.

JOB 19:25-27; PSALM 19:12-14; ISAIAH 44:6-8

*Related texts:* ISAIAH 44:24-28; 54; LUKE 24:13-36; GALATIANS 4:4-5;
TITUS 2:11-14

# Names of God: *Refuge*

**THE ONE
MINUTE
BIBLE**

The LORD also will be a refuge for the oppressed,
   a refuge in times of trouble.
And they that know thy name will put their trust in thee:
   for thou, LORD, hast not forsaken them that seek thee.

O LORD, thou *art* my God;
   I will exalt thee, I will praise thy name;
for thou hast done wonderful *things*;
   *thy* counsels of old *are* faithfulness *and* truth.
For thou hast made of a city an heap;
   *of* a defenced city a ruin:
a palace of strangers to be no city;
   it shall never be built.
Therefore shall the strong people glorify thee,
   the city of the terrible nations shall fear thee.
For thou hast been a strength to the poor,
   a strength to the needy in his distress,
a refuge from the storm,
   a shadow from the heat.

O LORD, my strength, and my fortress,
   and my refuge in the day of affliction,
the Gentiles shall come unto thee
   from the ends of the earth, and shall say,
Surely our fathers have inherited lies, vanity,
   and *things* wherein *there is* no profit.
Shall a man make gods unto himself,
   and they *are* no gods?
Therefore, behold, I will this once cause them to know,
   I will cause them to know mine hand and my might;
and they shall know
   that my name *is* The LORD.

PSALMS 9:9-10; ISAIAH 25:1-4a; JEREMIAH 16:19-21

*Related texts:* 2 SAMUEL 22:3, 31; PSALMS 46; 59:16-17; 71; 91

# Names of God: *Rock*

Give ear, O ye heavens, and I will speak;
   and hear, O earth, the words of my mouth.
My doctrine shall drop as the rain,
   my speech shall distil as the dew,
as the small rain upon the tender herb,
   and as the showers upon the grass:
because I will publish the name of the LORD:
   ascribe ye greatness unto our God.
*He is* the Rock, his work *is* perfect:
   for all his ways *are* judgment:
a God of truth and without iniquity,
   just and right *is* he.

And Hannah prayed, and said,

   My heart rejoiceth in the LORD,
      mine horn is exalted in the LORD:
   my mouth is enlarged over mine enemies;
      because I rejoice in thy salvation.
   *There is* none holy as the LORD:
      for *there is* none beside thee:
      neither *is there* any rock like our God.

The LORD *is* my rock, and my fortress, and my deliverer;
   my God, my strength, in whom I will trust;
   my buckler, and the horn of my salvation, *and* my
      high tower.
I will call upon the LORD, *who is worthy* to be praised:
   so shall I be saved from mine enemies.

DEUTERONOMY 32:1-4; 1 SAMUEL 2:1-2; PSALM 18:2-3

---

*Related texts:* DEUTERONOMY 32; 2 SAMUEL 22; PSALM 62;
ROMANS 9:30-33; 1 CORINTHIANS 10:1-4; 1 PETER 2:1-8

# Names of God: *Savior*

**THE ONE
MINUTE
BIBLE**

Ye *are* my witnesses, saith the LORD,
    and my servant whom I have chosen:
that ye may know and believe me,
    and understand that I *am* he:
before me there was no God formed,
    neither shall there be after me.
I, *even* I, *am* the LORD;
    and beside me *there is* no saviour.
I have declared, and have saved, and I have showed,
    when *there was* no strange *god* among you:
therefore ye *are* my witnesses, saith the LORD,
        that I *am* God.

Verily thou *art* a God that hidest thyself,
    O God of Israel, the Saviour.
They shall be ashamed, and also confounded, all of them:
    they shall go to confusion together
        *that are* makers of idols.
*But* Israel shall be saved in the LORD
    with an everlasting salvation:
ye shall not be ashamed nor confounded
    world without end.

For the grace of God that bringeth salvation hath
appeared to all men, teaching us that, denying
ungodliness and worldly lusts, we should live soberly,
righteously, and godly, in this present world; looking for
that blessed hope, and the glorious appearing of the
great God and our Saviour Jesus Christ; who gave
himself for us, that he might redeem us from all
iniquity, and purify unto himself a peculiar people,
zealous of good works.

ISAIAH 43:10-13; 45:15-17; TITUS 2:11-14

***Related texts:*** PSALM 68:19-20; MICAH 7:1-7; HABAKKUK 3:16-19;
LUKE 1:47-55; 2:8-20; JOHN 4:40-42; ACTS 5:29-32

# Names of God: *Shepherd*

The L ORD *is* my shepherd; I shall not want.

Behold, the Lord G OD will come with strong *hand*,
  and his arm shall rule for him:
behold, his reward *is* with him,
  and his work before him.
He shall feed his flock like a shepherd:
  he shall gather the lambs with his arm,
and carry *them* in his bosom,
  *and* shall gently lead those that are with young.

Now the God of peace, that brought again from the
dead our Lord Jesus, that great shepherd of the sheep,
through the blood of the everlasting covenant, make you
perfect in every good work to do his will, working in you
that which is wellpleasing in his sight, through Jesus
Christ; to whom *be* glory for ever and ever. Amen.

Therefore are they before the throne of God,
  and serve him day and night in his temple:
and he that sitteth on the throne shall dwell among them.
They shall hunger no more,
  neither thirst any more;
neither shall the sun light on them,
  nor any heat.
For the Lamb which is in the midst of the throne shall
    feed them,
  and shall lead them unto living fountains of waters:
and God shall wipe away all tears from their eyes.

P SALM 23:1; I SAIAH 40:10-11; H EBREWS 13:20-21; R EVELATION 7:15-17

*Related texts:* P SALMS 23; 80:1-7; E ZEKIEL 34; M ICAH 5:2-5;
J OHN 10:11-15; 1 P ETER 2:21-25; 5:1-4

## The Fruit of the Spirit

**THE ONE
MINUTE
BIBLE**

Now the works of the flesh are manifest, which are *these*; adultery, fornication, uncleanness, lasciviousness, idolatry, witchcraft, hatred, variance, emulations, wrath, strife, seditions, heresies, envyings, murders, drunkenness, revellings, and such like: of the which I tell you before, as I have also told *you* in time past, that they which do such things shall not inherit the kingdom of God.

But the fruit of the Spirit is love, joy, peace, longsuffering, gentleness, goodness, faith, meekness, temperance: against such there is no law.

For ye were sometimes darkness, but now *are ye* light in the Lord: walk as children of light: (for the fruit of the Spirit *is* in all goodness and righteousness and truth;) proving what is acceptable unto the Lord. And have no fellowship with the unfruitful works of darkness, but rather reprove *them*.

For a good tree bringeth not forth corrupt fruit; neither doth a corrupt tree bring forth good fruit. For every tree is known by his own fruit. For of thorns men do not gather figs, nor of a bramble bush gather they grapes. A good man out of the good treasure of his heart bringeth forth that which is good; and an evil man out of the evil treasure of his heart bringeth forth that which is evil: for of the abundance of the heart his mouth speaketh.

GALATIANS 5:19-23; EPHESIANS 5:8-11; LUKE 6:43-45

*Related texts:* PSALMS 1; 112; ISAIAH 27:2-3; JOHN 15:1-16; ROMANS 7:1-6

# The Fruit of the Spirit: *Love*

And Jesus answered him, The first of all the commandments *is*, Hear, O Israel; The Lord our God is one Lord: and thou shalt love the Lord thy God with all thy heart, and with all thy soul, and with all thy mind, and with all thy strength: this *is* the first commandment. And the second *is* like, *namely* this, Thou shalt love thy neighbour as thyself. There is none other commandment greater than these.

A new commandment I give unto you, That ye love one another; as I have loved you, that ye also love one another. By this shall all *men* know that ye are my disciples, if ye have love one to another.

Ye have heard that it hath been said, Thou shalt love thy neighbour, and hate thine enemy. But I say unto you, Love your enemies, bless them that curse you, do good to them that hate you, and pray for them which despitefully use you, and persecute you; that ye may be the children of your Father which is in heaven: for he maketh his sun to rise on the evil and on the good, and sendeth rain on the just and on the unjust. For if ye love them which love you, what reward have ye? Do not even the publicans the same?

Put on therefore, as the elect of God, holy and beloved, bowels of mercies, kindness, humbleness of mind, meekness, longsuffering; forbearing one another, and forgiving one another, if any man have a quarrel against any: even as Christ forgave you, so also *do* ye. And above all these things *put on* charity, which is the bond of perfectness.

MARK 12:29-31; JOHN 13:34-35; MATTHEW 5:43-46; COLOSSIANS 3:12-14

*Related texts:* DEUTERONOMY 6:4-6; PSALM 18:1; JOHN 14-15; 21:15-17; 1 CORINTHIANS 13; 1 JOHN 4:7-21; 1 PETER 4:7-8

## *God Is Love*

**THE ONE
MINUTE
BIBLE**

He loveth righteousness and judgment:
  the earth is full of the goodness of the LORD.

The LORD hath appeared of old unto me, *saying,*

Yea, I have loved thee with an everlasting love:
    therefore with lovingkindness have I drawn thee.
Again I will build thee,
    and thou shalt be built, O virgin of Israel:
thou shalt again be adorned with thy tabrets,
    and shalt go forth in the dances of them that make
      merry.

For God so loved the world, that he gave his only
begotten Son, that whosoever believeth in him should
not perish, but have everlasting life. For God sent not
his Son into the world to condemn the world; but that
the world through him might be saved.

But God commendeth his love toward us, in that,
while we were yet sinners, Christ died for us.

For I am persuaded, that neither death, nor life, nor
angels, nor principalities, nor powers, nor things
present, nor things to come, nor height, nor depth, nor
any other creature, shall be able to separate us from the
love of God, which is in Christ Jesus our Lord.

God is love; and he that dwelleth in love dwelleth in
God, and God in him.

PSALM 33:5; JEREMIAH 31:3-4; JOHN 3:16-17; ROMANS 5:8; 8:38-39;
1 JOHN 4:16b

*Related texts:* PSALM 136; ISAIAH 63:7; JEREMIAH 9:23-24;
ZEPHANIAH 3:16-17; TITUS 3:3-5a; 1 JOHN 4:7-21

# The Fruit of the Spirit: *Joy*

Rejoice in the LORD, O ye righteous:
  *for* praise is comely for the upright.
Praise the LORD with harp:
  sing unto him with the psaltery *and* an instrument of
    ten strings.
Sing unto him a new song;
  play skilfully with a loud noise.
For the word of the LORD *is* right;
  and all his works *are done* in truth.

When it goeth well with the righteous, the city rejoiceth:
  and when the wicked perish, *there is* shouting.

Although the fig tree shall not blossom,
  neither *shall* fruit *be* in the vines;
the labour of the olive shall fail,
  and the fields shall yield no meat;
the flock shall be cut off from the fold,
  and *there shall be* no herd in the stalls:
yet I will rejoice in the LORD,
  I will joy in the God of my salvation.

Now the God of hope fill you with all joy and peace in
believing, that ye may abound in hope, through the
power of the Holy Ghost.

Rejoice in the Lord alway: *and* again I say, Rejoice.

Beloved, think it not strange concerning the fiery trial
which is to try you, as though some strange thing
happened unto you: but rejoice, inasmuch as ye are
partakers of Christ's sufferings; that, when his glory
shall be revealed, ye may be glad also with exceeding joy.

PSALM 33:1-4; PROVERBS 11:10; HABAKKUK 3:17-18; ROMANS 15:13;
PHILIPPIANS 4:4; 1 PETER 4:12-13

*Related texts:* NEHEMIAH 8:1-12; PSALMS 28:6-9; 30:4-5; ISAIAH 61

## God Is Joyful

**THE ONE
MINUTE
BIBLE**

The glory of the Lord shall endure for ever:
    the Lord shall rejoice in his works.
He looketh on the earth, and it trembleth:
    he toucheth the hills, and they smoke.

I will sing unto the Lord as long as I live:
    I will sing praise to my God while I have my being.
My meditation of him shall be sweet:
    I will be glad in the Lord.

In that day it shall be said to Jerusalem, Fear thou not:
    *and to* Zion, Let not thine hands be slack.
The Lord thy God in the midst of thee *is* mighty;
    he will save,
he will rejoice over thee with joy;
    he will rest in his love,
    he will joy over thee with singing.

Wherefore seeing we also are compassed about with so great a cloud of witnesses, let us lay aside every weight, and the sin which doth so easily beset *us*, and let us run with patience the race that is set before us, looking unto Jesus the author and finisher of *our* faith; who for the joy that was set before him endured the cross, despising the shame, and is set down at the right hand of the throne of God. For consider him that endured such contradiction of sinners against himself, lest ye be wearied and faint in your minds.

Psalm 104:31-34; Zephaniah 3:16-17; Hebrews 12:1-3

***Related texts:*** 1 Chronicles 16:23-33; Nehemiah 8:1-12; Psalm 21:1-7; Isaiah 62:4-7

# The Fruit of the Spirit: *Peace*

The LORD bless thee,
  and keep thee:
the LORD make his face shine upon thee,
  and be gracious unto thee:
the LORD lift up his countenance upon thee,
  and give thee peace.

Great peace have they which love thy law:
  and nothing shall offend them.

Thou wilt keep *him* in perfect peace,
  *whose* mind *is* stayed *on* thee:
  because he trusteth in thee.
Trust ye in the LORD for ever:
  for in the LORD JEHOVAH *is* everlasting strength.

Peace I leave with you, my peace I give unto you: not
as the world giveth, give I unto you. Let not your heart
be troubled, neither let it be afraid.

Be careful for nothing; but in every thing by prayer
and supplication with thanksgiving let your requests be
made known unto God. And the peace of God, which
passeth all understanding, shall keep your hearts and
minds through Christ Jesus.

And let the peace of God rule in your hearts, to the
which also ye are called in one body; and be ye thankful.

NUMBERS 6:24-26; PSALM 119:165; ISAIAH 26:3-4; JOHN 14:27;
PHILIPPIANS 4:6-7; COLOSSIANS 3:15

*Related texts:* PROVERBS 12:20; ISAIAH 32:17; 57:21; MICAH 4:1-5;
LUKE 2:13-14; ROMANS 8:1-6

## *God Is Peaceful*

**THE ONE
MINUTE
BIBLE**

The LORD will give strength unto his people;
the LORD will bless his people with peace.

For unto us a child is born,
unto us a son is given:
and the government shall be upon his shoulder:
and his name shall be called
Wonderful, Counsellor, The mighty God,
The everlasting Father, The Prince of Peace.
Of the increase of *his* government and peace
*there shall be* no end,
upon the throne of David,
and upon his kingdom,
to order it, and to establish it
with judgment and with justice
from henceforth even for ever.
The zeal of the LORD of hosts will perform this.

Therefore being justified by faith, we have peace with God through our Lord Jesus Christ: by whom also we have access by faith into this grace wherein we stand, and rejoice in hope of the glory of God.

And the very God of peace sanctify you wholly; and *I pray God* your whole spirit and soul and body be preserved blameless unto the coming of our Lord Jesus Christ.

Now the Lord of peace himself give you peace always by all means. The Lord *be* with you all.

PSALM 29:11; ISAIAH 9:6-7; ROMANS 5:1-2; 1 THESSALONIANS 5:23;
2 THESSALONIANS 3:16

***Related texts:*** ECCLESIASTES 3:1-8; ROMANS 15:33; 16:20;
2 CORINTHIANS 13:11; PHILIPPIANS 4:6-9

# The Fruit of the Spirit: *Longsuffering*

Rest in the LORD, and wait patiently for him:
    fret not thyself because of him who prospereth in his
        way,
    because of the man who bringeth wicked devices to
        pass.
Cease from anger, and forsake wrath:
    fret not thyself in any wise to do evil.
For evildoers shall be cut off:
    but those that wait upon the LORD,
        they shall inherit the earth.

I waited patiently for the LORD;
    and he inclined unto me, and heard my cry.
He brought me up also out of an horrible pit,
    out of the miry clay,
and set my feet upon a rock,
    *and* established my goings.
And he hath put a new song in my mouth,
    *even* praise unto our God:
many shall see *it*, and fear,
    and shall trust in the LORD.

*He that is* slow to wrath *is* of great understanding:
    but *he that is* hasty of spirit exalteth folly.

Charity suffereth long, *and* is kind; charity envieth
not; charity vaunteth not itself, is not puffed up.

Be patient therefore, brethren, unto the coming of
the Lord. Behold, the husbandman waiteth for the
precious fruit of the earth, and hath long patience for it,
until he receive the early and latter rain. Be ye also
patient; stablish your hearts: for the coming of the Lord
draweth nigh.

PSALMS 37:7-9; 40:1-3; PROVERBS 14:29; 1 CORINTHIANS 13:4; JAMES 5:7-8

*Related texts:* PROVERBS 15:18; 16:32; 19:11; 25:15; ECCLESIASTES 7:8;
ROMANS 12:9-12

## God Is Longsuffering

**THE ONE
MINUTE
BIBLE**

This *is* a faithful saying, and worthy of all acceptation, that Christ Jesus came into the world to save sinners; of whom I am chief. Howbeit for this cause I obtained mercy, that in me first Jesus Christ might show forth all longsuffering, for a pattern to them which should hereafter believe on him to life everlasting.

The Lord is not slack concerning his promise, as some men count slackness; but is longsuffering to us-ward, not willing that any should perish, but that all should come to repentance.

But the day of the Lord will come as a thief in the night; in the which the heavens shall pass away with a great noise, and the elements shall melt with fervent heat, the earth also and the works that are therein shall be burned up.

*Seeing* then *that* all these things shall be dissolved, what manner *of persons* ought ye to be in *all* holy conversation and godliness, looking for and hasting unto the coming of the day of God, wherein the heavens being on fire shall be dissolved, and the elements shall melt with fervent heat? Nevertheless we, according to his promise, look for new heavens and a new earth, wherein dwelleth righteousness.

Wherefore, beloved, seeing that ye look for such things, be diligent that ye may be found of him in peace, without spot, and blameless. And account *that* the longsuffering of our Lord *is* salvation; even as our beloved brother Paul also according to the wisdom given unto him hath written unto you.

1 TIMOTHY 1:15-16; 2 PETER 3:9-15

*Related texts:* ISAIAH 7:13; 65:17-25; ROMANS 2:1-4; 3:21-28; 1 PETER 3:18-20; REVELATION 21:1-8

# The Fruit of the Spirit: *Gentleness*

Flee also youthful lusts: but follow righteousness, faith, charity, peace, with them that call on the Lord out of a pure heart. But foolish and unlearned questions avoid, knowing that they do gender strifes. And the servant of the Lord must not strive; but be gentle unto all *men*, apt to teach, patient, in meekness instructing those that oppose themselves; if God peradventure will give them repentance to the acknowledging of the truth; and *that* they may recover themselves out of the snare of the devil, who are taken captive by him at his will.

**THE ONE MINUTE BIBLE**

Who *is* a wise man and endued with knowledge among you? Let him show out of a good conversation his works with meekness of wisdom. But if ye have bitter envying and strife in your hearts, glory not, and lie not against the truth. This wisdom descendeth not from above, but *is* earthly, sensual, devilish. For where envying and strife *is*, there *is* confusion and every evil work.

But the wisdom that is from above is first pure, then peaceable, gentle, *and* easy to be entreated, full of mercy and good fruits, without partiality, and without hypocrisy. And the fruit of righteousness is sown in peace of them that make peace.

2 TIMOTHY 2:22-26; JAMES 3:13-18

---

***Related texts:*** RUTH 1:1–3:10; PROVERBS 11:16-17; 14:21, 31; 1 THESSALONIANS 2:1-8; 5:15; COLOSSIANS 3:12-14

## God Is Gentle

**THE ONE**
**MINUTE**
**BIBLE**

*As for* God, his way *is* perfect;
    the word of the LORD *is* tried:
he *is* a buckler
    to all them that trust in him.
For who is God, save the LORD?
    And who *is* a rock, save our God?
God *is* my strength and power:
    *and* he maketh my way perfect.
He maketh my feet like hinds' *feet*:
    and setteth me upon my high places.
He teacheth my hands to war;
    so that a bow of steel is broken by mine arms.
Thou hast also given me the shield of thy salvation:
    and thy gentleness hath made me great.
Thou hast enlarged my steps under me;
    so that my feet did not slip.

Behold, the Lord GOD will come with strong *hand*,
    and his arm shall rule for him:
behold, his reward *is* with him,
    and his work before him.
He shall feed his flock like a shepherd:
    he shall gather the lambs with his arm,
and carry *them* in his bosom,
    *and* shall gently lead those that are with young.

2 SAMUEL 22:31-37; ISAIAH 40:10-11

***Related texts:*** PSALM 18:30-36; ISAIAH 53:1-9; 2 CORINTHIANS 10:1

# The Fruit of the Spirit: *Goodness*

A good *man* obtaineth favour of the LORD:
but a man of wicked devices will he condemn.

I know that *there is* no good in them, but for *a man* to
rejoice, and to do good in his life. And also that every
man should eat and drink, and enjoy the good of all his
labour, it *is* the gift of God.

For a good tree bringeth not forth corrupt fruit;
neither doth a corrupt tree bring forth good fruit. For
every tree is known by his own fruit. For of thorns men
do not gather figs, nor of a bramble bush gather they
grapes. A good man out of the good treasure of his heart
bringeth forth that which is good; and an evil man out
of the evil treasure of his heart bringeth forth that
which is evil: for of the abundance of the heart his
mouth speaketh.

And let us not be weary in well doing: for in due
season we shall reap, if we faint not. As we have
therefore opportunity, let us do good unto all *men*,
especially unto them who are of the household of faith.

For we are his workmanship, created in Christ Jesus
unto good works, which God hath before ordained that
we should walk in them.

Beloved, follow not that which is evil, but that which
is good. He that doeth good is of God: but he that doeth
evil hath not seen God.

PROVERBS 12:2; ECCLESIASTES 3:12-13; LUKE 6:43-45; GALATIANS 6:9-10;
EPHESIANS 2:10; 3 JOHN 11

*Related texts:* PSALM 34:8-14; PROVERBS 3:27; 11:27; 1 PETER 2:12-15

## *God Is Good*

**THE ONE
MINUTE
BIBLE**

O taste and see that the LORD *is* good:
    blessed *is* the man *that* trusteth in him.

I will praise thee for ever, because thou hast done *it*:
    and I will wait on thy name;
    for *it is* good before thy saints.

Truly God *is* good to Israel,
    *even* to such as are of a clean heart.

For the LORD *is* good; his mercy *is* everlasting;
    and his truth *endureth* to all generations.

O give thanks unto the LORD; for *he is* good:
    for his mercy *endureth* for ever.

Thou *art* good, and doest good;
    teach me thy statutes.

Praise the LORD; for the LORD *is* good:
    sing praises unto his name; for *it is* pleasant.

The LORD *is* good to all:
    and his tender mercies *are* over all his works.

PSALMS 34:8; 52:9; 73:1; 100:5; 118:29; 119:68; 135:3; 145:9

***Related texts:*** 2 CHRONICLES 6:41; PSALM 84:9-12; MARK 10:17-18;
ROMANS 8:18-28; 3 JOHN 11

# The Fruit of the Spirit: *Faithfulness*

O love the LORD, all ye his saints:
   *for* the LORD preserveth the faithful,
   and plentifully rewardeth the proud doer.
Be of good courage, and he shall strengthen your heart,
   all ye that hope in the LORD.

Most men will proclaim every one his own goodness:
   but a faithful man who can find?
The just *man* walketh in his integrity:
   his children *are* blessed after him.

Faithful *are* the wounds of a friend;
   but the kisses of an enemy *are* deceitful.

A faithful man shall abound with blessings:
   but he that maketh haste to be rich shall not be
      innocent.

*It is* a faithful saying:

   For if we be dead with *him*,
      we shall also live with *him*:
   if we suffer,
      we shall also reign with *him*:
   if we deny *him*,
      he also will deny us:
   if we believe not,
      *yet* he abideth faithful:
      he cannot deny himself.

PSALM 31:23-24; PROVERBS 20:6-7; 27:6; 2 TIMOTHY 2:11-13

**THE ONE MINUTE BIBLE**

---

*Related texts:* PSALM 101; PROVERBS 3:1-4; MATTHEW 24:45-51; 25:14-30

## God Is Faithful

**THE ONE**
**M I N U T E**
**B I B L E**

Know therefore that the LORD thy God, he *is* God, the faithful God, which keepeth covenant and mercy with them that love him and keep his commandments to a thousand generations; and repayeth them that hate him to their face, to destroy them: he will not be slack to him that hateth him, he will repay him to his face.

I will sing of the mercies of the LORD for ever:
    with my mouth will I make known thy faithfulness to
        all generations.
For I have said, Mercy shall be built up for ever:
    thy faithfulness shalt thou establish in the very
        heavens.

This I recall to my mind,
    therefore have I hope.
*It is of* the LORD's mercies that we are not consumed,
    because his compassions fail not.
*They are* new every morning:
    great *is* thy faithfulness.

Wherefore let him that thinketh he standeth take heed lest he fall. There hath no temptation taken you but such as is common to man: but God *is* faithful, who will not suffer you to be tempted above that ye are able; but will with the temptation also make a way to escape, that ye may be able to bear *it*.

If we confess our sins, he is faithful and just to forgive us *our* sins, and to cleanse us from all unrighteousness.

DEUTERONOMY 7:9-10; PSALM 89:1-2; LAMENTATIONS 3:21-23;
1 CORINTHIANS 10:12-13; 1 JOHN 1:9

***Related texts:*** DEUTERONOMY 31:30–32:4; 2 THESSALONIANS 3:3;
2 TIMOTHY 2:11-13; REVELATION 19:11-16

# The Fruit of the Spirit: *Meekness*

Good and upright *is* the LORD:
  therefore will he teach sinners in the way.
The meek will he guide in judgment:
  and the meek will he teach his way.

A soft answer turneth away wrath:
  but grievous words stir up anger.

Seek ye the LORD, all ye meek of the earth,
  which have wrought his judgment;
seek righteousness, seek meekness:
  it may be ye shall be hid
  in the day of the LORD's anger.

I therefore, the prisoner of the Lord, beseech you that
ye walk worthy of the vocation wherewith ye are called,
with all lowliness and meekness, with longsuffering,
forbearing one another in love; endeavouring to keep
the unity of the Spirit in the bond of peace.

And who *is* he that will harm you, if ye be followers of
that which is good? But and if ye suffer for
righteousness' sake, happy *are ye*: and be not afraid of
their terror, neither be troubled; but sanctify the Lord
God in your hearts: and *be* ready always to *give* an
answer to every man that asketh you a reason of the
hope that is in you with meekness and fear: having a
good conscience; that, whereas they speak evil of you,
as of evildoers, they may be ashamed that falsely accuse
your good conversation in Christ.

PSALM 25:8-9; PROVERBS 15:1; ZEPHANIAH 2:3; EPHESIANS 4:1-3;
1 PETER 3:13-16

*Related texts:* ISAIAH 8:12-15; 1 TIMOTHY 6:3-11; 2 TIMOTHY 2:24-25;
1 PETER 3:1-6

## *God Is Meek*

**THE ONE
MINUTE
BIBLE**

My heart is inditing a good matter:
    I speak of the things which I have made touching the
        king:
    my tongue *is* the pen of a ready writer.

Thou art fairer than the children of men:
    grace is poured into thy lips:
    therefore God hath blessed thee for ever.
Gird thy sword upon *thy* thigh, O *most* mighty,
    with thy glory and thy majesty.
And in thy majesty ride prosperously
    because of truth and meekness *and* righteousness;
    and thy right hand shall teach thee terrible things.

Rejoice greatly, O daughter of Zion;
    shout, O daughter of Jerusalem:
behold, thy King cometh unto thee:
    he *is* just, and having salvation;
    lowly, and riding upon an ass,
    and upon a colt the foal of an ass.

[Jesus said,] Come unto me, all *ye* that labour and
are heavy laden, and I will give you rest. Take my yoke
upon you, and learn of me; for I am meek and lowly in
heart: and ye shall find rest unto your souls. For my yoke
*is* easy, and my burden is light.

PSALM 45:1-4; ZECHARIAH 9:9; MATTHEW 11:28-30

---

***Related texts:*** 1 KINGS 19:9-12; 2 CORINTHIANS 10:1; MATTHEW 21:1-12

# The Fruit of the Spirit: *Temperance*

He that *hath* no rule over his own spirit
 *is like* a city *that is* broken down, and without walls.

But speak thou the things which become sound
doctrine: that the aged men be sober, grave, temperate,
sound in faith, in charity, in patience.

The aged women likewise, that *they be* in behaviour
as becometh holiness, not false accusers, not given to
much wine, teachers of good things; that they may
teach the young women to be sober, to love their
husbands, to love their children, *to be* discreet, chaste,
keepers at home, good, obedient to their own husbands,
that the word of God be not blasphemed.

Young men likewise exhort to be sober minded.

And beside this, giving all diligence, add to your faith
virtue; and to virtue knowledge; and to knowledge
temperance; and to temperance patience; and to
patience godliness; and to godliness brotherly kindness;
and to brotherly kindness charity. For if these things be
in you, and abound, they make *you that ye shall* neither
*be* barren nor unfruitful in the knowledge of our Lord
Jesus Christ.

PROVERBS 25:28; TITUS 2:1-6; 2 PETER 1:5-8

**THE ONE
MINUTE
BIBLE**

---

*Related texts:* PROVERBS 1:1-7; 23:23; 1 CORINTHIANS 9:24-27;
1 THESSALONIANS 5:5-10; 2 TIMOTHY 1:7; TITUS 2:11-14; 1 PETER 4:7

## *God Is Slow to Anger*

**THE ONE
MINUTE
BIBLE**

The LORD *is* merciful and gracious,
  slow to anger, and plenteous in mercy.
He will not always chide:
  neither will he keep *his anger* for ever.
He hath not dealt with us after our sins;
  nor rewarded us according to our iniquities.
For as the heaven is high above the earth,
  *so* great is his mercy toward them that fear him.
As far as the east is from the west,
  *so* far hath he removed our transgressions from us.

The LORD *is* gracious, and full of compassion;
  slow to anger, and of great mercy.
The LORD *is* good to all:
  and his tender mercies *are* over all his works.

God *is* jealous, and the LORD revengeth;
  the LORD revengeth, and *is* furious;
the LORD will take vengeance on his adversaries,
  and he reserveth *wrath* for his enemies.
The LORD *is* slow to anger, and great in power,
  and will not at all acquit *the wicked*:
the LORD *hath* his way in the whirlwind and in the
      storm,
  and the clouds *are* the dust of his feet.

PSALMS 103:8-12; 145:8-9; NAHUM 1:2-3

---

***Related texts:*** EXODUS 34:5-7; PSALM 86:15-17; JOEL 2:12-14;
JONAH 3–4; 2 PETER 3:8-15

## God Sends Moses to Egypt

**THE ONE
MINUTE
BIBLE**

And God said moreover unto Moses, Thus shalt thou say unto the children of Israel, The LORD God of your fathers, the God of Abraham, the God of Isaac, and the God of Jacob, hath sent me unto you: this *is* my name for ever, and this *is* my memorial unto all generations.

Go, and gather the elders of Israel together, and say unto them, The LORD God of your fathers, the God of Abraham, of Isaac, and of Jacob, appeared unto me, saying, I have surely visited you, and *seen* that which is done to you in Egypt: and I have said, I will bring you up out of the affliction of Egypt unto the land of the Canaanites, and the Hittites, and the Amorites, and the Perizzites, and the Hivites, and the Jebusites, unto a land flowing with milk and honey.

And they shall hearken to thy voice: and thou shalt come, thou and the elders of Israel, unto the king of Egypt, and ye shall say unto him, The LORD God of the Hebrews hath met with us: and now let us go, we beseech thee, three days' journey into the wilderness, that we may sacrifice to the LORD our God. And I am sure that the king of Egypt will not let you go, no, not by a mighty hand. And I will stretch out my hand, and smite Egypt with all my wonders which I will do in the midst thereof: and after that he will let you go.

And I will give this people favour in the sight of the Egyptians: and it shall come to pass, that, when ye go, ye shall not go empty: but every woman shall borrow of her neighbour, and of her that sojourneth in her house, jewels of silver, and jewels of gold, and raiment: and ye shall put *them* upon your sons, and upon your daughters; and ye shall spoil the Egyptians.

EXODUS 3:15-22

*Related texts:* GENESIS 13:12-17; 15:12-16; HAGGAI 2:4-8; ACTS 7:30-36

# Moses Confronts Pharaoh

**THE ONE
MINUTE
BIBLE**

And the LORD said unto Moses, When thou goest to return into Egypt, see that thou do all those wonders before Pharaoh, which I have put in thine hand: but I will harden his heart, that he shall not let the people go. And thou shalt say unto Pharaoh, Thus saith the LORD, Israel *is* my son, *even* my firstborn: and I say unto thee, Let my son go, that he may serve me: and if thou refuse to let him go, behold, I will slay thy son, *even* thy firstborn.

And the LORD said to Aaron, Go into the wilderness to meet Moses. And he went, and met him in the mount of God, and kissed him. And Moses told Aaron all the words of the LORD who had sent him, and all the signs which he had commanded him.

And Moses and Aaron went and gathered together all the elders of the children of Israel: and Aaron spake all the words which the LORD had spoken unto Moses, and did the signs in the sight of the people. And the people believed: and when they heard that the LORD had visited the children of Israel, and that he had looked upon their affliction, then they bowed their heads and worshipped.

And afterward Moses and Aaron went in, and told Pharaoh, Thus saith the LORD God of Israel, Let my people go, that they may hold a feast unto me in the wilderness.

And Pharaoh said, Who *is* the LORD, that I should obey his voice to let Israel go? I know not the LORD, neither will I let Israel go.

EXODUS 4:21-23, 27-31; 5:1-2

*Related texts:* EXODUS 1:8-13; 9:13-16; PROVERBS 29:1-2; JOHN 10:33-38

## *God Hardens Pharaoh's Heart*

And the LORD said unto Moses, See, I have made thee a god to Pharaoh: and Aaron thy brother shall be thy prophet. Thou shalt speak all that I command thee: and Aaron thy brother shall speak unto Pharaoh, that he send the children of Israel out of his land. And I will harden Pharaoh's heart, and multiply my signs and my wonders in the land of Egypt. But Pharaoh shall not hearken unto you, that I may lay my hand upon Egypt, and bring forth mine armies, *and* my people the children of Israel, out of the land of Egypt by great judgments. And the Egyptians shall know that I *am* the LORD, when I stretch forth mine hand upon Egypt, and bring out the children of Israel from among them.

And the LORD spake unto Moses and unto Aaron, saying, When Pharaoh shall speak unto you, saying, Show a miracle for you: then thou shalt say unto Aaron, Take thy rod, and cast *it* before Pharaoh, *and* it shall become a serpent.

And Moses and Aaron went in unto Pharaoh, and they did so as the LORD had commanded: and Aaron cast down his rod before Pharaoh, and before his servants, and it became a serpent. Then Pharaoh also called the wise men and the sorcerers: now the magicians of Egypt, they also did in like manner with their enchantments. For they cast down every man his rod, and they became serpents: but Aaron's rod swallowed up their rods. And he hardened Pharaoh's heart, that he hearkened not unto them; as the LORD had said.

EXODUS 7:1-5, 8-13

**THE ONE MINUTE BIBLE**

*Related texts:* EXODUS 8:7, 18-19; ROMANS 9:14-21; 2 TIMOTHY 3:8-9

## The Plagues Against Egypt

**THE ONE
MINUTE
BIBLE**

Give ear, O my people, *to* my law:
   incline your ears to the words of my mouth.
I will open my mouth in a parable:
   I will utter dark sayings of old:
which we have heard and known,
   and our fathers have told us.
We will not hide *them* from their children,
   showing to the generation to come
the praises of the LORD, and his strength,
   and his wonderful works that he hath done.

How he had wrought his signs in Egypt,
   and his wonders in the field of Zoan:
and had turned their rivers into blood;
   and their floods, that they could not drink.
He sent divers sorts of flies among them,
      which devoured them;
   and frogs, which destroyed them.
He gave also their increase unto the caterpillar,
   and their labour unto the locust.
He destroyed their vines with hail,
   and their sycamore trees with frost.
He gave up their cattle also to the hail,
   and their flocks to hot thunderbolts.
He cast upon them the fierceness of his anger,
   wrath, and indignation, and trouble,
   by sending evil angels *among them.*
He made a way to his anger;
   he spared not their soul from death,
   but gave their life over to the pestilence;
and smote all the firstborn in Egypt;
   the chief of *their* strength in the tabernacles of Ham.

PSALM 78:1-4, 43-51

*Related texts:* EXODUS 7:15–10:29; DEUTERONOMY 4:32-38;
1 SAMUEL 4:2-8; ACTS 7:30-36

96

## God Kills the Firstborn in Egypt

And the LORD said unto Moses, Yet will I bring one plague *more* upon Pharaoh, and upon Egypt; afterwards he will let you go hence: when he shall let *you* go, he shall surely thrust you out hence altogether. Speak now in the ears of the people, and let every man borrow of his neighbour, and every woman of her neighbour, jewels of silver, and jewels of gold. And the LORD gave the people favour in the sight of the Egyptians. Moreover the man Moses *was* very great in the land of Egypt, in the sight of Pharaoh's servants, and in the sight of the people.

And Moses said, Thus saith the LORD, About midnight will I go out into the midst of Egypt: and all the firstborn in the land of Egypt shall die, from the firstborn of Pharaoh that sitteth upon his throne, even unto the firstborn of the maidservant that *is* behind the mill; and all the firstborn of beasts. And there shall be a great cry throughout all the land of Egypt, such as there was none like it, nor shall be like it any more. But against any of the children of Israel shall not a dog move his tongue, against man or beast: that ye may know how that the LORD doth put a difference between the Egyptians and Israel. And all these thy servants shall come down unto me, and bow down themselves unto me, saying, Get thee out, and all the people that follow thee: and after that I will go out. And he went out from Pharaoh in a great anger.

And the LORD said unto Moses, Pharaoh shall not hearken unto you; that my wonders may be multiplied in the land of Egypt. And Moses and Aaron did all these wonders before Pharaoh: and the LORD hardened Pharaoh's heart, so that he would not let the children of Israel go out of his land.

EXODUS 11:1-10

*Related texts:* EXODUS 4:22-23; PSALMS 105:23-38; 135:8-9; 136:10-12; ROMANS 9:14-21; HEBREWS 11:28

*I never omit to read it, and every
day with the same pleasure....
The soul can never go astray with
this book for its guide.*
**Napoleon Bonaparte (1769-1821)**
EMPEROR OF FRANCE

*It ain't those parts of the Bible
that I can't understand
that bother me, it is the parts
that I do understand.*
**Mark Twain (1835-1910)**
AMERICAN AUTHOR

*No sciences are better attested
than the religion of the Bible.*
**Sir Isaac Newton (1642-1727)**
ENGLISH SCIENTIST

## The First Passover

Then Moses called for all the elders of Israel, and said unto them, Draw out and take you a lamb according to your families, and kill the passover. And ye shall take a bunch of hyssop, and dip *it* in the blood that *is* in the basin, and strike the lintel and the two side posts with the blood that *is* in the basin; and none of you shall go out at the door of his house until the morning. For the LORD will pass through to smite the Egyptians; and when he seeth the blood upon the lintel, and on the two side posts, the LORD will pass over the door, and will not suffer the destroyer to come in unto your houses to smite *you*.

And ye shall observe this thing for an ordinance to thee and to thy sons for ever. And it shall come to pass, when ye be come to the land which the LORD will give you, according as he hath promised, that ye shall keep this service. And it shall come to pass, when your children shall say unto you, What mean ye by this service? That ye shall say, It *is* the sacrifice of the LORD's passover, who passed over the houses of the children of Israel in Egypt, when he smote the Egyptians, and delivered our houses. And the people bowed the head and worshipped. And the children of Israel went away, and did as the LORD had commanded Moses and Aaron, so did they.

EXODUS 12:21-28

*Related texts:* NUMBERS 9:1-14; DEUTERONOMY 16:1-8; 2 CHRONICLES 30; 1 CORINTHIANS 5:6-8

## The Prophecy of the Suffering Servant

**THE ONE
MINUTE
BIBLE**

Behold, my servant shall deal prudently,
    he shall be exalted and extolled, and be very high.

He is despised and rejected of men;
    a man of sorrows, and acquainted with grief:
and we hid as it were *our* faces from him;
    he was despised, and we esteemed him not.

Surely he hath borne our griefs,
    and carried our sorrows:
yet we did esteem him stricken,
    smitten of God, and afflicted.
But he *was* wounded for our transgressions,
    *he was* bruised for our iniquities:
the chastisement of our peace *was* upon him;
    and with his stripes we are healed.
All we like sheep have gone astray;
    we have turned every one to his own way;
and the LORD hath laid on him
    the iniquity of us all.

He was oppressed, and he was afflicted,
    yet he opened not his mouth:
he is brought as a lamb to the slaughter,
    and as a sheep before her shearers is dumb,
    so he openeth not his mouth.

Yet it pleased the LORD to bruise him; he hath put *him*
    to grief:
    when thou shalt make his soul an offering for sin,
he shall see *his* seed, he shall prolong *his* days,
    and the pleasure of the LORD shall prosper in his hand.

ISAIAH 52:13; 53:3-7, 10

*Related texts:* PSALM 22; MARK 10:45; ACTS 8:26-39; 1 PETER 2:21-25

## *Jesus: The Lamb of God*

THE ONE
MINUTE
BIBLE

The next day John seeth Jesus coming unto him, and saith, Behold the Lamb of God, which taketh away the sin of the world. This is he of whom I said, After me cometh a man which is preferred before me: for he was before me. And I knew him not: but that he should be made manifest to Israel, therefore am I come baptizing with water.

And John bare record, saying, I saw the Spirit descending from heaven like a dove, and it abode upon him. And I knew him not: but he that sent me to baptize with water, the same said unto me, Upon whom thou shalt see the Spirit descending, and remaining on him, the same is he which baptizeth with the Holy Ghost. And I saw, and bare record that this is the Son of God.

And I beheld, and I heard the voice of many angels round about the throne and the beasts and the elders: and the number of them was ten thousand times ten thousand, and thousands of thousands; saying with a loud voice,

> Worthy is the Lamb that was slain
> to receive power, and riches, and wisdom,
> and strength, and honour, and glory, and blessing.

JOHN 1:29-34; REVELATION 5:11-12

*Related texts:* GENESIS 22:1-19; HEBREWS 9:11-28; 1 PETER 1:18-20; REVELATION 5–7; 21:9–22:4

103

## Jesus Predicts His Resurrection

**THE ONE
MINUTE
BIBLE**

Jesus called the disciples *to him*, and saith unto them, Ye know that they which are accounted to rule over the Gentiles exercise lordship over them; and their great ones exercise authority upon them. But so shall it not be among you: but whosoever will be great among you, shall be your minister: and whosoever of you will be the chiefest, shall be servant of all. For even the Son of man came not to be ministered unto, but to minister, and to give his life a ransom for many.

And it came to pass, as Jesus was alone praying, his disciples were with him: and he asked them, saying, Whom say the people that I am?

They answering said, John the Baptist; but some *say*, Elias; and others *say*, that one of the old prophets is risen again.

He said unto them, But whom say ye that I am?

Peter answering said, The Christ of God.

And he straitly charged them, and commanded *them* to tell no man that thing; saying, The Son of man must suffer many things, and be rejected of the elders and chief priests and scribes, and be slain, and be raised the third day.

MARK 10:42-45; LUKE 9:18-22

---

***Related texts:*** PSALM 16; ISAIAH 53; MATTHEW 12:38-41;
MARK 10:32-34; LUKE 24:13-32; ACTS 2:14-40

## *Jesus' Triumphal Entry*

And when they drew nigh unto Jerusalem, and were come to Bethphage, unto the mount of Olives, then sent Jesus two disciples, saying unto them, Go into the village over against you, and straightway ye shall find an ass tied, and a colt with her: loose *them*, and bring *them* unto me. And if any *man* say ought unto you, ye shall say, The Lord hath need of them; and straightway he will send them.

All this was done, that it might be fulfilled which was spoken by the prophet, saying,

Tell ye the daughter of Sion,
   Behold, thy King cometh unto thee,
meek, and sitting upon an ass,
   and a colt the foal of an ass.

And the disciples went, and did as Jesus commanded them, and brought the ass, and the colt, and put on them their clothes, and they set *him* thereon. And a very great multitude spread their garments in the way; others cut down branches from the trees, and strawed *them* in the way. And the multitudes that went before, and that followed, cried, saying,

Hosanna to the son of David:
Blessed *is* he that cometh in the name of the Lord;
Hosanna in the highest.

And when he was come into Jerusalem, all the city was moved, saying, Who is this?

And the multitude said, This is Jesus the prophet of Nazareth of Galilee.

MATTHEW 21:1-11

*Related texts:* PSALM 118; ZECHARIAH 9:9; MARK 11:1-11; LUKE 19:28-40; JOHN 12:12-16

## Jesus Cleanses the Temple

**THE ONE
MINUTE
BIBLE**

And when Jesus was come near, he beheld the city, and wept over it, saying, If thou hadst known, even thou, at least in this thy day, the things *which belong* unto thy peace! But now they are hid from thine eyes. For the days shall come upon thee, that thine enemies shall cast a trench about thee, and compass thee round, and keep thee in on every side, and shall lay thee even with the ground, and thy children within thee; and they shall not leave in thee one stone upon another; because thou knewest not the time of thy visitation.

And Jesus went into the temple of God, and cast out all them that sold and bought in the temple, and overthrew the tables of the moneychangers, and the seats of them that sold doves, and said unto them, It is written, My house shall be called the house of prayer; but ye have made it a den of thieves.

And the blind and the lame came to him in the temple; and he healed them. And when the chief priests and scribes saw the wonderful things that he did, and the children crying in the temple, and saying, Hosanna to the son of David; they were sore displeased, and said unto him, Hearest thou what these say?

And Jesus saith unto them, Yea; have ye never read,

Out of the mouth of babes and sucklings
    thou hast perfected praise?

LUKE 19:41-44; MATTHEW 21:12-16

---

*Related texts:* PSALM 8; ISAIAH 56; JEREMIAH 7:9-11; MARK 11:15-18; JOHN 2:13-17

## *Whose Son Is the Messiah?*

While the Pharisees were gathered together, Jesus asked them, saying, What think ye of Christ? Whose son is he?

They say unto him, *The son* of David.

He saith unto them, How then doth David in spirit call him Lord, saying,

The LORD said unto my Lord,
Sit thou on my right hand,
till I make thine enemies
thy footstool?

If David then call him Lord, how is he his son? And no man was able to answer him a word, neither durst any *man* from that day forth ask him any more *questions*.

And after six days Jesus taketh *with him* Peter, and James, and John, and leadeth them up into an high mountain apart by themselves: and he was transfigured before them.

And there was a cloud that overshadowed them: and a voice came out of the cloud, saying, This is my beloved Son: hear him.

For we have not followed cunningly devised fables, when we made known unto you the power and coming of our Lord Jesus Christ, but were eyewitnesses of his majesty. For he received from God the Father honour and glory, when there came such a voice to him from the excellent glory, This is my beloved Son, in whom I am well pleased.

MATTHEW 22:41-46; MARK 9:2, 7; 2 PETER 1:16-17

*Related texts:* PSALM 110; MATTHEW 27:45-54; MARK 1:9-11; LUKE 9:28-36; ACTS 2

# The Last Supper

**THE ONE MINUTE BIBLE**

Then came the day of unleavened bread, when the passover must be killed. And Jesus sent Peter and John, saying, Go and prepare us the passover, that we may eat.

And when the hour was come, he sat down, and the twelve apostles with him. And he said unto them, With desire I have desired to eat this passover with you before I suffer: for I say unto you, I will not any more eat thereof, until it be fulfilled in the kingdom of God.

And he took the cup, and gave thanks, and said, Take this, and divide *it* among yourselves: for I say unto you, I will not drink of the fruit of the vine, until the kingdom of God shall come.

And he took bread, and gave thanks, and brake *it*, and gave unto them, saying, This is my body which is given for you: this do in remembrance of me.

Likewise also the cup after supper, saying, This cup *is* the new testament in my blood, which is shed for you. But, behold, the hand of him that betrayeth me *is* with me on the table. And truly the Son of man goeth, as it was determined: but woe unto that man by whom he is betrayed!

LUKE 22:7-8, 14-22

*Related texts:* JEREMIAH 31:31-36; MATTHEW 26:17-30; MARK 14:12-26; REVELATION 19:4-9

## *Jesus Is Betrayed*

THE ONE
MINUTE
BIBLE

When Jesus had spoken these words, he went forth with his disciples over the brook Cedron, where was a garden, into the which he entered, and his disciples.

And Judas also, which betrayed him, knew the place: for Jesus ofttimes resorted thither with his disciples. Judas then, having received a band *of men* and officers from the chief priests and Pharisees, cometh thither with lanterns and torches and weapons.

Jesus therefore, knowing all things that should come upon him, went forth, and said unto them, Whom seek ye?

They answered him, Jesus of Nazareth.

Jesus saith unto them, I am *he*. And Judas also, which betrayed him, stood with them. As soon then as he had said unto them, I am *he*, they went backward, and fell to the ground.

Then asked he them again, Whom seek ye?

And they said, Jesus of Nazareth.

Jesus answered, I have told you that I am *he*: if therefore ye seek me, let these go their way: that the saying might be fulfilled, which he spake, Of them which thou gavest me have I lost none.

JOHN 18:1-9

***Related texts:*** GENESIS 37; MATTHEW 26:47-56; MARK 14:43-50; LUKE 22:47-54; JOHN 6:35-40; 17:1-12

## Jesus Is Condemned to Death

**THE ONE
MINUTE
BIBLE**

Now the chief priests, and elders, and all the council, sought false witness against Jesus, to put him to death; but found none: yea, though many false witnesses came, *yet* found they none.

At the last came two false witnesses, and said, This *fellow* said, I am able to destroy the temple of God, and to build it in three days.

And the high priest arose, and said unto him, Answerest thou nothing? What *is it which* these witness against thee? But Jesus held his peace.

And the high priest answered and said unto him, I adjure thee by the living God, that thou tell us whether thou be the Christ, the Son of God.

Jesus saith unto him, Thou hast said: nevertheless I say unto you, Hereafter shall ye see the Son of man sitting on the right hand of power, and coming in the clouds of heaven.

Then the high priest rent his clothes, saying, He hath spoken blasphemy; what further need have we of witnesses? Behold, now ye have heard his blasphemy. What think ye?

They answered and said, He is guilty of death.

Then did they spit in his face, and buffeted him; and others smote *him* with the palms of their hands, saying, Prophesy unto us, thou Christ, Who is he that smote thee?

MATTHEW 26:59-68

***Related texts:*** LEVITICUS 24:13-16; DANIEL 7:13-14; MARK 14:55-65; LUKE 23:63-71

## *Jesus Is Crucified*

THE ONE
MINUTE
BIBLE

And they bring him unto the place Golgotha, which is, being interpreted, The place of a skull. And they gave him to drink wine mingled with myrrh: but he received *it* not. And when they had crucified him, they parted his garments, casting lots upon them, what every man should take.

And it was the third hour, and they crucified him. And the superscription of his accusation was written over, THE KING OF THE JEWS. And with him they crucify two thieves; the one on his right hand, and the other on his left. And the scripture was fulfilled, which saith, And he was numbered with the transgressors. And they that passed by railed on him, wagging their heads, and saying, Ah, thou that destroyest the temple, and buildest *it* in three days, save thyself, and come down from the cross.

Likewise also the chief priests mocking said among themselves with the scribes, He saved others; himself he cannot save. Let Christ the King of Israel descend now from the cross, that we may see and believe. And they that were crucified with him reviled him.

And Jesus cried with a loud voice, and gave up the ghost.

And the veil of the temple was rent in twain from the top to the bottom. And when the centurion, which stood over against him, saw that he so cried out, and gave up the ghost, he said, Truly this man was the Son of God.

MARK 15:22-32, 37-39

---

***Related texts:*** PSALM 22; ISAIAH 53; MATTHEW 27:33-56; LUKE 23:26-48; JOHN 3:13-16; 19:16-37

## *Alive Again!*

**THE ONE
MINUTE
BIBLE**

In the end of the sabbath, as it began to dawn toward the first *day* of the week, came Mary Magdalene and the other Mary to see the sepulchre.

And, behold, there was a great earthquake: for the angel of the Lord descended from heaven, and came and rolled back the stone from the door, and sat upon it. His countenance was like lightning, and his raiment white as snow: and for fear of him the keepers did shake, and became as dead *men*.

And the angel answered and said unto the women, Fear not ye: for I know that ye seek Jesus, which was crucified. He is not here: for he is risen, as he said. Come, see the place where the Lord lay. And go quickly, and tell his disciples that he is risen from the dead; and, behold, he goeth before you into Galilee; there shall ye see him: lo, I have told you.

And they departed quickly from the sepulchre with fear and great joy; and did run to bring his disciples word. And as they went to tell his disciples, behold, Jesus met them, saying, All hail. And they came and held him by the feet, and worshipped him. Then said Jesus unto them, Be not afraid: go tell my brethren that they go into Galilee, and there shall they see me.

MATTHEW 28:1-10

*Related texts:* PSALM 16:8-11; MARK 16:1-8; LUKE 24:1-10; JOHN 20:1-18; 1 CORINTHIANS 15

# The All-Importance of the Resurrection

Now if Christ be preached that he rose from the dead, how say some among you that there is no resurrection of the dead? But if there be no resurrection of the dead, then is Christ not risen: and if Christ be not risen, then *is* our preaching vain, and your faith *is* also vain. Yea, and we are found false witnesses of God; because we have testified of God that he raised up Christ: whom he raised not up, if so be that the dead rise not. For if the dead rise not, then is not Christ raised: and if Christ be not raised, your faith *is* vain; ye are yet in your sins. Then they also which are fallen asleep in Christ are perished. If in this life only we have hope in Christ, we are of all men most miserable.

But now is Christ risen from the dead, *and* become the firstfruits of them that slept. For since by man *came* death, by man *came* also the resurrection of the dead. For as in Adam all die, even so in Christ shall all be made alive.

1 CORINTHIANS 15:12-22

**THE ONE MINUTE BIBLE**

*Related texts:* JOB 19:23-27; 1 CORINTHIANS 15:23-58; ROMANS 6:1-11; ACTS 2:22-36

113

## Jesus Christ: Our Passover

**THE ONE
MINUTE
BIBLE**

Your glorying *is* not good. Know ye not that a little leaven leaveneth the whole lump? Purge out therefore the old leaven, that ye may be a new lump, as ye are unleavened. For even Christ our passover is sacrificed for us: therefore let us keep the feast, not with old leaven, neither with the leaven of malice and wickedness; but with the unleavened *bread* of sincerity and truth.

And if ye call on the Father, who without respect of persons judgeth according to every man's work, pass the time of your sojourning *here* in fear: forasmuch as ye know that ye were not redeemed with corruptible things, *as* silver and gold, from your vain conversation *received* by tradition from your fathers; but with the precious blood of Christ, as of a lamb without blemish and without spot: who verily was foreordained before the foundation of the world, but was manifest in these last times for you, who by him do believe in God, that raised him up from the dead, and gave him glory; that your faith and hope might be in God.

Seeing ye have purified your souls in obeying the truth through the Spirit unto unfeigned love of the brethren, *see that ye* love one another with a pure heart fervently.

1 Corinthians 5:6-8; 1 Peter 1:17-22

***Related texts:*** Exodus 12–13; John 1:19-36; Hebrews 2:11-18; Revelation 13:8

## The Israelites Leave Egypt

And it came to pass, that at midnight the Lord smote all the firstborn in the land of Egypt, from the firstborn of Pharaoh that sat on his throne unto the firstborn of the captive that *was* in the dungeon; and all the firstborn of cattle. And Pharaoh rose up in the night, he, and all his servants, and all the Egyptians; and there was a great cry in Egypt; for *there was* not a house where *there was* not one dead.

And he called for Moses and Aaron by night, and said, Rise up, *and* get you forth from among my people, both ye and the children of Israel; and go, serve the Lord, as ye have said. Also take your flocks and your herds, as ye have said, and be gone; and bless me also.

And the Egyptians were urgent upon the people, that they might send them out of the land in haste; for they said, We *be* all dead *men*. And the people took their dough before it was leavened, their kneadingtroughs being bound up in their clothes upon their shoulders. And the children of Israel did according to the word of Moses; and they borrowed of the Egyptians jewels of silver, and jewels of gold, and raiment: and the Lord gave the people favour in the sight of the Egyptians, so that they lent unto them *such things as they required*. And they spoiled the Egyptians.

And the Lord went before them by day in a pillar of a cloud, to lead them the way; and by night in a pillar of fire, to give them light; to go by day and night: he took not away the pillar of the cloud by day, nor the pillar of fire by night, *from* before the people.

Exodus 12:29-36; 13:21-22

*Related texts:* Deuteronomy 16:1-8; Psalm 78:41-52; 105:26-38; 2 Thessalonians 1:5-10

## *Pharaoh Pursues the Israelites*

**THE ONE
MINUTE
BIBLE**

But the Egyptians pursued after them, all the horses *and* chariots of Pharaoh, and his horsemen, and his army, and overtook them encamping by the sea, beside Pi-hahiroth, before Baal-zephon.

And when Pharaoh drew nigh, the children of Israel lifted up their eyes, and, behold, the Egyptians marched after them; and they were sore afraid: and the children of Israel cried out unto the LORD. And they said unto Moses, Because *there were* no graves in Egypt, hast thou taken us away to die in the wilderness? Wherefore hast thou dealt thus with us, to carry us forth out of Egypt? *Is* not this the word that we did tell thee in Egypt, saying, Let us alone, that we may serve the Egyptians? For *it had been* better for us to serve the Egyptians, than that we should die in the wilderness.

And Moses said unto the people, Fear ye not, stand still, and see the salvation of the LORD, which he will show to you to day: for the Egyptians whom ye have seen to day, ye shall see them again no more for ever. The LORD shall fight for you, and ye shall hold your peace.

And the LORD said unto Moses, Wherefore criest thou unto me? Speak unto the children of Israel, that they go forward: but lift thou up thy rod, and stretch out thine hand over the sea, and divide it: and the children of Israel shall go on dry *ground* through the midst of the sea. And I, behold, I will harden the hearts of the Egyptians, and they shall follow them: and I will get me honour upon Pharaoh, and upon all his host, upon his chariots, and upon his horsemen. And the Egyptians shall know that I *am* the LORD, when I have gotten me honour upon Pharaoh, upon his chariots, and upon his horsemen.

EXODUS 14:9-18

*Related texts:* PSALM 37:7; 46:10; ISAIAH 59:1; ROMANS 9:14-24; HEBREWS 11:1-2

## Crossing the Red Sea

**THE ONE
MINUTE
BIBLE**

And Moses stretched out his hand over the sea; and the LORD caused the sea to go *back* by a strong east wind all that night, and made the sea dry *land*, and the waters were divided. And the children of Israel went into the midst of the sea upon the dry *ground*: and the waters *were* a wall unto them on their right hand, and on their left.

And the Egyptians pursued, and went in after them to the midst of the sea, *even* all Pharaoh's horses, his chariots, and his horsemen. And it came to pass, that in the morning watch the LORD looked unto the host of the Egyptians through the pillar of fire and of the cloud, and troubled the host of the Egyptians, and took off their chariot wheels, that they drave them heavily: so that the Egyptians said, Let us flee from the face of Israel; for the LORD fighteth for them against the Egyptians.

And the LORD said unto Moses, Stretch out thine hand over the sea, that the waters may come again upon the Egyptians, upon their chariots, and upon their horsemen. And Moses stretched forth his hand over the sea, and the sea returned to his strength when the morning appeared; and the Egyptians fled against it; and the LORD overthrew the Egyptians in the midst of the sea. And the waters returned, and covered the chariots, and the horsemen, *and* all the host of Pharaoh that came into the sea after them; there remained not so much as one of them.

EXODUS 14:21-28

*Related texts:* PSALMS 114; 136:13-15; DEUTERONOMY 11:1-4; JOSHUA 24:5-7; HEBREWS 11:23-29

**THE ONE
MINUTE
BIBLE**

## *The LORD Is a Warrior*

Thus the LORD saved Israel that day out of the hand of the Egyptians; and Israel saw the Egyptians dead upon the sea shore. And Israel saw that great work which the LORD did upon the Egyptians: and the people feared the LORD, and believed the LORD, and his servant Moses.

Then sang Moses and the children of Israel this song unto the LORD, and spake, saying,

I will sing unto the LORD,
    for he hath triumphed gloriously:
the horse and his rider
    hath he thrown into the sea.
The LORD *is* my strength and song,
    and he is become my salvation:
he *is* my God, and I will prepare him an habitation;
    my father's God, and I will exalt him.
The LORD *is* a man of war:
    the LORD *is* his name.
Pharaoh's chariots and his host
    hath he cast into the sea:
his chosen captains
    also are drowned in the Red sea.
Who *is* like unto thee, O LORD, among the gods?
    Who *is* like thee,
        glorious in holiness,
        fearful *in* praises,
        doing wonders?
Thou in thy mercy hast led forth
    the people *which* thou hast redeemed:
thou hast guided *them* in thy strength
    unto thy holy habitation.
The LORD shall reign
    for ever and ever.

EXODUS 14:30-31; 15:1-4, 11, 13, 18

*Related texts:* PSALM 136; EPHESIANS 5:19-20; REVELATION 15:2-4

## God's Care in the Desert

O give thanks unto the LORD; call upon his name:
make known his deeds among the people.
Sing unto him, sing psalms unto him:
talk ye of all his wondrous works.
Glory ye in his holy name:
let the heart of them rejoice that seek the LORD.
Seek the LORD, and his strength:
seek his face evermore.

Remember his marvellous works that he hath done;
his wonders, and the judgments of his mouth;
O ye seed of Abraham his servant,
ye children of Jacob his chosen.

He brought them forth also with silver and gold:
and *there was* not one feeble *person* among their tribes.
Egypt was glad when they departed:
for the fear of them fell upon them.
He spread a cloud for a covering;
and fire to give light in the night.
*The* people asked, and he brought quails,
and satisfied them with the bread of heaven.
He opened the rock, and the waters gushed out;
they ran in the dry places *like* a river.
For he remembered his holy promise,
*and* Abraham his servant.
And he brought forth his people with joy,
*and* his chosen with gladness:
and gave them the lands of the heathen:
and they inherited the labour of the people;
that they might observe his statutes,
and keep his laws.
Praise ye the LORD.

PSALM 105:1-6, 37-45

**THE ONE**
**MINUTE**
**BIBLE**

*Related texts:* GENESIS 15; EXODUS 15:19–18:27; JOHN 6; ACTS 7:36-38;
1 CORINTHIANS 10:1-4

## God Makes a Covenant With Israel

**THE ONE
MINUTE
BIBLE**

In the third month, when the children of Israel were gone forth out of the land of Egypt, the same day came they *into* the wilderness of Sinai. For they were departed from Rephidim, and were come *to* the desert of Sinai, and had pitched in the wilderness; and there Israel camped before the mount.

And Moses went up unto God, and the LORD called unto him out of the mountain, saying, Thus shalt thou say to the house of Jacob, and tell the children of Israel; Ye have seen what I did unto the Egyptians, and *how* I bare you on eagles' wings, and brought you unto myself. Now therefore, if ye will obey my voice indeed, and keep my covenant, then ye shall be a peculiar treasure unto me above all people: for all the earth *is* mine: and ye shall be unto me a kingdom of priests, and an holy nation. These *are* the words which thou shalt speak unto the children of Israel.

And Moses came and called for the elders of the people, and laid before their faces all these words which the LORD commanded him. And all the people answered together, and said, All that the LORD hath spoken we will do. And Moses returned the words of the people unto the LORD.

And the LORD said unto Moses, Lo, I come unto thee in a thick cloud, that the people may hear when I speak with thee, and believe thee for ever. And Moses told the words of the people unto the LORD.

EXODUS 19:1-9

---

*Related texts:* DEUTERONOMY 4:1-20; JEREMIAH 31:31-34; HEBREWS 8

# The Ten Commandments: *No Other Gods*

I *am* the LORD thy God, which have brought thee out
of the land of Egypt, out of the house of bondage.
Thou shalt have no other gods before me.

Sing unto the LORD, all the earth;
  show forth from day to day his salvation.
Declare his glory among the heathen;
  his marvellous works among all nations.
For great *is* the LORD, and greatly to be praised:
  he also *is* to be feared above all gods.
For all the gods of the people *are* idols:
  but the LORD made the heavens.
Glory and honour *are* in his presence;
  strength and gladness *are* in his place.
Give unto the LORD, ye kindreds of the people,
  give unto the LORD glory and strength.
  Give unto the LORD the glory *due* unto his name:
bring an offering, and come before him:
  worship the LORD in the beauty of holiness.
Fear before him, all the earth:
  the world also shall be stable, that it be not moved.
Let the heavens be glad, and let the earth rejoice:
  and let *men* say among the nations,
    The LORD reigneth.

EXODUS 20:2-3; 1 CHRONICLES 16:23-31

THE ONE
MINUTE
BIBLE

---

***Related texts:*** EXODUS 18:8-10; DEUTERONOMY 4:32-39; 5:1-21; 13:1-16;
ISAIAH 37:15-20; EPHESIANS 4:4-6

**THE ONE
MINUTE
BIBLE**

*April 22*

# The Ten Commandments: *No Idols*

Thou shalt not make unto thee any graven image, or any likeness *of* any thing that *is* in heaven above, or that *is* in the earth beneath, or that *is* in the water under the earth: thou shalt not bow down thyself to them, nor serve them: for I the LORD thy God *am* a jealous God, visiting the iniquity of the fathers upon the children unto the third and fourth *generation* of them that hate me; and showing mercy unto thousands of them that love me, and keep my commandments.

Not unto us, O LORD, not unto us,
    but unto thy name give glory,
    for thy mercy, *and* for thy truth's sake.

Wherefore should the heathen say,
    Where *is* now their God?
But our God *is* in the heavens:
    he hath done whatsoever he hath pleased.
Their idols *are* silver and gold,
    the work of men's hands.
They have mouths, but they speak not:
    eyes have they, but they see not:
they have ears, but they hear not:
    noses have they, but they smell not:
they have hands, but they handle not:
    feet have they, but they walk not:
    neither speak they through their throat.
They that make them are like unto them;
    *so is* every one that trusteth in them.

EXODUS 20:4-6; PSALM 115:1-8

***Related texts:*** DEUTERONOMY 7; ISAIAH 44:6-19; JEREMIAH 10:1-16; 16:19-21; MATTHEW 6:19-24; 1 JOHN 5:21

122

# The Ten Commandments: *God's Name*

THE ONE
MINUTE
BIBLE

Thou shalt not take the name of the LORD thy God in vain; for the LORD will not hold him guiltless that taketh his name in vain.

And the son of an Israelitish woman, whose father *was* an Egyptian, went out among the children of Israel: and this son of the Israelitish *woman* and a man of Israel strove together in the camp; and the Israelitish woman's son blasphemed the name *of the LORD*, and cursed. And they brought him unto Moses: (and his mother's name *was* Shelomith, the daughter of Dibri, of the tribe of Dan:) and they put him in ward, that the mind of the LORD might be showed them.

And the LORD spake unto Moses, saying, Bring forth him that hath cursed without the camp; and let all that heard *him* lay their hands upon his head, and let all the congregation stone him. And thou shalt speak unto the children of Israel, saying, Whosoever curseth his God shall bear his sin. And he that blasphemeth the name of the LORD, he shall surely be put to death, *and* all the congregation shall certainly stone him: as well the stranger, as he that is born in the land, when he blasphemeth the name *of the LORD*, shall be put to death.

The name of the LORD *is* a strong tower:
the righteous runneth into it, and is safe.

EXODUS 20:7; LEVITICUS 24:10-16; PROVERBS 18:10

*Related texts:* EXODUS 3:13-15; PSALMS 20; 86:5-12; ACTS 4:5-12

# The Ten Commandments: *The Sabbath*

**THE ONE MINUTE BIBLE**

Remember the sabbath day, to keep it holy. Six days shalt thou labour, and do all thy work: but the seventh day *is* the sabbath of the Lord thy God: *in it* thou shalt not do any work, thou, nor thy son, nor thy daughter, thy manservant, nor thy maidservant, nor thy cattle, nor thy stranger that *is* within thy gates: for *in* six days the Lord made heaven and earth, the sea, and all that in them *is*, and rested the seventh day: wherefore the Lord blessed the sabbath day, and hallowed it.

And when Jesus was departed thence, he went into their synagogue: and, behold, there was a man which had *his* hand withered. And they asked him, saying, Is it lawful to heal on the sabbath days? That they might accuse him.

And he said unto them, What man shall there be among you, that shall have one sheep, and if it fall into a pit on the sabbath day, will he not lay hold on it, and lift *it* out? How much then is a man better than a sheep? Wherefore it is lawful to do well on the sabbath days.

Then saith he to the man, Stretch forth thine hand. And he stretched *it* forth; and it was restored whole, like as the other.

Exodus 20:8-11; Matthew 12:9-13

***Related texts:*** Genesis 2:1-3; Exodus 16:11-30; Psalm 62:1-5; Mark 2:23-28; Hebrews 4:1-4

124

# The Ten Commandments: *Parents*

Honour thy father and thy mother: that thy days may be long upon the land which the LORD thy God giveth thee.

And he that smiteth his father, or his mother, shall be surely put to death.

For every one that curseth his father or his mother shall be surely put to death: he hath cursed his father or his mother; his blood *shall be* upon him.

The proverbs of Solomon.

A wise son maketh a glad father:
 but a foolish son *is* the heaviness of his mother.

Hearken unto thy father that begat thee,
 and despise not thy mother when she is old.
Buy the truth, and sell *it* not;
 *also* wisdom, and instruction, and understanding.
The father of the righteous shall greatly rejoice:
 and he that begetteth a wise *child* shall have joy
  of him.
Thy father and thy mother shall be glad,
 and she that bare thee shall rejoice.

Children, obey your parents in the Lord: for this is right. Honour thy father and mother; which is the first commandment with promise; that it may be well with thee, and thou mayest live long on the earth.

EXODUS 20:12; 21:15; LEVITICUS 20:9; PROVERBS 10:1; 23:22-25;
EPHESIANS 6:1-3

***Related texts:*** MALACHI 4:5-6; COLOSSIANS 3:20-21; 2 TIMOTHY 3:1-5;
TITUS 1:6-9

# The Ten Commandments: *Murder*

**THE ONE
MINUTE
BIBLE**

Thou shalt not kill.

Whoso sheddeth man's blood,
    by man shall his blood be shed:
for in the image of God
    made he man.

[Jesus said,] Ye have heard that it was said by them of old time, Thou shalt not kill; and whosoever shall kill shall be in danger of the judgment: but I say unto you, That whosoever is angry with his brother without a cause shall be in danger of the judgment: and whosoever shall say to his brother, Raca, shall be in danger of the council: but whosoever shall say, Thou fool, shall be in danger of hell fire.

For this is the message that ye heard from the beginning, that we should love one another. Not as Cain, *who* was of that wicked one, and slew his brother. And wherefore slew he him? Because his own works were evil, and his brother's righteous. Marvel not, my brethren, if the world hate you. We know that we have passed from death unto life, because we love the brethren. He that loveth not *his* brother abideth in death. Whosoever hateth his brother is a murderer: and ye know that no murderer hath eternal life abiding in him.

Hereby perceive we the love *of God*, because he laid down his life for us: and we ought to lay down *our* lives for the brethren.

EXODUS 20:13; GENESIS 9:6; MATTHEW 5:21-22; 1 JOHN 3:11-16

***Related texts:*** GENESIS 4:1-16; NUMBERS 35:9-34; MATTHEW 15:10-20; JOHN 8:42-44; ROMANS 1:28-32

# The Ten Commandments: *Adultery*

Thou shalt not commit adultery.

And why wilt thou, my son, be ravished with a strange
woman,
and embrace the bosom of a stranger?
For the ways of man *are* before the eyes of the LORD,
and he pondereth all his goings.
His own iniquities shall take the wicked himself,
and he shall be holden with the cords of his sins.
He shall die without instruction;
and in the greatness of his folly he shall go astray.

**THE ONE
MINUTE
BIBLE**

[Jesus said,] Ye have heard that it was said by them
of old time, Thou shalt not commit adultery: but I say
unto you, That whosoever looketh on a woman to lust
after her hath committed adultery with her already in
his heart.

Know ye not that the unrighteous shall not inherit
the kingdom of God? Be not deceived: neither
fornicators, nor idolaters, nor adulterers, nor
effeminate, nor abusers of themselves with mankind,
nor thieves, nor covetous, nor drunkards, nor revilers,
nor extortioners, shall inherit the kingdom of God. And
such were some of you: but ye are washed, but ye are
sanctified, but ye are justified in the name of the Lord
Jesus, and by the Spirit of our God.

Marriage is honourable in all, and the bed undefiled:
but whoremongers and adulterers God will judge.

EXODUS 20:14; PROVERBS 5:20-23; MATTHEW 5:27-28;
1 CORINTHIANS 6:9-11; HEBREWS 13:4

*Related texts:* PROVERBS 5:1-19; 6:20-35; ROMANS 1:18-27;
EPHESIANS 4:17-24; COLOSSIANS 3:1-7; 1 THESSALONIANS 4:3-8

# The Ten Commandments: *Stealing*

**THE ONE
MINUTE
BIBLE**

Thou shalt not steal.

Trust not in oppression,
    and become not vain in robbery:
if riches increase,
    set not your heart *upon them*.

God hath spoken once;
    twice have I heard this;
that power *belongeth* unto God.
    Also unto thee, O Lord, *belongeth* mercy:
for thou renderest to every man
    according to his work.

Charge them that are rich in this world, that they be
not highminded, nor trust in uncertain riches, but in
the living God, who giveth us richly all things to enjoy;
that they do good, that they be rich in good works, ready
to distribute, willing to communicate; laying up in store
for themselves a good foundation against the time to
come, that they may lay hold on eternal life.

Let him that stole steal no more: but rather let him
labour, working with *his* hands the thing which is good,
that he may have to give to him that needeth.

EXODUS 20:15; PSALM 62:10-12; 1 TIMOTHY 6:17-19; EPHESIANS 4:28

***Related texts:*** PROVERBS 1:10-19; 10:2; ISAIAH 10:1-4; MALACHI 3:6-12;
TITUS 2:9-10

# The Ten Commandments: *False Witness*

Thou shalt not bear false witness against thy
neighbour.

If a false witness rise up against any man to testify
against him *that which is* wrong; then both the men,
between whom the controversy *is*, shall stand before the
LORD, before the priests and the judges, which shall be
in those days; and the judges shall make diligent
inquisition: and, behold, *if* the witness *be* a false
witness, *and* hath testified falsely against his brother;
then shall ye do unto him, as he had thought to have
done unto his brother: so shalt thou put the evil away
from among you. And those which remain shall hear,
and fear, and shall henceforth commit no more any such
evil among you.

**THE ONE
MINUTE
BIBLE**

LORD, who shall abide in thy tabernacle?
　　Who shall dwell in thy holy hill?
He that walketh uprightly,
　　and worketh righteousness,
and speaketh the truth in his heart.
　　*He that* backbiteth not with his tongue,
nor doeth evil to his neighbour,
　　nor taketh up a reproach against his neighbour.
In whose eyes a vile person is contemned;
　　but he honoureth them that fear the LORD.
*He that* sweareth to *his own* hurt,
　　and changeth not.
*He that* putteth not out his money to usury,
　　nor taketh reward against the innocent.
He that doeth these *things*
　　shall never be moved.
　　　　　　EXODUS 20:16; DEUTERONOMY 19:16-20; PSALM 15

*Related texts:* PROVERBS 12:17-18; 25:18; ISAIAH 29:19-21;
MATTHEW 15:10-20; MARK 14:53-64

# The Ten Commandments: *Coveting*

**THE ONE
MINUTE
BIBLE**

Thou shalt not covet thy neighbour's house, thou shalt not covet thy neighbour's wife, nor his manservant, nor his maidservant, nor his ox, nor his ass, nor any thing that *is* thy neighbour's.

Owe no man any thing, but to love one another: for he that loveth another hath fulfilled the law. For this, Thou shalt not commit adultery, Thou shalt not kill, Thou shalt not steal, Thou shalt not bear false witness, Thou shalt not covet; and if *there be* any other commandment, it is briefly comprehended in this saying, namely, Thou shalt love thy neighbour as thyself. Love worketh no ill to his neighbour: therefore love *is* the fulfilling of the law.

But godliness with contentment is great gain. For we brought nothing into *this* world, *and it is* certain we can carry nothing out. And having food and raiment let us be therewith content.

*Let your* conversation *be* without covetousness; *and be* content with such things as ye have: for he hath said,

I will never leave thee,
nor forsake thee.

EXODUS 20:17; ROMANS 13:8-10; 1 TIMOTHY 6:6-8; HEBREWS 13:5

---

***Related texts:*** DEUTERONOMY 31:6; PROVERBS 1:10-19;
PHILIPPIANS 4:11-12; 1 TIMOTHY 6:9-11; JAMES 4:1-3; 1 JOHN 2:15-17

*When I read...the Holy Scriptures...
all seems luminous, a single
word opens up infinite horizons
to my soul.*
**St. Terese of Lisieux (1873-1897)**
FRENCH NUN

*The highest earthly enjoyments
are but a shadow of the joy I
find in reading God's word.*
**Lady Jane Grey (1537-1554)**
QUEEN OF ENGLAND FOR NINE DAYS

*The most stupendous book, the most
sublime literature, even apart from
its sacred character, in the history
of the world.*
**Blanche Mary Kelly (1881-1966)**
AMERICAN AUTHOR

## *The Greatest Commandment*

Hear, O Israel: The Lord our God *is* one Lord: and thou shalt love the Lord thy God with all thine heart, and with all thy soul, and with all thy might. And these words, which I command thee this day, shall be in thine heart: and thou shalt teach them diligently unto thy children, and shalt talk of them when thou sittest in thine house, and when thou walkest by the way, and when thou liest down, and when thou risest up. And thou shalt bind them for a sign upon thine hand, and they shall be as frontlets between thine eyes. And thou shalt write them upon the posts of thy house, and on thy gates.

**THE ONE MINUTE BIBLE**

Thou shalt not avenge, nor bear any grudge against the children of thy people, but thou shalt love thy neighbour as thyself: I *am* the Lord.

And if a stranger sojourn with thee in your land, ye shall not vex him. but the stranger that dwelleth with you shall be unto you as one born among you, and thou shalt love him as thyself; for ye were strangers in the land of Egypt: I *am* the Lord your God.

Master, which *is* the great commandment in the law? Jesus said unto him, Thou shalt love the Lord thy God with all thy heart, and with all thy soul, and with all thy mind. This is the first and great commandment. And the second *is* like unto it, Thou shalt love thy neighbour as thyself. On these two commandments hang all the law and the prophets.

DEUTERONOMY 6:4-9; LEVITICUS 19:18, 33-34; MATTHEW 22:36-40

*Related texts:* MICAH 6:8; MARK 12:28-31; LUKE 10:25-37; ACTS 4:32-35; ROMANS 13:8-10; 2 CORINTHIANS 8:13-15

**THE ONE
MINUTE
BIBLE**

# The Law: *Widows, Orphans and Foreigners*

Ye shall not afflict any widow, or fatherless child. If thou afflict them in any wise, and they cry at all unto me, I will surely hear their cry; and my wrath shall wax hot, and I will kill you with the sword; and your wives shall be widows, and your children fatherless.

Thou shalt not pervert the judgment of the stranger, *nor* of the fatherless; nor take a widow's raiment to pledge: but thou shalt remember that thou wast a bondman in Egypt, and the LORD thy God redeemed thee thence: therefore I command thee to do this thing.
When thou cuttest down thine harvest in thy field, and hast forgot a sheaf in the field, thou shalt not go again to fetch it: it shall be for the stranger, for the fatherless, and for the widow: that the LORD thy God may bless thee in all the work of thine hands. When thou beatest thine olive tree, thou shalt not go over the boughs again: it shall be for the stranger, for the fatherless, and for the widow. When thou gatherest the grapes of thy vineyard, thou shalt not glean *it* afterward: it shall be for the stranger, for the fatherless, and for the widow. And thou shalt remember that thou wast a bondman in the land of Egypt: therefore I command thee to do this thing.

Pure religion and undefiled before God and the Father is this, To visit the fatherless and widows in their affliction, *and* to keep himself unspotted from the world.

EXODUS 22:22-24; DEUTERONOMY 24:17-22; JAMES 1:27

*Related texts:* DEUTERONOMY 10:17-20; PSALMS 68:5; 146:9; 1 TIMOTHY 5:3-16

# The Law: *Restitution*

If a man shall steal an ox, or a sheep, and kill it, or sell it; he shall restore five oxen for an ox, and four sheep for a sheep.

If a thief be found breaking up, and be smitten that he die, *there shall* no blood *be shed* for him. If the sun be risen upon him, *there shall be* blood *shed* for him; *for* he should make full restitution; if he have nothing, then he shall be sold for his theft.

If the theft be certainly found in his hand alive, whether it be ox, or ass, or sheep; he shall restore double.

If a man shall cause a field or vineyard to be eaten, and shall put in his beast, and shall feed in another man's field; of the best of his own field, and of the best of his own vineyard, shall he make restitution.

If fire break out, and catch in thorns, so that the stacks of corn, or the standing corn, or the field, be consumed *therewith*; he that kindled the fire shall surely make restitution.

If a man shall deliver unto his neighbour money or stuff to keep, and it be stolen out of the man's house; if the thief be found, let him pay double. If the thief be not found, then the master of the house shall be brought unto the judges, *to see* whether he have put his hand unto his neighbour's goods. For all manner of trespass, *whether it be* for ox, for ass, for sheep, for raiment, *or* for any manner of lost thing, which *another* challengeth to be his, the cause of both parties shall come before the judges; *and* whom the judges shall condemn, he shall pay double unto his neighbour.

EXODUS 22:1-9

*Related texts:* NUMBERS 5:5-8; MATTHEW 5:23,24; LUKE 19:1-10;
1 CORINTHIANS 6:1-11

**THE ONE
MINUTE
BIBLE**

# The Law: *Eye for Eye*

If men strive, and hurt a woman with child, so that her fruit depart *from her*, and yet no mischief follow: he shall be surely punished, according as the woman's husband will lay upon him; and he shall pay as the judges *determine*. And if *any* mischief follow, then thou shalt give life for life, eye for eye, tooth for tooth, hand for hand, foot for foot, burning for burning, wound for wound, stripe for stripe.

And he that killeth any man shall surely be put to death. And he that killeth a beast shall make it good; beast for beast. And if a man cause a blemish in his neighbour; as he hath done, so shall it be done to him; breach for breach, eye for eye, tooth for tooth: as he hath caused a blemish in a man, so shall it be done to him *again*. And he that killeth a beast, he shall restore it: and he that killeth a man, he shall be put to death. Ye shall have one manner of law, as well for the stranger, as for one of your own country: for I *am* the Lᴏʀᴅ your God.

[Jesus said,] Ye have heard that it hath been said, An eye for an eye, and a tooth for a tooth: but I say unto you, That ye resist not evil: but whosoever shall smite thee on thy right cheek, turn to him the other also.

Exᴏᴅᴜs 21:22-25; Lᴇᴠɪᴛɪᴄᴜs 24:17-22; Mᴀᴛᴛʜᴇᴡ 5:38-39

*Related texts:* Exᴏᴅᴜs 21:22-25; Dᴇᴜᴛᴇʀᴏɴᴏᴍʏ 19:16-21; Psᴀʟᴍ 103:8-12; Mᴀᴛᴛʜᴇᴡ 5:38-42

# The Law: *Capital Punishment*

THE ONE
MINUTE
BIBLE

He that smiteth a man, so that he die, shall be surely put to death.

And he that smiteth his father, or his mother, shall be surely put to death.

And he that stealeth a man, and selleth him, or if he be found in his hand, he shall surely be put to death.

Thou shalt not suffer a witch to live.

Whosoever lieth with a beast shall surely be put to death.

He that sacrificeth unto *any* god, save unto the LORD only, he shall be utterly destroyed.

Ye shall keep the sabbath therefore; for it *is* holy unto you: every one that defileth it shall surely be put to death: for whosoever doeth *any* work therein, that soul shall be cut off from among his people.

For every one that curseth his father or his mother shall be surely put to death: he hath cursed his father or his mother; his blood *shall be* upon him.

And the man that committeth adultery with *another* man's wife, *even he* that committeth adultery with his neighbour's wife, the adulterer and the adulteress shall surely be put to death.

And the man that lieth with his father's wife hath uncovered his father's nakedness: both of them shall surely be put to death; their blood *shall be* upon them.

And if a man lie with his daughter in law, both of them shall surely be put to death: they have wrought confusion; their blood *shall be* upon them. If a man also lie with mankind, as he lieth with a woman, both of them have committed an abomination: they shall surely be put to death; their blood *shall be* upon them.

EXODUS 21:12, 15-16; 22:18-20; 31:14; LEVITICUS 20:9-13

*Related texts:* GENESIS 9:6; LEVITICUS 24:17-22; DEUTERONOMY 24:16; MATTHEW 21:33-44

**THE ONE
MINUTE
BIBLE**

# The Law: *Clean and Unclean*

And the LORD spake unto Moses and to Aaron, saying unto them, Speak unto the children of Israel, saying, These *are* the beasts which ye shall eat among all the beasts that *are* on the earth. Whatsoever parteth the hoof, and is clovenfooted, *and* cheweth the cud, among the beasts, that shall ye eat.

These shall ye eat of all that *are* in the waters: whatsoever hath fins and scales in the waters, in the seas, and in the rivers, them shall ye eat. And all that have not fins and scales in the seas, and in the rivers, of all that move in the waters, and of any living thing which *is* in the waters, they *shall be* an abomination unto you: they shall be even an abomination unto you; ye shall not eat of their flesh, but ye shall have their carcases in abomination.

All fowls that creep, going upon *all* four, *shall be* an abomination unto you. Yet these may ye eat of every flying creeping thing that goeth upon *all* four, which have legs above their feet, to leap withal upon the earth.

For I *am* the LORD your God: ye shall therefore sanctify yourselves, and ye shall be holy; for I *am* holy: neither shall ye defile yourselves with any manner of creeping thing that creepeth upon the earth. For I *am* the LORD that bringeth you up out of the land of Egypt, to be your God: ye shall therefore be holy, for I *am* holy.

LEVITICUS 11:1-3, 9-11, 20-21, 44-45

***Related texts:*** GENESIS 7:1-4; MATTHEW 15:1-20; MARK 7:1-23; ACTS 10; ROMANS 14

# The Law: *The Festivals*

Observe the month of Abib, and keep the passover unto the LORD thy God: for in the month of Abib the LORD thy God brought thee forth out of Egypt by night. Thou shalt therefore sacrifice the passover unto the LORD thy God, of the flock and the herd, in the place which the LORD shall choose to place his name there.

Six days thou shalt eat unleavened bread: and on the seventh day *shall be* a solemn assembly to the LORD thy God: thou shalt do no work *therein.*

Seven weeks shalt thou number unto thee: begin to number the seven weeks from *such time as* thou beginnest *to put* the sickle to the corn. And thou shalt keep the feast of weeks unto the LORD thy God with a tribute of a freewill offering of thine hand, which thou shalt give *unto* the LORD thy God, according as the LORD thy God hath blessed thee.

Thou shalt observe the feast of tabernacles seven days, after that thou hast gathered in thy corn and thy wine: seven days shalt thou keep a solemn feast unto the LORD thy God in the place which the LORD shall choose: because the LORD thy God shall bless thee in all thine increase, and in all the works of thine hands, therefore thou shalt surely rejoice.

Three times in a year shall all thy males appear before the LORD thy God in the place which he shall choose; in the feast of unleavened bread, and in the feast of weeks, and in the feast of tabernacles: and they shall not appear before the LORD empty: every man *shall give* as he is able, according to the blessing of the LORD thy God which he hath given thee.

DEUTERONOMY 16:1-2, 8-10, 13, 15-17

*Related texts:* EXODUS 12; 23:14-17; LEVITICUS 23; COLOSSIANS 2:16-23

## Honor Your Mother

**THE ONE
MINUTE
BIBLE**

Honour thy father and thy mother, as the LORD thy God hath commanded thee; that thy days may be prolonged, and that it may go well with thee, in the land which the LORD thy God giveth thee.

Then came to Jesus scribes and Pharisees, which were of Jerusalem, saying, Why do thy disciples transgress the tradition of the elders? For they wash not their hands when they eat bread.

But he answered and said unto them, Why do ye also transgress the commandment of God by your tradition? For God commanded, saying, Honour thy father and mother: and, He that curseth father or mother, let him die the death. But ye say, Whosoever shall say to *his* father or *his* mother, *It is* a gift, by whatsoever thou mightest be profited by me; and honour not his father or his mother, *he shall be free.* Thus have ye made the commandment of God of none effect by your tradition. *Ye* hypocrites, well did Esaias prophesy of you, saying,

This people draweth nigh unto me with their mouth,
    and honoureth me with *their* lips;
  but their heart is far from me.
But in vain they do worship me,
    teaching *for* doctrines the commandments of men.

DEUTERONOMY 5:16; MATTHEW 15:1-9

**Related texts:** EXODUS 20:12; 21:15; LEVITICUS 20:9; EPHESIANS 6:1-2

## *The LORD Has a Mother's Compassion*

Sing, O heavens;
 and be joyful, O earth;
 and break forth into singing, O mountains:
for the LORD hath comforted his people,
 and will have mercy upon his afflicted.

But Zion said, The LORD hath forsaken me,
 and my Lord hath forgotten me.

Can a woman forget her sucking child,
 that she should not have compassion on the son
  of her womb?
Yea, they may forget,
 yet will I not forget thee.
Behold, I have graven thee upon the palms of *my* hands;
 thy walls *are* continually before me.
Thy children shall make haste;
 thy destroyers and they that made thee waste
  shall go forth of thee.
Lift up thine eyes round about,and behold:
 all these gather themselves together,
  *and* come to thee.
*As* I live, saith the LORD,
 thou shalt surely clothe thee with them all, as with an
  ornament,
 and bind them *on thee*, as a bride *doeth*.

For thy waste and thy desolate places,
 and the land of thy destruction,
shall even now be too narrow by reason of the
  inhabitants,
 and they that swallowed thee up shall be far away.

ISAIAH 49:13-19

*Related texts:* PSALMS 51:1-9; 77:1-8; 103:1-18; ISAIAH 66:12-14;
LAMENTATIONS 3:22-33; COLOSSIANS 3:12-14

## A Happy Mother

**THE ONE
MINUTE
BIBLE**

Praise ye the LORD.

Praise, O ye servants of the LORD,
    praise the name of the LORD.
Blessed be the name of the LORD
    from this time forth and for evermore.
From the rising of the sun unto the going down
        of the same
    the LORD's name *is* to be praised.

The LORD *is* high above all nations,
    *and* his glory above the heavens.
Who *is* like unto the LORD our God,
    who dwelleth on high,
who humbleth *himself* to behold
    *the* things that are in heaven, and in the earth!

He raiseth up the poor out of the dust,
    *and* lifteth the needy out of the dunghill;
that he may set *him* with princes,
    *even* with the princes of his people.
He maketh the barren woman to keep house,
    *and to be* a joyful mother of children.

Praise ye the LORD.

PSALM 113

*Related texts:* 1 SAMUEL 2:1-10; JOB 42:12-16; PSALM 127:3-5;
PROVERBS 17:6; ISAIAH 54:1-8; LUKE 1

## *A Mother's Teaching*

My son, hear the instruction of thy father,
    and forsake not the law of thy mother:
for they *shall be* an ornament of grace unto thy head,
    and chains about thy neck.

The words of king Lemuel, the prophecy that his mother
taught him.

    What, my son? And what, the son of my womb?
        And what, the son of my vows?
    Give not thy strength unto women,
        nor thy ways to that which destroyeth kings.

    *It is* not for kings, O Lemuel,
        *it is* not for kings to drink wine;
        nor for princes strong drink:
    lest they drink, and forget the law,
        and pervert the judgment of any of the afflicted.
    Give strong drink unto him that is ready to perish,
        and wine unto those that be of heavy hearts.
    Let him drink, and forget his poverty,
        and remember his misery no more.

    Open thy mouth for the dumb
        in the cause of all such as are appointed
            to destruction.
    Open thy mouth, judge righteously,
        and plead the cause of the poor and needy.

PROVERBS 1:8-9; 31:1-9

*Related texts:* EXODUS 2:1-9; PROVERBS 6:20-24; 2 TIMOTHY 1:5; 3:14-17

# The Virtuous Wife: Part 1

**THE ONE
MINUTE
BIBLE**

A virtuous woman *is* a crown to her husband:
    but she that maketh ashamed *is* as rottenness
        in his bones.


Who can find a virtuous woman?
    For her price *is* far above rubies.
The heart of her husband doth safely trust in her,
    so that he shall have no need of spoil.
She will do him good and not evil
    all the days of her life.
She seeketh wool, and flax,
    and worketh willingly with her hands.
She is like the merchants' ships;
    she bringeth her food from afar.
She riseth also while it is yet night,
    and giveth meat to her household,
    and a portion to her maidens.
She considereth a field, and buyeth it:
    with the fruit of her hands she planteth a vineyard.
She girdeth her loins with strength,
    and strengtheneth her arms.
She perceiveth that her merchandise *is* good:
    her candle goeth not out by night.
She layeth her hands to the spindle,
    and her hands hold the distaff.
She stretcheth out her hand to the poor;
    yea, she reacheth forth her hands to the needy.

PROVERBS 12:4; 31:10-20

***Related texts:*** GENESIS 24; ACTS 18:23-26; ROMANS 16:1-6

# *The Virtuous Wife: Part 2*

THE ONE
MINUTE
BIBLE

Who can find a virtuous woman?
For her price *is* far above rubies.

She is not afraid of the snow for her household:
for all her household *are* clothed with scarlet.
She maketh herself coverings of tapestry;
her clothing *is* silk and purple.
Her husband is known in the gates,
when he sitteth among the elders of the land.
She maketh fine linen, and selleth *it*;
and delivereth girdles unto the merchant.
Strength and honour *are* her clothing;
and she shall rejoice in time to come.
She openeth her mouth with wisdom;
and in her tongue *is* the law of kindness.
She looketh well to the ways of her household,
and eateth not the bread of idleness.
Her children arise up, and call her blessed;
her husband *also*, and he praiseth her.
Many daughters have done virtuously,
but thou excellest them all.
Favour *is* deceitful, and beauty *is* vain:
*but* a woman *that* feareth the LORD,
she shall be praised.
Give her of the fruit of her hands;
and let her own works praise her in the gates.

*Whoso* findeth a wife findeth a good *thing*,
and obtaineth favour of the LORD.

PROVERBS 31:10, 21-31; 18:22

*Related texts:* 1 SAMUEL 25:1-42; PROVERBS 19:14; LUKE 1:26-55;
EPHESIANS 5:21-24; 1 PETER 3:1-6

**THE ONE
MINUTE
BIBLE**

# *Your Maker Is Your Husband*

Sing, O barren,
    thou *that* didst not bear;
break forth into singing, and cry aloud,
    thou *that* didst not travail with child:
for more *are* the children of the desolate
    than the children of the married wife, saith the LORD.
Enlarge the place of thy tent,
    and let them stretch forth the curtains of thine
        habitations:
spare not, lengthen thy cords,
    and strengthen thy stakes.
Fear not; for thou shalt not be ashamed:
    neither be thou confounded;
    for thou shalt not be put to shame:
for thou shalt forget the shame of thy youth,
    and shalt not remember the reproach of thy
        widowhood any more.
For thy Maker *is* thine husband;
    the LORD of hosts *is* his name;
and thy Redeemer the Holy One of Israel;
    the God of the whole earth shall he be called.
For the LORD hath called thee
    as a woman forsaken and grieved in spirit,
and a wife of youth,
    when thou wast refused, saith thy God.
For a small moment have I forsaken thee;
    but with great mercies will I gather thee.
In a little wrath
    I hid my face from thee for a moment;
but with everlasting kindness
    will I have mercy on thee,
        saith the LORD thy Redeemer.

ISAIAH 54:1-2, 4-8

***Related texts:*** PSALM 45; SONG OF SONGS 4; ISAIAH 62:1-7;
REVELATION 19:5-9; 21:1-4

# The Law: *Women's Rights*

THE ONE
MINUTE
BIBLE

And if a man sell his daughter to be a maidservant, she shall not go out as the menservants do. If she please not her master, who hath betrothed her to himself, then shall he let her be redeemed: to sell her unto a strange nation he shall have no power, seeing he hath dealt deceitfully with her. And if he have betrothed her unto his son, he shall deal with her after the manner of daughters. If he take him another *wife*; her food, her raiment, and her duty of marriage, shall he not diminish. And if he do not these three unto her, then shall she go out free without money.

Do not prostitute thy daughter, to cause her to be a whore; lest the land fall to whoredom, and the land become full of wickedness.

If brethren dwell together, and one of them die, and have no child, the wife of the dead shall not marry without unto a stranger: her husband's brother shall go in unto her, and take her to him to wife, and perform the duty of an husband's brother unto her. And it shall be, *that* the firstborn which she beareth shall succeed in the name of his brother *which* is dead, that his name be not put out of Israel.

EXODUS 21:7-11; LEVITICUS 19:29; DEUTERONOMY 25:5-6

*Related texts:* EXODUS 22:16,17; NUMBERS 27; 30; 36;
DEUTERONOMY 21:10-17; 22:13-30; 25:7-10; RUTH 3–4; 1 TIMOTHY 3:2, 12

# The Law: *The Tabernacle*

**THE ONE
MINUTE
BIBLE**

Then verily the first *covenant* had also ordinances of divine service, and a worldly sanctuary. For there was a tabernacle made; the first, wherein *was* the candlestick, and the table, and the showbread; which is called the sanctuary. And after the second veil, the tabernacle which is called the Holiest of all; which had the golden censer, and the ark of the covenant overlaid round about with gold, wherein *was* the golden pot that had manna, and Aaron's rod that budded, and the tables of the covenant; and over it the cherubims of glory shadowing the mercyseat; of which we cannot now speak particularly.

Now when these things were thus ordained, the priests went always into the first tabernacle, accomplishing the service *of God*. But into the second *went* the high priest alone once every year, not without blood, which he offered for himself, and *for* the errors of the people.

But Christ being come an high priest of good things to come, by a greater and more perfect tabernacle, not made with hands, that is to say, not of this building; neither by the blood of goats and calves, but by his own blood he entered in once into the holy place, having obtained eternal redemption *for us*.

HEBREWS 9:1-7, 11-12

*Related texts:* EXODUS 25–27; 35–40; MARK 15:37-38; HEBREWS 9:13-28; 10:19-23

# The Law: *The Priesthood*

And the Lord said unto Aaron, Thou and thy sons and thy father's house with thee shall bear the iniquity of the sanctuary: and thou and thy sons with thee shall bear the iniquity of your priesthood. And thy brethren also of the tribe of Levi, the tribe of thy father, bring thou with thee, that they may be joined unto thee, and minister unto thee: but thou and thy sons with thee *shall minister* before the tabernacle of witness.

And ye shall keep the charge of the sanctuary, and the charge of the altar: that there be no wrath any more upon the children of Israel. And I, behold, I have taken your brethren the Levites from among the children of Israel: to you *they are* given *as* a gift for the Lord, to do the service of the tabernacle of the congregation. Therefore thou and thy sons with thee shall keep your priest's office for every thing of the altar, and within the veil; and ye shall serve: I have given your priest's office *unto* you as a service of gift: and the stranger that cometh nigh shall be put to death.

All the heave offerings of the holy things, which the children of Israel offer unto the Lord, have I given thee, and thy sons and thy daughters with thee, by a statute for ever: it *is* a covenant of salt for ever before the Lord unto thee and to thy seed with thee.

And the Lord spake unto Aaron, Thou shalt have no inheritance in their land, neither shalt thou have any part among them: I *am* thy part and thine inheritance among the children of Israel.

NUMBERS 18:1-2, 5-7, 19-20

*Related texts:* LEVITICUS 1–7; 21–22; NUMBERS 3; HEBREWS 7–9; 1 PETER 2:4-10

# The Law: *Driving Out the Nations*

**THE ONE
MINUTE
BIBLE**

When the Lord thy God shall bring thee into the land whither thou goest to possess it, and hath cast out many nations before thee, the Hittites, and the Girgashites, and the Amorites, and the Canaanites, and the Perizzites, and the Hivites, and the Jebusites, seven nations greater and mightier than thou; and when the Lord thy God shall deliver them before thee; thou shalt smite them, *and* utterly destroy them; thou shalt make no covenant with them, nor show mercy unto them: neither shalt thou make marriages with them; thy daughter thou shalt not give unto his son, nor his daughter shalt thou take unto thy son. For they will turn away thy son from following me, that they may serve other gods: so will the anger of the Lord be kindled against you, and destroy thee suddenly.

But thus shall ye deal with them; ye shall destroy their altars, and break down their images, and cut down their groves, and burn their graven images with fire. For thou *art* an holy people unto the Lord thy God: the Lord thy God hath chosen thee to be a special people unto himself, above all people that *are* upon the face of the earth.

The Lord did not set his love upon you, nor choose you, because ye were more in number than any people; for ye *were* the fewest of all people: but because the Lord loved you, and because he would keep the oath which he had sworn unto your fathers, hath the Lord brought you out with a mighty hand, and redeemed you out of the house of bondmen, from the hand of Pharaoh king of Egypt.

DEUTERONOMY 7:1-8

*Related texts:* DEUTERONOMY 8:18–9:5; JUDGES 2:10-23; 2 CORINTHIANS 6:14–7:1; COLOSSIANS 4:4-6; 1 PETER 2:1-12

# The Law: *Not Too Difficult*

For this commandment which I command thee this day, it *is* not hidden from thee, neither *is* it far off. It *is* not in heaven, that thou shouldest say, Who shall go up for us to heaven, and bring it unto us, that we may hear it, and do it? Neither *is* it beyond the sea, that thou shouldest say, Who shall go over the sea for us, and bring it unto us, that we may hear it, and do it? But the word *is* very nigh unto thee, in thy mouth, and in thy heart, that thou mayest do it.

See, I have set before thee this day life and good, and death and evil; in that I command thee this day to love the LORD thy God, to walk in his ways, and to keep his commandments and his statutes and his judgments, that thou mayest live and multiply: and the LORD thy God shall bless thee in the land whither thou goest to possess it.

But if thine heart turn away, so that thou wilt not hear, but shalt be drawn away, and worship other gods, and serve them; I denounce unto you this day, that ye shall surely perish, *and that* ye shall not prolong *your* days upon the land, whither thou passest over Jordan to go to possess it.

I call heaven and earth to record this day against you, *that* I have set before you life and death, blessing and cursing: therefore choose life, that both thou and thy seed may live: that thou mayest love the LORD thy God, *and* that thou mayest obey his voice, and that thou mayest cleave unto him: for he *is* thy life, and the length of thy days: that thou mayest dwell in the land which the LORD sware unto thy fathers, to Abraham, to Isaac, and to Jacob, to give them.

DEUTERONOMY 30:11-20

*Related texts:* DEUTERONOMY 7:9-15; 10:12-13; MICAH 6:6-8;
JOHN 14:15; ROMANS 10:5-13; 1 JOHN 5:3

## Sermon on the Mount: *The Beatitudes*

**THE ONE
MINUTE
BIBLE**

And seeing the multitudes, Jesus went up into a mountain: and when he was set, his disciples came unto him: and he opened his mouth, and taught them, saying,

Blessed *are* the poor in spirit:
  for theirs is the kingdom of heaven.
Blessed *are* they that mourn:
  for they shall be comforted.
Blessed *are* the meek:
  for they shall inherit the earth.
Blessed *are* they which do hunger and thirst after
    righteousness:
  for they shall be filled.
Blessed *are* the merciful:
  for they shall obtain mercy.
Blessed *are* the pure in heart:
  for they shall see God.
Blessed *are* the peacemakers:
  for they shall be called the children of God.
Blessed *are* they which are persecuted for
    righteousness' sake:
  for theirs is the kingdom of heaven.

MATTHEW 5:1-10

*Related texts:* GENESIS 12:1-3; PSALMS 1; 84; LUKE 6:17-26; 11:27-28; JOHN 20:24-29

# Sermon on the Mount: *Salt and Light*

Blessed are ye, when *men* shall revile you, and persecute *you*, and shall say all manner of evil against you falsely, for my sake. Rejoice, and be exceeding glad: for great *is* your reward in heaven: for so persecuted they the prophets which were before you.

Ye are the salt of the earth: but if the salt have lost his savour, wherewith shall it be salted? It is thenceforth good for nothing, but to be cast out, and to be trodden under foot of men.

Ye are the light of the world. A city that is set on an hill cannot be hid. Neither do men light a candle, and put it under a bushel, but on a candlestick; and it giveth light unto all that are in the house. Let your light so shine before men, that they may see your good works, and glorify your Father which is in heaven.

For ye were sometimes darkness, but now *are ye* light in the Lord: walk as children of light: (for the fruit of the Spirit *is* in all goodness and righteousness and truth;) proving what is acceptable unto the Lord.

MATTHEW 5:11-16; EPHESIANS 5:8-10

**THE ONE MINUTE BIBLE**

---

***Related texts:*** PROVERBS 13:9; MARK 9:50; LUKE 14:34-35; 1 PETER 4:12-19

153

**THE ONE
MINUTE
BIBLE**

# Sermon on the Mount: *Fulfilling the Law*

Think not that I am come to destroy the law, or the prophets: I am not come to destroy, but to fulfil. For verily I say unto you, Till heaven and earth pass, one jot or one tittle shall in no wise pass from the law, till all be fulfilled.

Whosoever therefore shall break one of these least commandments, and shall teach men so, he shall be called the least in the kingdom of heaven: but whosoever shall do and teach *them*, the same shall be called great in the kingdom of heaven. For I say unto you, That except your righteousness shall exceed *the righteousness* of the scribes and Pharisees, ye shall in no case enter into the kingdom of heaven.

*There is* therefore now no condemnation to them which are in Christ Jesus, who walk not after the flesh, but after the Spirit. For the law of the Spirit of life in Christ Jesus hath made me free from the law of sin and death. For what the law could not do, in that it was weak through the flesh, God sending his own Son in the likeness of sinful flesh, and for sin, condemned sin in the flesh: that the righteousness of the law might be fulfilled in us, who walk not after the flesh, but after the Spirit.

MATTHEW 5:17-20; ROMANS 8:1-4

***Related texts:*** PSALM 119:161-176; MATTHEW 22:34-40; ROMANS 3:21-31; 7-8

# Sermon on the Mount: *Murder and Hate*

Ye have heard that it was said by them of old time, Thou shalt not kill; and whosoever shall kill shall be in danger of the judgment: but I say unto you, That whosoever is angry with his brother without a cause shall be in danger of the judgment: and whosoever shall say to his brother, Raca, shall be in danger of the council: but whosoever shall say, Thou fool, shall be in danger of hell fire.

Therefore if thou bring thy gift to the altar, and there rememberest that thy brother hath ought against thee; leave there thy gift before the altar, and go thy way; first be reconciled to thy brother, and then come and offer thy gift.

Agree with thine adversary quickly, whiles thou art in the way with him; lest at any time the adversary deliver thee to the judge, and the judge deliver thee to the officer, and thou be cast into prison. Verily I say unto thee, Thou shalt by no means come out thence, till thou hast paid the uttermost farthing.

He that saith he is in the light, and hateth his brother, is in darkness even until now. He that loveth his brother abideth in the light, and there is none occasion of stumbling in him. But he that hateth his brother is in darkness, and walketh in darkness, and knoweth not whither he goeth, because that darkness hath blinded his eyes.

MATTHEW 5:21-26; 1 JOHN 2:9-11

*Related texts:* EXODUS 20:13; PROVERBS 8:12-13; MATTHEW 5:38-48; LUKE 6:22-36

# Sermon on the Mount: *Adultery*

**THE ONE MINUTE BIBLE**

Ye have heard that it was said by them of old time, Thou shalt not commit adultery: but I say unto you, That whosoever looketh on a woman to lust after her hath committed adultery with her already in his heart. And if thy right eye offend thee, pluck it out, and cast *it* from thee: for it is profitable for thee that one of thy members should perish, and not *that* thy whole body should be cast into hell. And if thy right hand offend thee, cut it off, and cast *it* from thee: for it is profitable for thee that one of thy members should perish, and not *that* thy whole body should be cast into hell.

It hath been said, Whosoever shall put away his wife, let him give her a writing of divorcement: but I say unto you, That whosoever shall put away his wife, saving for the cause of fornication, causeth her to commit adultery: and whosoever shall marry her that is divorced committeth adultery.

For this is the will of God, *even* your sanctification, that ye should abstain from fornication: that every one of you should know how to possess his vessel in sanctification and honour; not in the lust of concupiscence, even as the Gentiles which know not God: that no *man* go beyond and defraud his brother in *any* matter: because that the Lord *is* the avenger of all such, as we also have forewarned you and testified. For God hath not called us unto uncleanness, but unto holiness. He therefore that despiseth, despiseth not man, but God, who hath also given unto us his holy Spirit.

MATTHEW 5:27-32; 1 THESSALONIANS 4:3-8

*Related texts:* DEUTERONOMY 24:1-4; PROVERBS 5; MALACHI 2:10-16; MATTHEW 19:3-12; 1 CORINTHIANS 7

# Sermon on the Mount: *Love, Not Revenge*

THE ONE
MINUTE
BIBLE

Ye have heard that it hath been said, An eye for an eye, and a tooth for a tooth: but I say unto you, That ye resist not evil: but whosoever shall smite thee on thy right cheek, turn to him the other also. And if any man will sue thee at the law, and take away thy coat, let him have *thy* cloak also. And whosoever shall compel thee to go a mile, go with him twain. Give to him that asketh thee, and from him that would borrow of thee turn not thou away.

Ye have heard that it hath been said, Thou shalt love thy neighbour, and hate thine enemy. But I say unto you, Love your enemies, bless them that curse you, do good to them that hate you, and pray for them which despitefully use you, and persecute you; that ye may be the children of your Father which is in heaven: for he maketh his sun to rise on the evil and on the good, and sendeth rain on the just and on the unjust. For if ye love them which love you, what reward have ye? Do not even the publicans the same? And if ye salute your brethren only, what do ye more *than others*? Do not even the publicans so? Be ye therefore perfect, even as your Father which is in heaven is perfect.

Beloved, let us love one another: for love is of God; and every one that loveth is born of God, and knoweth God. He that loveth not knoweth not God; for God is love.

MATTHEW 5:38-48; 1 JOHN 4:7-8

---

*Related texts:* GENESIS 12:1-3; LEVITICUS 24:17-20; LUKE 6:27-37; ROMANS 12:14-18

**THE ONE MINUTE BIBLE**

# Sermon on the Mount: *Treasure in Heaven*

Take heed that ye do not your alms before men, to be seen of them: otherwise ye have no reward of your Father which is in heaven.

Therefore when thou doest *thine* alms, do not sound a trumpet before thee, as the hypocrites do in the synagogues and in the streets, that they may have glory of men. Verily I say unto you, They have their reward. But when thou doest alms, let not thy left hand know what thy right hand doeth: that thine alms may be in secret: and thy Father which seeth in secret himself shall reward thee openly.

Lay not up for yourselves treasures upon earth, where moth and rust doth corrupt, and where thieves break through and steal: but lay up for yourselves treasures in heaven, where neither moth nor rust doth corrupt, and where thieves do not break through nor steal: for where your treasure is, there will your heart be also.

The light of the body is the eye: if therefore thine eye be single, thy whole body shall be full of light. But if thine eye be evil, thy whole body shall be full of darkness. If therefore the light that is in thee be darkness, how great *is* that darkness!

No man can serve two masters: for either he will hate the one, and love the other; or else he will hold to the one, and despise the other. Ye cannot serve God and mammon.

MATTHEW 6:1-4, 19-24

*Related texts:* PROVERBS 11:24-25; MARK 10:17-31; LUKE 6:38; 12:32-34; ACTS 20:32-35; 2 CORINTHIANS 9:6-15

# Sermon on the Mount: *Prayer*

And when thou prayest, thou shalt not be as the hypocrites *are*: for they love to pray standing in the synagogues and in the corners of the streets, that they may be seen of men. Verily I say unto you, They have their reward. But thou, when thou prayest, enter into thy closet, and when thou hast shut thy door, pray to thy Father which is in secret; and thy Father which seeth in secret shall reward thee openly. But when ye pray, use not vain repetitions, as the heathen *do*: for they think that they shall be heard for their much speaking. Be not ye therefore like unto them: for your Father knoweth what things ye have need of, before ye ask him.

After this manner therefore pray ye:

Our Father which art in heaven,
Hallowed be thy name.
Thy kingdom come.
Thy will be done
    in earth, as *it is* in heaven.
Give us this day our daily bread.
And forgive us our debts,
    as we forgive our debtors.
And lead us not into temptation,
but deliver us from evil:
For thine is the kingdom,
    and the power, and the glory, for ever. Amen.

For if ye forgive men their trespasses, your heavenly Father will also forgive you: but if ye forgive not men their trespasses, neither will your Father forgive your trespasses.

MATTHEW 6:5-15

*Related texts:* PSALM 5; MARK 11:22-26; LUKE 11:1-13; 18:1-14; JAMES 5:13-20

# Sermon on the Mount: *Fasting*

**THE ONE
MINUTE
BIBLE**

Moreover when ye fast, be not, as the hypocrites, of a sad countenance: for they disfigure their faces, that they may appear unto men to fast. Verily I say unto you, They have their reward. But thou, when thou fastest, anoint thine head, and wash thy face; that thou appear not unto men to fast, but unto thy Father which is in secret: and thy Father, which seeth in secret, shall reward thee openly.

And the disciples of John and of the Pharisees used to fast: and they come and say unto him, Why do the disciples of John and of the Pharisees fast, but thy disciples fast not?

And Jesus said unto them, Can the children of the bridechamber fast, while the bridegroom is with them? *as* long as they have the bridegroom with them, they cannot fast. But the days will come, when the bridegroom shall be taken away from them, and then shall they fast in those days.

No man also seweth a piece of new cloth on an old garment: else the new piece that filled it up taketh away from the old, and the rent is made worse. And no man putteth new wine into old bottles: else the new wine doth burst the bottles, and the wine is spilled, and the bottles will be marred: but new wine must be put into new bottles.

MATTHEW 6:16-18; MARK 2:18-22

*Related texts:* ESTHER 3–4; ISAIAH 58; JONAH 3; ZECHARIAH 7–8; ACTS 14:21-23

# Sermon on the Mount: *Why Worry?*

Therefore I say unto you, Take no thought for your life, what ye shall eat, or what ye shall drink; nor yet for your body, what ye shall put on. Is not the life more than meat, and the body than raiment? Behold the fowls of the air: for they sow not, neither do they reap, nor gather into barns; yet your heavenly Father feedeth them. Are ye not much better than they? Which of you by taking thought can add one cubit unto his stature?

And why take ye thought for raiment? Consider the lilies of the field, how they grow; they toil not, neither do they spin: and yet I say unto you, That even Solomon in all his glory was not arrayed like one of these. Wherefore, if God so clothe the grass of the field, which to day is, and to morrow is cast into the oven, *shall he* not much more *clothe* you, O ye of little faith?

Therefore take no thought, saying, What shall we eat? or, What shall we drink? or, Wherewithal shall we be clothed? (For after all these things do the Gentiles seek:) for your heavenly Father knoweth that ye have need of all these things. But seek ye first the kingdom of God, and his righteousness; and all these things shall be added unto you. Take therefore no thought for the morrow: for the morrow shall take thought for the things of itself. Sufficient unto the day *is* the evil thereof.

Matthew 6:25-34

**THE ONE MINUTE BIBLE**

*Related texts:* Proverbs 12:25; Mark 13:11; Luke 12:11-34; Philippians 4:6-7

# Sermon on the Mount: *Judging and Asking*

**THE ONE
MINUTE
BIBLE**

Judge not, that ye be not judged. For with what judgment ye judge, ye shall be judged: and with what measure ye mete, it shall be measured to you again.

And why beholdest thou the mote that is in thy brother's eye, but considerest not the beam that is in thine own eye? Or how wilt thou say to thy brother, Let me pull out the mote out of thine eye; and, behold, a beam *is* in thine own eye? Thou hypocrite, first cast out the beam out of thine own eye; and then shalt thou see clearly to cast out the mote out of thy brother's eye.

Give not that which is holy unto the dogs, neither cast ye your pearls before swine, lest they trample them under their feet, and turn again and rend you.

Ask, and it shall be given you; seek, and ye shall find; knock, and it shall be opened unto you: for every one that asketh receiveth; and he that seeketh findeth; and to him that knocketh it shall be opened.

Or what man is there of you, whom if his son ask bread, will he give him a stone? Or if he ask a fish, will he give him a serpent? If ye then, being evil, know how to give good gifts unto your children, how much more shall your Father which is in heaven give good things to them that ask him? Therefore all things whatsoever ye would that men should do to you, do ye even so to them: for this is the law and the prophets.

MATTHEW 7:1-12

*Related texts:* ROMANS 14:1-13; JOHN 16:24; 1 CORINTHIANS 5; JAMES 4:1-3; 1 JOHN 3:21-22

# Sermon on the Mount: *The Two Ways*

**THE ONE
MINUTE
BIBLE**

Enter ye in at the strait gate: for wide *is* the gate, and broad *is* the way, that leadeth to destruction, and many there be which go in thereat: because strait *is* the gate, and narrow *is* the way, which leadeth unto life, and few there be that find it.

Not every one that saith unto me, Lord, Lord, shall enter into the kingdom of heaven; but he that doeth the will of my Father which is in heaven. Many will say to me in that day, Lord, Lord, have we not prophesied in thy name? And in thy name have cast out devils? And in thy name done many wonderful works? And then will I profess unto them, I never knew you: depart from me, ye that work iniquity.

Therefore whosoever heareth these sayings of mine, and doeth them, I will liken him unto a wise man, which built his house upon a rock: and the rain descended, and the floods came, and the winds blew, and beat upon that house; and it fell not: for it was founded upon a rock. And every one that heareth these sayings of mine, and doeth them not, shall be likened unto a foolish man, which built his house upon the sand: and the rain descended, and the floods came, and the winds blew, and beat upon that house; and it fell: and great was the fall of it.

And it came to pass, when Jesus had ended these sayings, the people were astonished at his doctrine: for he taught them as *one* having authority, and not as the scribes.

MATTHEW 7:13-14, 21-29

*Related texts:* PROVERBS 14:11-12; LUKE 13:22-30; JOHN 10:1-10; EPHESIANS 2:13-22

*By the reading of Scripture I am so renewed that all nature seems renewed around me and with me. The whole world is charged with the glory of God and I feel fire and music under my feet.*
**Thomas Merton (1915-1968)**
AMERICAN MONK

*The Scripture...dispels the darkness and gives us a clear view of the true God.*
**John Calvin (1509-1564)**
FRENCH THEOLOGIAN AND REFORMER

*Give me a used Bible and I will, I think, be able to tell you about a man by the places that are edged with the dirt of seeking fingers.*
**John Steinbeck (1902-1968)**
AMERICAN NOVELIST

# The Golden Calf

THE ONE
MINUTE
BIBLE

And when the people saw that Moses delayed to come down out of the mount, the people gathered themselves together unto Aaron, and said unto him, Up, make us gods, which shall go before us; for *as for* this Moses, the man that brought us up out of the land of Egypt, we wot not what is become of him.

And Aaron said unto them, Break off the golden earrings, which *are* in the ears of your wives, of your sons, and of your daughters, and bring *them* unto me. And he received *them* at their hand, and fashioned it with a graving tool, after he had made it a molten calf: and they said, These *be* thy gods, O Israel, which brought thee up out of the land of Egypt.

And when Aaron saw *it*, he built an altar before it; and Aaron made proclamation, and said, To morrow *is* a feast to the LORD. And they rose up early on the morrow, and offered burnt offerings, and brought peace offerings; and the people sat down to eat and to drink, and rose up to play.

And the LORD said unto Moses, Go, get thee down; for thy people, which thou broughtest out of the land of Egypt, have corrupted *themselves*: they have turned aside quickly out of the way which I commanded them: they have made them a molten calf, and have worshipped it, and have sacrificed thereunto, and said, These *be* thy gods, O Israel, which have brought thee up out of the land of Egypt.

And the LORD said unto Moses, I have seen this people, and, behold, it *is* a stiffnecked people: now therefore let me alone, that my wrath may wax hot against them, and that I may consume them: and I will make of thee a great nation.

EXODUS 32:1-2, 4-10

*Related texts:* DEUTERONOMY 9:7-15; NEHEMIAH 9:16-19; PSALM 106:19-22; ACTS 7:37-41

# Moses Pleads for the Israelites

**THE ONE
MINUTE
BIBLE**

And Moses besought the LORD his God, and said, LORD, why doth thy wrath wax hot against thy people, which thou hast brought forth out of the land of Egypt with great power, and with a mighty hand? Wherefore should the Egyptians speak, and say, For mischief did he bring them out, to slay them in the mountains, and to consume them from the face of the earth? Turn from thy fierce wrath, and repent of this evil against thy people. Remember Abraham, Isaac, and Israel, thy servants, to whom thou swarest by thine own self, and saidst unto them, I will multiply your seed as the stars of heaven, and all this land that I have spoken of will I give unto your seed, and they shall inherit *it* for ever. And the LORD repented of the evil which he thought to do unto his people.

And Moses turned, and went down from the mount, and the two tables of the testimony *were* in his hand: the tables *were* written on both their sides; on the one side and on the other *were* they written. And the tables *were* the work of God, and the writing *was* the writing of God, graven upon the tables.

And it came to pass, as soon as he came nigh unto the camp, that he saw the calf, and the dancing: and Moses' anger waxed hot, and he cast the tables out of his hands, and brake them beneath the mount. And he took the calf which they had made, and burnt *it* in the fire, and ground *it* to powder, and strawed *it* upon the water, and made the children of Israel drink *of it*.

EXODUS 32:11-16, 19-20

---

***Related texts:*** GENESIS 15:1-5; 22:15-18; 26:2-4; DEUTERONOMY 9:16-21; PSALM 106:23; JONAH 3; ACTS 7:40-42

168

## *Israel's History Is Our Warning*

Moreover, brethren, I would not that ye should be ignorant, how that all our fathers were under the cloud, and all passed through the sea; and were all baptized unto Moses in the cloud and in the sea; and did all eat the same spiritual meat; and did all drink the same spiritual drink: for they drank of that spiritual Rock that followed them: and that Rock was Christ. But with many of them God was not well pleased: for they were overthrown in the wilderness.

**THE ONE MINUTE BIBLE**

Now these things were our examples, to the intent we should not lust after evil things, as they also lusted. Neither be ye idolaters, as *were* some of them; as it is written, The people sat down to eat and drink, and rose up to play. Neither let us commit fornication, as some of them committed, and fell in one day three and twenty thousand.

Now all these things happened unto them for ensamples: and they are written for our admonition, upon whom the ends of the world are come. Wherefore let him that thinketh he standeth take heed lest he fall. There hath no temptation taken you but such as is common to man: but God *is* faithful, who will not suffer you to be tempted above that ye are able; but will with the temptation also make a way to escape, that ye may be able to bear *it*.

1 CORINTHIANS 10:1-8, 11-13

***Related texts:*** EXODUS 14; 17:1-7; 32; JOHN 6; HEBREWS 2:9-18; JAMES 1:12-15

## *God Forgives Those Who Repent*

**THE ONE
MINUTE
BIBLE**

And the LORD said unto Moses, Hew thee two tables of stone like unto the first: and I will write upon *these* tables the words that were in the first tables, which thou brakest.

And he hewed two tables of stone like unto the first; and Moses rose up early in the morning, and went up unto mount Sinai, as the LORD had commanded him, and took in his hand the two tables of stone. And the LORD descended in the cloud, and stood with him there, and proclaimed the name of the LORD. And the LORD passed by before him, and proclaimed, The LORD, The LORD God, merciful and gracious, longsuffering, and abundant in goodness and truth, keeping mercy for thousands, forgiving iniquity and transgression and sin, and that will by no means clear *the guilty*; visiting the iniquity of the fathers upon the children, and upon the children's children, unto the third and to the fourth *generation*.

And Moses made haste, and bowed his head toward the earth, and worshipped. And he said, If now I have found grace in thy sight, O Lord, let my Lord, I pray thee, go among us; for it *is* a stiffnecked people; and pardon our iniquity and our sin, and take us for thine inheritance.

And he said, Behold, I make a covenant: before all thy people I will do marvels, such as have not been done in all the earth, nor in any nation: and all the people among which thou *art* shall see the work of the LORD: for it *is* a terrible thing that I will do with thee.

EXODUS 34:1, 4-10

*Related texts:* PSALMS 86:15; 103:8; 145:8; JOHN 3:16-21; 1 JOHN 1:9

## *God Is Compassionate*

And be not ye like your fathers, and like your brethren, which trespassed against the LORD God of their fathers, *who* therefore gave them up to desolation, as ye see. Now be ye not stiffnecked, as your fathers *were*, *but* yield yourselves unto the LORD, and enter into his sanctuary, which he hath sanctified for ever: and serve the LORD your God, that the fierceness of his wrath may turn away from you. For if ye turn again unto the LORD, your brethren and your children *shall find* compassion before them that lead them captive, so that they shall come again into this land: for the LORD your God *is* gracious and merciful, and will not turn away *his* face from you, if ye return unto him.

The LORD *is* gracious, and full of compassion;
    slow to anger, and of great mercy.
The LORD *is* good to all:
    and his tender mercies *are* over all his works.

Blessed *be* God, even the Father of our Lord Jesus Christ, the Father of mercies, and the God of all comfort; who comforteth us in all our tribulation, that we may be able to comfort them which are in any trouble, by the comfort wherewith we ourselves are comforted of God. For as the sufferings of Christ abound in us, so our consolation also aboundeth by Christ.

2 CHRONICLES 30:7-9; PSALM 145:8-9; 2 CORINTHIANS 1:3-5

*Related texts:* EXODUS 33:19; 2 CHRONICLES 30:7-9; NEHEMIAH 9:16-19; PSALM 103; LAMENTATIONS 3:19-23; COLOSSIANS 3:12-14

## *God Is Forgiving*

**THE ONE
MINUTE
BIBLE**

Who *is* a God like unto thee,
    that pardoneth iniquity,
    and passeth by the transgression of the remnant
        of his heritage?
He retaineth not his anger for ever,
    because he delighteth *in* mercy.
He will turn again, he will have compassion upon us;
    he will subdue our iniquities;
    and thou wilt cast all their sins into the depths
        of the sea.
Thou wilt perform the truth to Jacob,
    *and* the mercy to Abraham,
which thou hast sworn unto our fathers
    from the days of old.

This then is the message which we have heard of
him, and declare unto you, that God is light, and in him
is no darkness at all. If we say that we have fellowship
with him, and walk in darkness, we lie, and do not the
truth: but if we walk in the light, as he is in the light, we
have fellowship one with another, and the blood of
Jesus Christ his Son cleanseth us from all sin.

If we say that we have no sin, we deceive ourselves,
and the truth is not in us. If we confess our sins, he is
faithful and just to forgive us *our* sins, and to cleanse us
from all unrighteousness. If we say that we have not
sinned, we make him a liar, and his word is not in us.

MICAH 7:18-20; 1 JOHN 1:5-10

***Related texts:*** NUMBERS 14:1-35; 1 KINGS 8:27-53; PSALM 32:1-5;
DANIEL 9:1-19; MATTHEW 6:14-15; 18:21-35

## *God Is Gracious*

THE ONE
MINUTE
BIBLE

Gracious *is* the L<small>ORD</small>, and righteous;
yea, our God *is* merciful.
The L<small>ORD</small> preserveth the simple:
I was brought low, and he helped me.
Return unto thy rest, O my soul;
for the L<small>ORD</small> hath dealt bountifully with thee.

And the Word was made flesh, and dwelt among us,
(and we beheld his glory, the glory as of the only begotten
of the Father,) full of grace and truth.
And of his fulness have all we received, and grace for
grace. For the law was given by Moses, *but* grace and
truth came by Jesus Christ.

But God, who is rich in mercy, for his great love
wherewith he loved us, even when we were dead in sins,
hath quickened us together with Christ, (by grace ye are
saved;) and hath raised *us* up together, and made *us* sit
together in heavenly *places* in Christ Jesus: that in the
ages to come he might show the exceeding riches of his
grace in *his* kindness toward us through Christ Jesus.
For by grace are ye saved through faith; and that not of
yourselves: *it is* the gift of God: not of works, lest any man
should boast.

P<small>SALM</small> 116:5-7; J<small>OHN</small> 1:14, 16-17; E<small>PHESIANS</small> 2:4-9

*Related texts:* N<small>UMBERS</small> 6:24-26; P<small>ROVERBS</small> 3:33-35; R<small>OMANS</small> 5:12-21

## *God Is Holy*

**THE ONE
MINUTE
BIBLE**

For I *am* the LORD that bringeth you up out of the land of Egypt, to be your God: ye shall therefore be holy, for I *am* holy.

In the year that king Uzziah died I saw also the Lord sitting upon a throne, high and lifted up, and his train filled the temple. Above it stood the seraphims: each one had six wings; with twain he covered his face, and with twain he covered his feet, and with twain he did fly. And one cried unto another, and said,

Holy, holy, holy, *is* the LORD of hosts:
   the whole earth *is* full of his glory.

For thus saith the high and lofty One
   that inhabiteth eternity, whose name *is* Holy;
I dwell in the high and holy *place*,
   with him also *that is* of a contrite and humble spirit,
to revive the spirit of the humble,
   and to revive the heart of the contrite ones.
For I will not contend for ever,
   neither will I be always wroth:
for the spirit should fail before me,
   and the souls *which* I have made.

As obedient children, not fashioning yourselves according to the former lusts in your ignorance: but as he which hath called you is holy, so be ye holy in all manner of conversation; because it is written, Be ye holy; for I am holy.

LEVITICUS 11:45; ISAIAH 6:1-3; 57:15-16; 1 PETER 1:14-16

*Related texts:* EXODUS 15:11; LEVITICUS 22:31-33; PSALM 99;
REVELATION 4; 15:2-4

174

## *God Is Merciful*

With the merciful thou wilt show thyself merciful,
*and* with the upright man thou wilt show thyself
   upright.
With the pure thou wilt show thyself pure;
   and with the froward thou wilt show thyself
      unsavoury.
And the afflicted people thou wilt save:
   but thine eyes *are* upon the haughty,
      *that* thou mayest bring *them* down.
For thou *art* my lamp, O Lord:
   and the Lord will lighten my darkness.
For by thee I have run through a troop:
   by my God have I leaped over a wall.


And you *hath he quickened*, who were dead in
trespasses and sins: wherein in time past ye walked
according to the course of this world, according to the
prince of the power of the air, the spirit that now
worketh in the children of disobedience: Among whom
also we all had our conversation in times past in the
lusts of our flesh, fulfilling the desires of the flesh and
of the mind; and were by nature the children of wrath,
even as others. But God, who is rich in mercy, for his
great love wherewith he loved us, even when we were
dead in sins, hath quickened us together with Christ,
(by grace ye are saved.)

2 Samuel 22:26-30; Ephesians 2:1-5

THE ONE
MINUTE
BIBLE

---

*Related texts:* Exodus 33:19; Deuteronomy 4:31; Nehemiah 9:29-31;
Micah 7:18-20; Romans 9:11-18

## *God Is All-Powerful*

**THE ONE
MINUTE
BIBLE**

Then Job answered the LORD, and said,
    I know that thou canst do every *thing*,
    and *that* no thought can be withholden from thee.


Ascribe ye strength unto God:
    his excellency *is* over Israel,
    and his strength *is* in the clouds.
O God, *thou art* terrible out of thy holy places:
    the God of Israel *is* he that giveth strength and power
        unto *his* people.
Blessed *be* God.


Ah Lord GOD! Behold, thou hast made the heaven and
the earth by thy great power and stretched out arm, *and*
there is nothing too hard for thee: thou showest
lovingkindness unto thousands, and recompensest the
iniquity of the fathers into the bosom of their children
after them: the Great, the Mighty God, the LORD of hosts,
is *his* name, great in counsel, and mighty in work: for
thine eyes *are* open upon all the ways of the sons of
men: to give every one according to his ways, and
according to the fruit of his doings.


Thou art worthy, O Lord,
    to receive glory and honour and power:
for thou hast created all things,
    and for thy pleasure they are
    and were created.

JOB 42:1-2; PSALM 68:34-35; JEREMIAH 32:17-19; REVELATION 4:11

---

***Related texts:*** GENESIS 18:14; EXODUS 15:1-18; PSALM 29; MARK 4:35-41

## *God Is Everywhere*

Whither shall I go from thy spirit?
Or whither shall I flee from thy presence?
If I ascend up into heaven, thou *art* there:
if I make my bed in hell, behold, thou *art there.*
*If* I take the wings of the morning,
*and* dwell in the uttermost parts of the sea;
even there shall thy hand lead me,
and thy right hand shall hold me.

If I say, Surely the darkness shall cover me;
even the night shall be light about me.
Yea, the darkness hideth not from thee;
but the night shineth as the day:
the darkness and the light *are* both alike *to thee.*

*Am* I a God at hand,
saith the Lord,
and not a God afar off?
Can any hide himself in secret places
that I shall not see him?
saith the Lord.
Do not I fill heaven and earth?
saith the Lord.

And Jesus came and spake unto them, saying, All
power is given unto me in heaven and in earth. Go ye
therefore, and teach all nations, baptizing them in the
name of the Father, and of the Son, and of the Holy
Ghost: teaching them to observe all things whatsoever I
have commanded you: and, lo, I am with you alway, *even*
unto the end of the world. Amen.

Psalm 139:7-12; Jeremiah 23:23-24; Matthew 28:18-20

**THE ONE
MINUTE
BIBLE**

*Related texts:* Deuteronomy 4:7; 1 Kings 8:27; John 1:45-49; 14:16-17

## *God Knows Everything*

**THE ONE
MINUTE
BIBLE**

O LORD, thou hast searched me,
   and known *me*.
Thou knowest my downsitting and mine uprising,
   thou understandest my thought afar off.
Thou compassest my path and my lying down,
   and art acquainted *with* all my ways.
For *there is* not a word in my tongue,
   *but*, lo, O LORD, thou knowest it altogether.

Thou hast beset me behind and before,
   and laid thine hand upon me.
*Such* knowledge *is* too wonderful for me;
   it is high, I cannot *attain* unto it.

O the depth of the riches both of the wisdom and
      knowledge of God!
   How unsearchable *are* his judgments,
   and his ways past finding out!
For who hath known the mind of the Lord?
   Or who hath been his counsellor?
Or who hath first given to him,
   and it shall be recompensed unto him again?
For of him, and through him, and to him, *are* all things:
   to whom *be* glory for ever. Amen.

   For the word of God *is* quick, and powerful, and
sharper than any twoedged sword, piercing even to the
dividing asunder of soul and spirit, and of the joints and
marrow, and *is* a discerner of the thoughts and intents of
the heart. Neither is there any creature that is not
manifest in his sight: but all things *are* naked and
opened unto the eyes of him with whom we have to do.

PSALM 139:1-6; ROMANS 11:33-36; HEBREWS 4:12-13

*Related texts:* PSALM 94:1-11; PROVERBS 5:21; 2 CHRONICLES 16:9;
1 CORINTHIANS 1:18-25; JOHN 3:19-20

## *God Is One*

Hear, O Israel: The LORD our God *is* one LORD: and thou shalt love the LORD thy God with all thine heart, and with all thy soul, and with all thy might.

And the LORD shall be king over all the earth: in that day shall there be one LORD, and his name one.

*Is he* the God of the Jews only? *Is he* not also of the Gentiles? Yes, of the Gentiles also: seeing *it is* one God, which shall justify the circumcision by faith, and uncircumcision through faith.

For though there be that are called gods, whether in heaven or in earth, (as there be gods many, and lords many,) but to us *there is but* one God, the Father, of whom *are* all things, and we in him; and one Lord Jesus Christ, by whom *are* all things, and we by him.

*There is* one body, and one Spirit, even as ye are called in one hope of your calling; one Lord, one faith, one baptism, one God and Father of all, who *is* above all, and through all, and in you all.

DEUTERONOMY 6:4-5; ZECHARIAH 14:9; ROMANS 3:29-30;
1 CORINTHIANS 8:5-6; EPHESIANS 4:4-6

**THE ONE
MINUTE
BIBLE**

*Related texts:* ISAIAH 44:6-8; MALACHI 2:10; MATTHEW 19:16-17;
23:1-10; MARK 12:28-34

## *God Is Righteous*

**THE ONE
MINUTE
BIBLE**

Arise, O Lᴏʀᴅ, in thine anger,
    lift up thyself because of the rage of mine enemies:
    and awake for me *to* the judgment *that* thou hast
        commanded.
So shall the congregation of the people compass thee about:
    for their sakes therefore return thou on high.
The Lᴏʀᴅ shall judge the people:
judge me, O Lᴏʀᴅ, according to my righteousness,
    and according to mine integrity *that is* in me.
Oh let the wickedness of the wicked come to an end;
    but establish the just:
for the righteous God
    trieth the hearts and reins.
My defence *is* of God,
    which saveth the upright in heart.
God judgeth the righteous,
    and God is angry *with the wicked* every day.

Behold, the days come, saith the Lᴏʀᴅ,
    that I will raise unto David a righteous Branch,
and a King shall reign and prosper,
    and shall execute judgment and justice in the earth.
In his days Judah shall be saved,
    and Israel shall dwell safely:
and this *is* his name whereby he shall be called,
    THE LORD OUR RIGHTEOUSNESS.

My little children, these things write I unto you, that ye
sin not. And if any man sin, we have an advocate with the
Father, Jesus Christ the righteous: and he is the
propitiation for our sins: and not for ours only, but also for
*the sins of* the whole world.

Psᴀʟᴍ 7:6-11; Jᴇʀᴇᴍɪᴀʜ 23:5-6; 1 Jᴏʜɴ 2:1-2

***Related texts:*** Eᴢʀᴀ 9; Psᴀʟᴍs 36:5-10; 71; Dᴀɴɪᴇʟ 9:1-19;
Mᴀᴛᴛʜᴇᴡ 6:28-33; Aᴄᴛs 3:12-16

## *Our Heavenly Father*

For ye are all the children of God by faith in Christ Jesus. For as many of you as have been baptized into Christ have put on Christ. There is neither Jew nor Greek, there is neither bond nor free, there is neither male nor female: for ye are all one in Christ Jesus. And if ye *be* Christ's, then are ye Abraham's seed, and heirs according to the promise.

Now I say, That the heir, as long as he is a child, differeth nothing from a servant, though he be lord of all; but is under tutors and governors until the time appointed of the father. Even so we, when we were children, were in bondage under the elements of the world: but when the fulness of the time was come, God sent forth his Son, made of a woman, made under the law, to redeem them that were under the law, that we might receive the adoption of sons. And because ye are sons, God hath sent forth the Spirit of his Son into your hearts, crying, Abba, Father. Wherefore thou art no more a servant, but a son; and if a son, then an heir of God through Christ.

Behold, what manner of love the Father hath bestowed upon us, that we should be called the sons of God: therefore the world knoweth us not, because it knew him not. Beloved, now are we the sons of God, and it doth not yet appear what we shall be: but we know that, when he shall appear, we shall be like him; for we shall see him as he is.

GALATIANS 3:26-29; 4:1-7; 1 JOHN 3:1-2

**THE ONE MINUTE BIBLE**

***Related texts:*** DEUTERONOMY 32:6; PSALM 2; ISAIAH 9:1-7; JOHN 1:12-13; ROMANS 8; HEBREWS 12:1-14

## *Honor Your Father*

**THE ONE
MINUTE
BIBLE**

Honour thy father and thy mother: that thy days may be long upon the land which the LORD thy God giveth thee.

He that begetteth a fool *doeth it* to his sorrow:
    and the father of a fool hath no joy.

My son, if thine heart be wise,
    my heart shall rejoice, even mine.
Yea, my reins shall rejoice,
    when thy lips speak right things.
Hear thou, my son, and be wise,
    and guide thine heart in the way.

Let the word of Christ dwell in you richly in all wisdom; teaching and admonishing one another in psalms and hymns and spiritual songs, singing with grace in your hearts to the Lord. And whatsoever ye do in word or deed, *do* all in the name of the Lord Jesus, giving thanks to God and the Father by him.

Wives, submit yourselves unto your own husbands, as it is fit in the Lord.

Husbands, love *your* wives, and be not bitter against them.

Children, obey *your* parents in all things: for this is well pleasing unto the Lord.

Fathers, provoke not your children *to* anger, lest they be discouraged.

EXODUS 20:12; PROVERBS 17:21; 23:15-16, 19; COLOSSIANS 3:16-21

---

***Related texts:*** EXODUS 21:15; LEVITICUS 19:3; PROVERBS 10:1; 23:22-25; EPHESIANS 6:1-3

## *A Father's Instruction*

Hear, ye children, the instruction of a father,
    and attend to know understanding.
For I give you good doctrine,
    forsake ye not my law.
For I was my father's son,
    tender and only *beloved* in the sight of my mother.
He taught me also, and said unto me,
    Let thine heart retain my words:
    keep my commandments, and live.
Get wisdom, get understanding:
    forget *it* not; neither decline from the words
        of my mouth.
Forsake her not, and she shall preserve thee:
    love her, and she shall keep thee.
Wisdom *is* the principal thing; *therefore* get wisdom:
    and with all thy getting get understanding.
Exalt her, and she shall promote thee:
    she shall bring thee to honour, when thou dost
        embrace her.
She shall give to thine head an ornament of grace:
    a crown of glory shall she deliver to thee.

Hear, O my son, and receive my sayings;
    and the years of thy life shall be many.
I have taught thee in the way of wisdom;
    I have led thee in right paths.
When thou goest, thy steps shall not be straitened;
    and when thou runnest, thou shalt not stumble.

PROVERBS 4:1-12

*Related texts:* DEUTERONOMY 6:1-9; PROVERBS 1:8; 6:20-24; 31:1-9;
2 TIMOTHY 1:2-3

## A Father's Discipline

Ye have not yet resisted unto blood, striving against sin. And ye have forgotten the exhortation which speaketh unto you as unto children,

My son, despise not thou the chastening of the Lord,
    nor faint when thou art rebuked of him:
for whom the Lord loveth he chasteneth,
    and scourgeth every son whom he receiveth.

If ye endure chastening, God dealeth with you as with sons; for what son is he whom the father chasteneth not? But if ye be without chastisement, whereof all are partakers, then are ye bastards, and not sons. Furthermore we have had fathers of our flesh which corrected *us*, and we gave *them* reverence: shall we not much rather be in subjection unto the Father of spirits, and live?

For they verily for a few days chastened *us* after their own pleasure; but he for *our* profit, that *we* might be partakers of his holiness. Now no chastening for the present seemeth to be joyous, but grievous: nevertheless afterward it yieldeth the peaceable fruit of righteousness unto them which are exercised thereby.

HEBREWS 12:4-11

*Related texts:* DEUTERONOMY 8:5; 1 SAMUEL 2:12-36; PROVERBS 3:11-12; 15:5; REVELATION 3:14-20

## *A Faithful Husband*

My son, attend unto my wisdom,
  *and* bow thine ear to my understanding:
that thou mayest regard discretion,
  and *that* thy lips may keep knowledge.
For the lips of a strange woman drop *as* an honeycomb,
  and her mouth *is* smoother than oil:
but her end is bitter as wormwood,
  sharp as a twoedged sword.

Drink waters out of thine own cistern,
  and running waters out of thine own well.
Let thy fountains be dispersed abroad,
  *and* rivers of waters in the streets.
Let them be only thine own,
  and not strangers' with thee.
Let thy fountain be blessed:
  and rejoice with the wife of thy youth.
*Let her be as* the loving hind and pleasant roe;
  let her breasts satisfy thee at all times;
  and be thou ravished always with her love.
And why wilt thou, my son, be ravished with a strange
    woman,
  and embrace the bosom of a stranger?

For the ways of man *are* before the eyes of the LORD,
  and he pondereth all his goings.
His own iniquities shall take the wicked himself,
  and he shall be holden with the cords of his sins.
He shall die without instruction;
  and in the greatness of his folly he shall go astray.

PROVERBS 5:1-4, 15-23

**THE ONE
MINUTE
BIBLE**

*Related texts:* EXODUS 20:14; LEVITICUS 20:10; PROVERBS 2:16-22;
6:23-35; 7; EPHESIANS 5:1-3

## *Love Song to a Husband*

**THE ONE
MINUTE
BIBLE**

As the apple tree among the trees of the wood,
    so *is* my beloved among the sons.
I sat down under his shadow with great delight,
    and his fruit *was* sweet to my taste.
He brought me to the banqueting house,
    and his banner over me *was* love.
Stay me with flagons,
    comfort me with apples:
    for I *am* sick of love.
His left hand *is* under my head,
    and his right hand doth embrace me.
The voice of my beloved!
    Behold, he cometh
leaping upon the mountains,
    skipping upon the hills.
My beloved is like a roe or a young hart:
    behold, he standeth behind our wall,
he looketh forth at the windows,
    showing himself through the lattice.
My beloved spake, and said unto me,
    Rise up, my love,
    my fair one, and come away.
For, lo, the winter is past,
    the rain is over *and* gone;
the flowers appear on the earth;
    the time of the singing *of birds* is come,
and the voice of the turtle
    is heard in our land;
the fig tree putteth forth her green figs,
    and the vines *with* the tender grape give a *good* smell.
Arise, my love,
    my fair one, and come away.

Song of Songs 2:3-6, 8-13

---

***Related texts:*** Psalm 45; Song of Songs 1–8; 2 Corinthians 11:2-3;
1 Peter 3:1-6

## Husbands, Love Your Wives

Husbands, love your wives, even as Christ also loved the church, and gave himself for it; that he might sanctify and cleanse it with the washing of water by the word, that he might present it to himself a glorious church, not having spot, or wrinkle, or any such thing; but that it should be holy and without blemish. So ought men to love their wives as their own bodies.

**THE ONE MINUTE BIBLE**

He that loveth his wife loveth himself. For no man ever yet hated his own flesh; but nourisheth and cherisheth it, even as the Lord the church: for we are members of his body, of his flesh, and of his bones. For this cause shall a man leave his father and mother, and shall be joined unto his wife, and they two shall be one flesh. This is a great mystery: but I speak concerning Christ and the church. Nevertheless let every one of you in particular so love his wife even as himself; and the wife *see* that she reverence *her* husband.

Likewise, ye husbands, dwell with *them* according to knowledge, giving honour unto the wife, as unto the weaker vessel, and as being heirs together of the grace of life; that your prayers be not hindered.

EPHESIANS 5:25-33; 1 PETER 3:7

*Related texts:* GENESIS 2:18-25; HOSEA 3:1-3; MALACHI 2:13-16; COLOSSIANS 3:19; REVELATION 21:1-4

## God's Daily Guidance for Israel

**THE ONE**
**MINUTE**
**BIBLE**

   And on the day that the tabernacle was reared up the cloud covered the tabernacle, *namely*, the tent of the testimony: and at even there was upon the tabernacle as it were the appearance of fire, until the morning. So it was alway: the cloud covered it *by day*, and the appearance of fire by night. And when the cloud was taken up from the tabernacle, then after that the children of Israel journeyed: and in the place where the cloud abode, there the children of Israel pitched their tents.

   At the commandment of the Lord the children of Israel journeyed, and at the commandment of the Lord they pitched: as long as the cloud abode upon the tabernacle they rested in their tents. And when the cloud tarried long upon the tabernacle many days, then the children of Israel kept the charge of the Lord, and journeyed not. And *so* it was, when the cloud was a few days upon the tabernacle; according to the commandment of the Lord they abode in their tents, and according to the commandment of the Lord they journeyed. And *so* it was, when the cloud abode from even unto the morning, and *that* the cloud was taken up in the morning, then they journeyed: whether *it was* by day or by night that the cloud was taken up, they journeyed. Or *whether it were* two days, or a month, or a year, that the cloud tarried upon the tabernacle, remaining thereon, the children of Israel abode in their tents, and journeyed not: but when it was taken up, they journeyed.

   At the commandment of the Lord they rested in the tents, and at the commandment of the Lord they journeyed: they kept the charge of the Lord, at the commandment of the Lord by the hand of Moses.

Numbers 9:15-23

*Related texts:* Exodus 13:22, 33; 40:34-38; Numbers 14:11-14; 1 Corinthians 10:1-2

## *Israel Puts God to the Test*

And they tempted God in their heart
  by asking meat for their lust.
Yea, they spake against God; they said,
  Can God furnish a table in the wilderness?
Behold, he smote the rock, that the waters gushed out,
  and the streams overflowed.
Can he give bread also?
  Can he provide flesh for his people?
Therefore the LORD heard *this*, and was wroth:
  so a fire was kindled against Jacob,
  and anger also came up against Israel;
because they believed not in God,
  and trusted not in his salvation:
though he had commanded the clouds from above,
  and opened the doors of heaven,
And had rained down manna upon them to eat,
  and had given them of the corn of heaven.
Man did eat angels' food:
  he sent them meat to the full.
He caused an east wind to blow in the heaven:
  and by his power he brought in the south wind.
He rained flesh also upon them as dust,
  and feathered fowls like as the sand of the sea:
and he let *it* fall in the midst of their camp,
  round about their habitations.
So they did eat, and were well filled:
  for he gave them their own desire;
they were not estranged from their lust.
  But while their meat *was* yet in their mouths,
the wrath of God came upon them,
  and slew the fattest of them,
  and smote down the chosen *men* of Israel.
For all this they sinned still,
  and believed not for his wondrous works.

PSALM 78:18-32

*Related texts:* NUMBERS 11; PSALM 106:1-15; LUKE 4:1-13; JAMES 4:1-4

# Israel Rejects the Promised Land

**THE ONE
MINUTE
BIBLE**

And the Lord spake unto Moses, saying, Send thou men, that they may search the land of Canaan, which I give unto the children of Israel: of every tribe of their fathers shall ye send a man, every one a ruler among them.

And they went and came to Moses, and to Aaron, and to all the congregation of the children of Israel, unto the wilderness of Paran, to Kadesh; and brought back word unto them, and unto all the congregation, and showed them the fruit of the land. And they told him, and said, We came unto the land whither thou sentest us, and surely it floweth with milk and honey; and this *is* the fruit of it. Nevertheless the people *be* strong that dwell in the land, and the cities *are* walled, *and* very great.

And Caleb stilled the people before Moses, and said, Let us go up at once, and possess it; for we are well able to overcome it.

But the men that went up with him said, We be not able to go up against the people; for they *are* stronger than we.

And all the congregation lifted up their voice, and cried; and the people wept that night. And all the children of Israel murmured against Moses and against Aaron: and the whole congregation said unto them, Would God that we had died in the land of Egypt! Or would God we had died in this wilderness! And wherefore hath the Lord brought us unto this land, to fall by the sword, that our wives and our children should be a prey? Were it not better for us to return into Egypt? And they said one to another, Let us make a captain, and let us return into Egypt.

Numbers 13:1-2, 26-28a, 30-31; 14:1-4

---

***Related texts:*** Deuteronomy 1:19-33; Psalm 106:24-27; Proverbs 29:25; Philippians 2:12-16

190

## Forty Years in the Desert

Then Moses and Aaron fell on their faces before all the assembly of the congregation of the children of Israel. And Joshua the son of Nun, and Caleb the son of Jephunneh, *which* were of them that searched the land, rent their clothes: and they spake unto all the company of the children of Israel, saying, The land, which we passed through to search it, *is* an exceeding good land. If the LORD delight in us, then he will bring us into this land, and give it us; a land which floweth with milk and honey. Only rebel not ye against the LORD, neither fear ye the people of the land; for they *are* bread for us: their defence is departed from them, and the LORD *is* with us: fear them not.

And the LORD spake unto Moses and unto Aaron, saying, How long *shall I bear with* this evil congregation, which murmur against me? I have heard the murmurings of the children of Israel, which they murmur against me. Say unto them, *As truly as* I live, saith the LORD, as ye have spoken in mine ears, so will I do to you: your carcases shall fall in this wilderness; and all that were numbered of you, according to your whole number, from twenty years old and upward, which have murmured against me, doubtless ye shall not come into the land, *concerning* which I sware to make you dwell therein, save Caleb the son of Jephunneh, and Joshua the son of Nun. After the number of the days in which ye searched the land, *even* forty days, each day for a year, shall ye bear your iniquities, *even* forty years, and ye shall know my breach of promise.

What shall we then say to these things? If God *be* for us, who *can be* against us?

NUMBERS 14:5-9, 26-30, 34; ROMANS 8:31

*Related texts:* JOSHUA 5:1-6; JOHN 6:48-51; 1 CORINTHIANS 10:1-6; HEBREWS 3:7–4:7

**THE ONE MINUTE BIBLE**

**June 26**

## Listen to God's Voice

Wherefore (as the Holy Ghost saith,

> To day if ye will hear his voice,
>> harden not your hearts,
> as in the provocation,
>> in the day of temptation in the wilderness:
> when your fathers tempted me, proved me,
>> and saw my works forty years.
> Wherefore I was grieved with that generation,
>> and said, They do alway err in *their* heart;
>> and they have not known my ways.
> So I sware in my wrath,
>> They shall not enter into my rest.)

Take heed, brethren, lest there be in any of you an evil heart of unbelief, in departing from the living God. But exhort one another daily, while it is called To day; lest any of you be hardened through the deceitfulness of sin. For we are made partakers of Christ, if we hold the beginning of our confidence stedfast unto the end; while it is said,

> To day if ye will hear his voice,
>> harden not your hearts,
> as in the provocation.

For some, when they had heard, did provoke: howbeit not all that came out of Egypt by Moses. But with whom was he grieved forty years? *Was it* not with them that had sinned, whose carcases fell in the wilderness? And to whom sware he that they should not enter into his rest, but to them that believed not? So we see that they could not enter in because of unbelief.

HEBREWS 3:7-19

---

***Related texts:*** PSALM 95; MATTHEW 17:1-5; JOHN 14:15-24; ACTS 3:19-23; HEBREWS 4

192

## God Crushes Rebellion

Now Korah, the son of Izhar, the son of Kohath, the son of Levi, and Dathan and Abiram, the sons of Eliab, and On, the son of Peleth, sons of Reuben, took *men*: and they rose up before Moses, with certain of the children of Israel, two hundred and fifty princes of the assembly, famous in the congregation, men of renown: and they gathered themselves together against Moses and against Aaron, and said unto them, *Ye take* too much upon you, seeing all the congregation *are* holy, every one of them, and the Lord *is* among them: wherefore then lift ye up yourselves above the congregation of the Lord?

And when Moses heard *it*, he fell upon his face: and he spake unto Korah and unto all his company, saying, Even to morrow the Lord will show who *are* his, and *who is* holy; and will cause *him* to come near unto him: even *him* whom he hath chosen will he cause to come near unto him. This do; Take you censers, Korah, and all his company; and put fire therein, and put incense in them before the Lord to morrow: and it shall be *that* the man whom the Lord doth choose, he *shall be* holy: *ye take* too much upon you, ye sons of Levi.

And Korah gathered all the congregation against them unto the door of the tabernacle of the congregation: and the glory of the Lord appeared unto all the congregation.

And the earth opened her mouth, and swallowed them up, and their houses, and all the men that *appertained* unto Korah, and all *their* goods. They, and all that *appertained* to them, went down alive into the pit, and the earth closed upon them: and they perished from among the congregation.

NUMBERS 16:1-7, 19, 32-33

*Related texts:* PSALM 106:16-17; HEBREWS 10:26-31; 12:23-29; 2 PETER 1:16–2:22; JUDE 1:11

## Moses Disobeys God

**THE ONE
MINUTE
BIBLE**

Then came the children of Israel, *even* the whole congregation, into the desert of Zin in the first month: and the people abode in Kadesh; and Miriam died there, and was buried there.

And there was no water for the congregation: and they gathered themselves together against Moses and against Aaron. And the people chode with Moses, and spake, saying, Would God that we had died when our brethren died before the LORD! And why have ye brought up the congregation of the LORD into this wilderness, that we and our cattle should die there? And wherefore have ye made us to come up out of Egypt, to bring us in unto this evil place? It *is* no place of seed, or of figs, or of vines, or of pomegranates; neither *is* there any water to drink.

And Moses and Aaron went from the presence of the assembly unto the door of the tabernacle of the congregation, and they fell upon their faces: and the glory of the LORD appeared unto them. And the LORD spake unto Moses, saying, Take the rod, and gather thou the assembly together, thou, and Aaron thy brother, and speak ye unto the rock before their eyes; and it shall give forth his water, and thou shalt bring forth to them water out of the rock: so thou shalt give the congregation and their beasts drink.

And Moses took the rod from before the LORD, as he commanded him. And Moses and Aaron gathered the congregation together before the rock, and he said unto them, Hear now, ye rebels; must we fetch you water out of this rock? And Moses lifted up his hand, and with his rod he smote the rock twice: and the water came out abundantly, and the congregation drank, and their beasts *also*.

And the LORD spake unto Moses and Aaron, Because ye believed me not, to sanctify me in the eyes of the children of Israel, therefore ye shall not bring this congregation into the land which I have given them.

NUMBERS 20:1-12

*Related texts:* EXODUS 7:19-21; 8:16-17; 17:1-6;
DEUTERONOMY 4:20-22; ACTS 5:1-11

## *Look Up and Live*

And they journeyed from mount Hor by the way of the Red sea, to compass the land of Edom: and the soul of the people was much discouraged because of the way. And the people spake against God, and against Moses, Wherefore have ye brought us up out of Egypt to die in the wilderness? For *there is* no bread, neither *is there any* water; and our soul loatheth this light bread.

And the LORD sent fiery serpents among the people, and they bit the people; and much people of Israel died. Therefore the people came to Moses, and said, We have sinned, for we have spoken against the LORD, and against thee; pray unto the LORD, that he take away the serpents from us. And Moses prayed for the people.

And the LORD said unto Moses, Make thee a fiery serpent, and set it upon a pole: and it shall come to pass, that every one that is bitten, when he looketh upon it, shall live. And Moses made a serpent of brass, and put it upon a pole, and it came to pass, that if a serpent had bitten any man, when he beheld the serpent of brass, he lived.

And as Moses lifted up the serpent in the wilderness, even so must the Son of man be lifted up: that whosoever believeth in him should not perish, but have eternal life.

For God so loved the world, that he gave his only begotten Son, that whosoever believeth in him should not perish, but have everlasting life. For God sent not his Son into the world to condemn the world; but that the world through him might be saved.

NUMBERS 21:4-9; JOHN 3:14-17

*Related texts:* EXODUS 16:6-12; NUMBERS 14:26-37; 2 KINGS 18:1-4; LAMENTATIONS 3:25-40; 1 CORINTHIANS 10:1-11

## Balaam Hired to Curse Israel

**THE ONE
MINUTE
BIBLE**

And the children of Israel set forward, and pitched in the plains of Moab on this side Jordan *by* Jericho.

And Balak the son of Zippor saw all that Israel had done to the Amorites. And Moab was sore afraid of the people, because they *were* many: and Moab was distressed because of the children of Israel.

And Balak the son of Zippor *was* king of the Moabites at that time. He sent messengers therefore unto Balaam the son of Beor to Pethor, which *is* by the river of the land of the children of his people, to call him, saying,

> Behold, there is a people come out from Egypt: behold, they cover the face of the earth, and they abide over against me: come now therefore, I pray thee, curse me this people; for they *are* too mighty for me: peradventure I shall prevail, *that* we may smite them, and *that* I may drive them out of the land: for I wot that he whom thou blessest *is* blessed, and he whom thou cursest is cursed.

An Ammonite or Moabite shall not enter into the congregation of the LORD; even to their tenth generation shall they not enter into the congregation of the LORD for ever: because they met you not with bread and with water in the way, when ye came forth out of Egypt; and because they hired against thee Balaam the son of Beor of Pethor of Mesopotamia, to curse thee. Nevertheless the LORD thy God would not hearken unto Balaam; but the LORD thy God turned the curse into a blessing unto thee, because the LORD thy God loved thee.

NUMBERS 22:1-3, 4b-6; DEUTERONOMY 23:3-5

---

***Related texts:*** GENESIS 12:1-3; NUMBERS 22–24; JOSHUA 24:8-10; 2 PETER 2:15-16

*This Bible is for the government
of the people, by the people,
and for the people.*
**John Wycliffe (1328-1384)**
ENGLISH THEOLOGIAN
(Preface to translation of the Bible)

*The more this Bible enters
into our national life the
grander and purer and better
will that life become.*
**David Josiah Brewer (1837-1910)**
UNITED STATES SUPREME COURT JUSTICE

*It is impossible to rightly
govern the world without
God and the Bible.*
**George Washington (1732-1799)**
UNITED STATES PRESIDENT

## *Balaam Blesses Israel*

And Balaam lifted up his eyes, and he saw Israel abiding *in his tents* according to their tribes; and the spirit of God came upon him. And he took up his parable, and said,

**THE ONE
MINUTE
BIBLE**

Balaam the son of Beor hath said,
and the man whose eyes are open hath said:
he hath said, which heard the words of God,
which saw the vision of the Almighty,
falling *into a trance*, but having his eyes open:

How goodly are thy tents, O Jacob,
*and* thy tabernacles, O Israel!

As the valleys are they spread forth,
as gardens by the river's side,
as the trees of lign aloes which the LORD hath planted,
*and* as cedar trees beside the waters.
He shall pour the water out of his buckets,
and his seed *shall be* in many waters,
and his king shall be higher than Agag,
and his kingdom shall be exalted.

God brought him forth out of Egypt;
he hath as it were the strength of an unicorn:
he shall eat up the nations his enemies,
and shall break their bones,
and pierce *them* through with his arrows.
He couched, he lay down as a lion,
and as a great lion: who shall stir him up?

Blessed *is* he that blesseth thee,
and cursed *is* he that curseth thee.

NUMBERS 24:2-9

*Related texts:* GENESIS 12:1-3; 22:15-18; 27:26-29; DEUTERONOMY 23:3-5;
JOSHUA 13:22; 24:8-10; REVELATION 2:12-14

# *Judgment for Immorality*

**THE ONE
MINUTE
BIBLE**

And Israel abode in Shittim, and the people began to commit whoredom with the daughters of Moab. And they called the people unto the sacrifices of their gods: and the people did eat, and bowed down to their gods. And Israel joined himself unto Baal-peor: and the anger of the LORD was kindled against Israel.

And the LORD said unto Moses, Take all the heads of the people, and hang them up before the LORD against the sun, that the fierce anger of the LORD may be turned away from Israel.

And Moses said unto the judges of Israel, Slay ye every one his men that were joined unto Baal-peor.

And, behold, one of the children of Israel came and brought unto his brethren a Midianitish woman in the sight of Moses, and in the sight of all the congregation of the children of Israel, who *were* weeping *before* the door of the tabernacle of the congregation. And when Phinehas, the son of Eleazar, the son of Aaron the priest, saw *it*, he rose up from among the congregation, and took a javelin in his hand; and he went after the man of Israel into the tent, and thrust both of them through, the man of Israel, and the woman through her belly. So the plague was stayed from the children of Israel. And those that died in the plague were twenty and four thousand.

Flee fornication. Every sin that a man doeth is without the body; but he that committeth fornication sinneth against his own body. What? Know ye not that your body is the temple of the Holy Ghost *which is* in you, which ye have of God, and ye are not your own? For ye are bought with a price: therefore glorify God in your body, and in your spirit, which are God's.

NUMBERS 25:1-9; 1 CORINTHIANS 6:18-20

*Related texts:* DEUTERONOMY 4:1-4; JOSHUA 22:16-20; PSALM 106:28-31; HOSEA 9:10; 1 CORINTHIANS 10:1-8

## *Vengeance Against Midian*

**THE ONE
MINUTE
BIBLE**

And the LORD spake unto Moses, saying, Avenge the children of Israel of the Midianites: afterward shalt thou be gathered unto thy people.

And Moses spake unto the people, saying, Arm some of yourselves unto the war, and let them go against the Midianites, and avenge the LORD of Midian. Of every tribe a thousand, throughout all the tribes of Israel, shall ye send to the war. So there were delivered out of the thousands of Israel, a thousand of *every* tribe, twelve thousand armed for war.

And they warred against the Midianites, as the LORD commanded Moses; and they slew all the males. And they slew the kings of Midian, beside the rest of them that were slain; *namely*, Evi, and Rekem, and Zur, and Hur, and Reba, five kings of Midian: Balaam also the son of Beor they slew with the sword. And the children of Israel took *all* the women of Midian captives, and their little ones, and took the spoil of all their cattle, and all their flocks, and all their goods. And they burnt all their cities wherein they dwelt, and all their goodly castles, with fire.

And Moses, and Eleazar the priest, and all the princes of the congregation, went forth to meet them without the camp. And Moses was wroth with the officers of the host, *with* the captains over thousands, and captains over hundreds, which came from the battle.

And Moses said unto them, Have ye saved all the women alive? Behold, these caused the children of Israel, through the counsel of Balaam, to commit trespass against the LORD in the matter of Peor, and there was a plague among the congregation of the LORD.

NUMBERS 31:1-5, 7-10, 13-16

---

***Related texts:*** NUMBERS 25; DEUTERONOMY 21:10-14; JOSHUA 13:16-22; JUDGES 6–8; ROMANS 12:16-21

**THE ONE
MINUTE
BIBLE**

## *Love the LORD Your God*

Now these *are* the commandments, the statutes, and the judgments, which the LORD your God commanded to teach you, that ye might do *them* in the land whither ye go to possess it: that thou mightest fear the LORD thy God, to keep all his statutes and his commandments, which I command thee, thou, and thy son, and thy son's son, all the days of thy life; and that thy days may be prolonged. Hear therefore, O Israel, and observe to do *it*; that it may be well with thee, and that ye may increase mightily, as the LORD God of thy fathers hath promised thee, in the land that floweth with milk and honey.

Hear, O Israel: The LORD our God *is* one LORD: and thou shalt love the LORD thy God with all thine heart, and with all thy soul, and with all thy might. And these words, which I command thee this day, shall be in thine heart: and thou shalt teach them diligently unto thy children, and shalt talk of them when thou sittest in thine house, and when thou walkest by the way, and when thou liest down, and when thou risest up. And thou shalt bind them for a sign upon thine hand, and they shall be as frontlets between thine eyes. And thou shalt write them upon the posts of thy house, and on thy gates.

O how love I thy law!
    *it is* my meditation all the day.

DEUTERONOMY 6:1-9; PSALM 119:97

***Related texts:*** DEUTERONOMY 10:12-16; 11:18-21; PSALMS 1; 119; PROVERBS 22:6; MARK 12:28-34; LUKE 10:25-28; 1 JOHN 5:1-4

## *Joshua Succeeds Moses*

And Moses went and spake these words unto all Israel. And he said unto them, I *am* an hundred and twenty years old this day; I can no more go out and come in: also the LORD hath said unto me, Thou shalt not go over this Jordan. The LORD thy God, he will go over before thee, *and* he will destroy these nations from before thee, and thou shalt possess them.

*And* Joshua, he shall go over before thee, as the LORD hath said. And the LORD shall do unto them as he did to Sihon and to Og, kings of the Amorites, and unto the land of them, whom he destroyed. And the LORD shall give them up before your face, that ye may do unto them according unto all the commandments which I have commanded you. Be strong and of a good courage, fear not, nor be afraid of them: for the LORD thy God, he *it is* that doth go with thee; he will not fail thee, nor forsake thee.

And Moses called unto Joshua, and said unto him in the sight of all Israel, Be strong and of a good courage: for thou must go with this people unto the land which the LORD hath sworn unto their fathers to give them; and thou shalt cause them to inherit it. And the LORD, he *it is* that doth go before thee; he will be with thee, he will not fail thee, neither forsake thee: fear not, neither be dismayed.

And Moses wrote this law, and delivered it unto the priests the sons of Levi, which bare the ark of the covenant of the LORD, and unto all the elders of Israel.

DEUTERONOMY 31:1-9

**THE ONE MINUTE BIBLE**

*Related texts:* NUMBERS 21:21-35; DEUTERONOMY 2:24–3:17; 1 KINGS 8:54-57; HEBREWS 13:5-6

**THE ONE
MINUTE
BIBLE**

## Be Strong and Courageous

Now after the death of Moses the servant of the LORD it came to pass, that the LORD spake unto Joshua the son of Nun, Moses' minister, saying, Moses my servant is dead; now therefore arise, go over this Jordan, thou, and all this people, unto the land which I do give to them, *even* to the children of Israel. Every place that the sole of your foot shall tread upon, that have I given unto you, as I said unto Moses. From the wilderness and this Lebanon even unto the great river, the river Euphrates, all the land of the Hittites, and unto the great sea toward the going down of the sun, shall be your coast. There shall not any man be able to stand before thee all the days of thy life: as I was with Moses, *so* I will be with thee: I will not fail thee, nor forsake thee.

Be strong and of a good courage: for unto this people shalt thou divide for an inheritance the land, which I sware unto their fathers to give them. Only be thou strong and very courageous, that thou mayest observe to do according to all the law, which Moses my servant commanded thee: turn not from it *to* the right hand or *to* the left, that thou mayest prosper whithersoever thou goest. This book of the law shall not depart out of thy mouth; but thou shalt meditate therein day and night, that thou mayest observe to do according to all that is written therein: for then thou shalt make thy way prosperous, and then thou shalt have good success. Have not I commanded thee? Be strong and of a good courage; be not afraid, neither be thou dismayed: for the LORD thy God *is* with thee whithersoever thou goest.

JOSHUA 1:1-9

---

***Related texts:*** DEUTERONOMY 11:22-25; PSALMS 1; 19; 119;
1 CORINTHIANS 16:13-14; HEBREWS 3:1-6

## Rahab Hides the Israelite Spies

THE ONE
MINUTE
BIBLE

And Joshua the son of Nun sent out of Shittim two men to spy secretly, saying, Go view the land, even Jericho. And they went, and came into an harlot's house, named Rahab, and lodged there.

And it was told the king of Jericho, saying, Behold, there came men in hither to night of the children of Israel to search out the country. And the king of Jericho sent unto Rahab, saying, Bring forth the men that are come to thee, which are entered into thine house: for they be come to search out all the country.

And the woman took the two men, and hid them, and said thus, There came men unto me, but I wist not whence they *were*: And it came to pass *about the time* of shutting of the gate, when it was dark, that the men went out: whither the men went I wot not: pursue after them quickly; for ye shall overtake them. But she had brought them up to the roof of the house, and hid them with the stalks of flax, which she had laid in order upon the roof.

And they went, and came unto the mountain, and abode there three days, until the pursuers were returned: and the pursuers sought *them* throughout all the way, but found *them* not. So the two men returned, and descended from the mountain, and passed over, and came to Joshua the son of Nun, and told him all *things* that befell them: and they said unto Joshua, Truly the LORD hath delivered into our hands all the land; for even all the inhabitants of the country do faint because of us.

JOSHUA 2:1-6, 22-24

*Related texts:* MATTHEW 1:1-6; HEBREWS 11:31; JAMES 2:25

**THE ONE
MINUTE
BIBLE**

## The Israelites Conquer Jericho

Now Jericho was straitly shut up because of the children of Israel: none went out, and none came in.

And the LORD said unto Joshua, See, I have given into thine hand Jericho, and the king thereof, *and* the mighty men of valour. And ye shall compass the city, all *ye* men of war, *and* go round about the city once. Thus shalt thou do six days. And seven priests shall bear before the ark seven trumpets of rams' horns: and the seventh day ye shall compass the city seven times, and the priests shall blow with the trumpets. And it shall come to pass, that when they make a long *blast* with the ram's horn, *and* when ye hear the sound of the trumpet, all the people shall shout with a great shout; and the wall of the city shall fall down flat, and the people shall ascend up every man straight before him.

So the people shouted when *the* priests blew with the trumpets: and it came to pass, when the people heard the sound of the trumpet, and the people shouted with a great shout, that the wall fell down flat, so that the people went up into the city, every man straight before him, and they took the city. And they utterly destroyed all that *was* in the city, both man and woman, young and old, and ox, and sheep, and ass, with the edge of the sword.

And Joshua saved Rahab the harlot alive, and her father's household, and all that she had; and she dwelleth in Israel *even* unto this day; because she hid the messengers, which Joshua sent to spy out Jericho.

JOSHUA 6:1-5, 20-21, 25

---

***Related texts:*** NUMBERS 10:1-10; JUDGES 7:1-22; MATTHEW 1:1-6

## *Joshua Conquers the Land of Canaan*

THE ONE
MINUTE
BIBLE

As the LORD commanded Moses his servant, so did Moses command Joshua, and so did Joshua; he left nothing undone of all that the LORD commanded Moses.

So Joshua took all that land, the hills, and all the south country, and all the land of Goshen, and the valley, and the plain, and the mountain of Israel, and the valley of the same; *even* from the mount Halak, that goeth up to Seir, even unto Baal-gad in the valley of Lebanon under mount Hermon: and all their kings he took, and smote them, and slew them. Joshua made war a long time with all those kings. There was not a city that made peace with the children of Israel, save the Hivites the inhabitants of Gibeon: all *other* they took in battle. For it was of the LORD to harden their hearts, that they should come against Israel in battle, that he might destroy them utterly, *and* that they might have no favour, but that he might destroy them, as the LORD commanded Moses.

So Joshua took the whole land, according to all that the LORD said unto Moses; and Joshua gave it for an inheritance unto Israel according to their divisions by their tribes.

And the land rested from war.

JOSHUA 11:15-20, 23

*Related texts:* DEUTERONOMY 7; 9:1-6; 18:9-14; 20:16-18; JOSHUA 7–10

# Joshua's Farewell Address

**THE ONE
MINUTE
BIBLE**

[Joshua said,] Now therefore fear the Lord, and serve him in sincerity and in truth: and put away the gods which your fathers served on the other side of the flood, and in Egypt; and serve ye the Lord. And if it seem evil unto you to serve the Lord, choose you this day whom ye will serve; whether the gods which your fathers served that *were* on the other side of the flood, or the gods of the Amorites, in whose land ye dwell: but as for me and my house, we will serve the Lord.

And the people answered and said, God forbid that we should forsake the Lord, to serve other gods; for the Lord our God, he *it is* that brought us up and our fathers out of the land of Egypt, from the house of bondage, and which did those great signs in our sight, and preserved us in all the way wherein we went, and among all the people through whom we passed: and the Lord drave out from before us all the people, even the Amorites which dwelt in the land: *therefore* will we also serve the Lord; for he *is* our God.

And Joshua said unto the people, Ye cannot serve the Lord: for he *is* an holy God; he *is* a jealous God; he will not forgive your transgressions nor your sins. If ye forsake the Lord, and serve strange gods, then he will turn and do you hurt, and consume you, after that he hath done you good.

And the people said unto Joshua, Nay; but we will serve the Lord.

JOSHUA 24:14-21

---

***Related texts:*** EXODUS 24:3-8; LEVITICUS 26; ROMANS 6; HEBREWS 3–4

# The Days of the Judges

And the people served the LORD all the days of Joshua, and all the days of the elders that outlived Joshua, who had seen all the great works of the LORD, that he did for Israel.

And also all that generation were gathered unto their fathers: and there arose another generation after them, which knew not the LORD, nor yet the works which he had done for Israel. And the children of Israel did evil in the sight of the LORD, and served Baalim.

And the anger of the LORD was hot against Israel, and he delivered them into the hands of spoilers that spoiled them, and he sold them into the hands of their enemies round about, so that they could not any longer stand before their enemies. Whithersoever they went out, the hand of the LORD was against them for evil, as the LORD had said, and as the LORD had sworn unto them: and they were greatly distressed.

Nevertheless the LORD raised up judges, which delivered them out of the hand of those that spoiled them. And when the LORD raised them up judges, then the LORD was with the judge, and delivered them out of the hand of their enemies all the days of the judge: for it repented the LORD because of their groanings by reason of them that oppressed them and vexed them. And it came to pass, when the judge was dead, *that* they returned, and corrupted *themselves* more than their fathers, in following other gods to serve them, and to bow down unto them; they ceased not from their own doings, nor from their stubborn way.

JUDGES 2:7, 10-11, 14-16, 18-19

---

*Related texts:* DEUTERONOMY 4:1-10; 11:18-25; JUDGES 2:19–3:31; PSALM 78:1-6; EPHESIANS 2:1-10

## Deborah: Prophetess and Judge

**THE ONE
MINUTE
BIBLE**

And the children of Israel again did evil in the sight of the LORD, when Ehud was dead. And the LORD sold them into the hand of Jabin king of Canaan, that reigned in Hazor; the captain of whose host *was* Sisera, which dwelt in Harosheth of the Gentiles. And the children of Israel cried unto the LORD: for Sisera had nine hundred chariots of iron; and twenty years he mightily oppressed the children of Israel.

And Deborah, a prophetess, the wife of Lapidoth, she judged Israel at that time. And she dwelt under the palm tree of Deborah between Ramah and Beth-el in mount Ephraim: and the children of Israel came up to her for judgment. And she sent and called Barak the son of Abinoam out of Kedesh-naphtali, and said unto him, Hath not the LORD God of Israel commanded, *saying*, Go and draw toward mount Tabor, and take with thee ten thousand men of the children of Naphtali and of the children of Zebulun? And I will draw unto thee to the river Kishon Sisera, the captain of Jabin's army, with his chariots and his multitude; and I will deliver him into thine hand.

And Barak said unto her, If thou wilt go with me, then I will go: but if thou wilt not go with me, *then* I will not go.

And she said, I will surely go with thee: notwithstanding the journey that thou takest shall not be for thine honour; for the LORD shall sell Sisera into the hand of a woman.

JUDGES 4:1-9a

---

***Related texts:*** EXODUS 15:19-21; JUDGES 5:1-12; 2 KINGS 22:11-20; 2 CHRONICLES 34:19-28; LUKE 2:21-38

## *Victory From a Woman's Hand*

THE ONE
MINUTE
BIBLE

And Deborah said unto Barak, Up; for this *is* the day in which the Lord hath delivered Sisera into thine hand: is not the Lord gone out before thee? So Barak went down from mount Tabor, and ten thousand men after him. And the Lord discomfited Sisera, and all *his* chariots, and all *his* host, with the edge of the sword before Barak; so that Sisera lighted down off *his* chariot, and fled away on his feet. But Barak pursued after the chariots, and after the host, unto Harosheth of the Gentiles: and all the host of Sisera fell upon the edge of the sword; *and* there was not a man left.

Howbeit Sisera fled away on his feet to the tent of Jael the wife of Heber the Kenite: for *there was* peace between Jabin the king of Hazor and the house of Heber the Kenite.

And Jael went out to meet Sisera, and said unto him, Turn in, my lord, turn in to me; fear not. And when he had turned in unto her into the tent, she covered him with a mantle.

And he said unto her, Give me, I pray thee, a little water to drink; for I am thirsty. And she opened a bottle of milk, and gave him drink, and covered him.

Again he said unto her, Stand in the door of the tent, and it shall be, when any man doth come and inquire of thee, and say, Is there any man here? That thou shalt say, No.

Then Jael Heber's wife took a nail of the tent, and took an hammer in her hand, and went softly unto him, and smote the nail into his temples, and fastened it into the ground: for he was fast asleep and weary. So he died.

Judges 4:14-21

*Related texts:* Judges 3:12-30; 5:13-31; 1 Samuel 12:8-11; Hebrews 11:32-34

211

## *The Birth of Samson the Strongman*

**THE ONE MINUTE BIBLE**

And the children of Israel did evil again in the sight of the LORD; and the LORD delivered them into the hand of the Philistines forty years.

And there was a certain man of Zorah, of the family of the Danites, whose name *was* Manoah; and his wife *was* barren, and bare not. And the angel of the LORD appeared unto the woman, and said unto her, Behold now, thou *art* barren, and bearest not: but thou shalt conceive, and bear a son. Now therefore beware, I pray thee, and drink not wine nor strong drink, and eat not any unclean *thing*: for, lo, thou shalt conceive, and bear a son; and no razor shall come on his head: for the child shall be a Nazarite unto God from the womb: and he shall begin to deliver Israel out of the hand of the Philistines.

And the woman bare a son, and called his name Samson: and the child grew, and the LORD blessed him. And the spirit of the LORD began to move him at times in the camp of Dan between Zorah and Eshtaol.

And Samson judged Israel in the days of the Philistines twenty years.

JUDGES 13:1-5, 24-25; 15:20

*Related texts:* GENESIS 25:21-24; NUMBERS 6:1-21; JUDGES 14-15; LUKE 1

## Samson and Delilah

Then went Samson to Gaza, and saw there an harlot, and went in unto her. *And it was told* the Gazites, saying, Samson is come hither. And they compassed *him* in, and laid wait for him all night in the gate of the city, and were quiet all the night, saying, In the morning, when it is day, we shall kill him.

And Samson lay till midnight, and arose at midnight, and took the doors of the gate of the city, and the two posts, and went away with them, bar and all, and put *them* upon his shoulders, and carried them up to the top of an hill that *is* before Hebron.

And it came to pass afterward, that he loved a woman in the valley of Sorek, whose name *was* Delilah. And the lords of the Philistines came up unto her, and said unto her, Entice him, and see wherein his great strength *lieth*, and by what *means* we may prevail against him, that we may bind him to afflict him: and we will give thee every one of us eleven hundred *pieces* of silver.

And Delilah said to Samson, Tell me, I pray thee, wherein thy great strength *lieth*, and wherewith thou mightest be bound to afflict thee.

And Samson said unto her, If they bind me with seven green withs that were never dried, then shall I be weak, and be as another man.

Then the lords of the Philistines brought up to her seven green withs which had not been dried, and she bound him with them. Now *there were* men lying in wait, abiding with her in the chamber. And she said unto him, The Philistines *be* upon thee, Samson. And he brake the withs, as a thread of tow is broken when it toucheth the fire. So his strength was not known.

JUDGES 16:1-9

*Related texts:* JUDGES 14–15; PROVERBS 5; 6:20–7:27; 31:1-3;
2 TIMOTHY 2:20-23

**THE ONE
MINUTE
BIBLE**

*July 16*

## The Philistines Blind Samson

And Delilah said unto Samson, How canst thou say, I love thee, when thine heart *is* not with me? Thou hast mocked me these three times, and hast not told me wherein thy great strength *lieth*.

And it came to pass, when she pressed him daily with her words, and urged him, *so* that his soul was vexed unto death; that he told her all his heart, and said unto her, There hath not come a razor upon mine head; for I *have been* a Nazarite unto God from my mother's womb: if I be shaven, then my strength will go from me, and I shall become weak, and be like any *other* man.

And when Delilah saw that he had told her all his heart, she sent and called for the lords of the Philistines, saying, Come up this once, for he hath showed me all his heart. Then the lords of the Philistines came up unto her, and brought money in their hand. And she made him sleep upon her knees; and she called for a man, and she caused him to shave off the seven locks of his head; and she began to afflict him, and his strength went from him.

And she said, The Philistines *be* upon thee, Samson.

And he awoke out of his sleep, and said, I will go out as at other times before, and shake myself. And he wist not that the LORD was departed from him.

But the Philistines took him, and put out his eyes, and brought him down to Gaza, and bound him with fetters of brass; and he did grind in the prison house.

JUDGES 16:15-21

***Related texts:*** NUMBERS 6:2-21; 30:1-2; PROVERBS 11:13; 20:19; ECCLESIASTES 5:4-6; LUKE 12:47-48

214

## Samson's Revenge

Then the lords of the Philistines gathered them together for to offer a great sacrifice unto Dagon their god, and to rejoice: for they said, Our god hath delivered Samson our enemy into our hand.

And it came to pass, when their hearts were merry, that they said, Call for Samson, that he may make us sport. And they called for Samson out of the prison house; and he made them sport: and they set him between the pillars.

And Samson said unto the lad that held him by the hand, Suffer me that I may feel the pillars whereupon the house standeth, that I may lean upon them. Now the house was full of men and women; and all the lords of the Philistines *were* there; and *there were* upon the roof about three thousand men and women, that beheld while Samson made sport.

And Samson called unto the Lord, and said, O Lord God, remember me, I pray thee, and strengthen me, I pray thee, only this once, O God, that I may be at once avenged of the Philistines for my two eyes. And Samson took hold of the two middle pillars upon which the house stood, and on which it was borne up, of the one with his right hand, and of the other with his left. And Samson said, Let me die with the Philistines. And he bowed himself with *all his* might; and the house fell upon the lords, and upon all the people that *were* therein. So the dead which he slew at his death were more than they which he slew in his life.

Judges 16:23, 25-30

**THE ONE MINUTE BIBLE**

---

***Related texts:*** Psalm 3; Isaiah 1:24; Jeremiah 5:7-9, 29; 9:9; Hebrews 11:32-34

# Naomi and Ruth: Love and Loyalty

**THE ONE
MINUTE
BIBLE**

Now it came to pass in the days when the judges ruled, that there was a famine in the land. And a certain man of Beth-lehem-judah went to sojourn in the country of Moab, he, and his wife, and his two sons. And the name of the man *was* Elimelech, and the name of his wife Naomi, and the name of his two sons Mahlon and Chilion.

And Elimelech Naomi's husband died; and she was left, and her two sons. And they took them wives of the women of Moab; the name of the one *was* Orpah, and the name of the other Ruth: and they dwelled there about ten years. And Mahlon and Chilion died also both of them; and the woman was left of her two sons and her husband.

And Naomi said unto her two daughters in law, Go, return each to her mother's house: the LORD deal kindly with you, as ye have dealt with the dead, and with me. The LORD grant you that ye may find rest, each *of you* in the house of her husband.

And Ruth said, Entreat me not to leave thee, *or* to return from following after thee: for whither thou goest, I will go; and where thou lodgest, I will lodge: thy people *shall be* my people, and thy God my God: where thou diest, will I die, and there will I be buried: the LORD do so to me, and more also, *if ought* but death part thee and me.

So Naomi returned, and Ruth the Moabitess, her daughter in law, with her, which returned out of the country of Moab: and they came to Beth-lehem in the beginning of barley harvest.

RUTH 1:1-2a, 3-5, 8-9a, 16-17, 22

---

*Related texts:* 2 SAMUEL 3:14-16; PROVERBS 20:6; SONG OF SONGS 8:6-7; 1 CORINTHIANS 13

## *Ruth Meets Boaz*

And Naomi had a kinsman of her husband's, a mighty man of wealth, of the family of Elimelech; and his name *was* Boaz.

And Ruth the Moabitess said unto Naomi, Let me now go to the field, and glean ears of corn after *him* in whose sight I shall find grace.

And she said unto her, Go, my daughter. And she went, and came, and gleaned in the field after the reapers: and her hap was to light on a part of the field *belonging* unto Boaz, who *was* of the kindred of Elimelech.

Then said Boaz unto Ruth, Hearest thou not, my daughter? Go not to glean in another field, neither go from hence, but abide here fast by my maidens.

Then she fell on her face, and bowed herself to the ground, and said unto him, Why have I found grace in thine eyes, that thou shouldest take knowledge of me, seeing I *am* a stranger?

And Boaz answered and said unto her, It hath fully been showed me, all that thou hast done unto thy mother in law since the death of thine husband: and *how* thou hast left thy father and thy mother, and the land of thy nativity, and art come unto a people which thou knewest not heretofore. The LORD recompense thy work, and a full reward be given thee of the LORD God of Israel, under whose wings thou art come to trust.

RUTH 2:1-3, 8, 10-12

**THE ONE MINUTE BIBLE**

*Related texts:* LEVITICUS 25:25-27, 49-50; PSALM 91; JEREMIAH 32:6-14

**THE ONE
MINUTE
BIBLE**

## Ruth Proposes Marriage to Boaz

Then Naomi her mother in law said unto her, My daughter, shall I not seek rest for thee, that it may be well with thee? And now *is* not Boaz of our kindred, with whose maidens thou wast? Behold, he winnoweth barley to night in the threshingfloor. Wash thy self therefore, and anoint thee, and put thy raiment upon thee, and get thee down to the floor: *but* make not thyself known unto the man, until he shall have done eating and drinking. And it shall be, when he lieth down, that thou shalt mark the place where he shall lie, and thou shalt go in, and uncover his feet, and lay thee down; and he will tell thee what thou shalt do.

And when Boaz had eaten and drunk, and his heart was merry, he went to lie down at the end of the heap of corn: and she came softly, and uncovered his feet, and laid her down. And it came to pass at midnight, that the man was afraid, and turned himself: and, behold, a woman lay at his feet.

And he said, Who *art* thou?

And she answered, I *am* Ruth thine handmaid: spread therefore thy skirt over thine handmaid; for thou *art* a near kinsman.

And he said, Blessed *be* thou of the LORD, my daughter: *for* thou hast showed more kindness in the latter end than at the beginning, inasmuch as thou followedst not young men, whether poor or rich. And now, my daughter, fear not; I will do to thee all that thou requirest: for all the city of my people doth know that thou *art* a virtuous woman.

RUTH 3:1-4, 7-11

***Related texts:*** GENESIS 38:8-10; DEUTERONOMY 25:5-10; HEBREWS 13:4

## Ruth Marries Boaz

And Boaz said unto the elders, and *unto* all the people, Ye *are* witnesses this day, that I have bought all that *was* Elimelech's, and all that *was* Chilion's and Mahlon's, of the hand of Naomi. Moreover Ruth the Moabitess, the wife of Mahlon, have I purchased to be my wife, to raise up the name of the dead upon his inheritance, that the name of the dead be not cut off from among his brethren, and from the gate of his place: ye *are* witnesses this day.

And all the people that *were* in the gate, and the elders, said, *We are* witnesses. The LORD make the woman that is come into thine house like Rachel and like Leah, which two did build the house of Israel: and do thou worthily in Ephratah, and be famous in Bethlehem: and let thy house be like the house of Pharez, whom Tamar bare unto Judah, of the seed which the LORD shall give thee of this young woman.

So Boaz took Ruth, and she was his wife: and when he went in unto her, the LORD gave her conception, and she bare a son. And the women said unto Naomi, Blessed *be* the LORD, which hath not left thee this day without a kinsman, that his name may be famous in Israel. And he shall be unto thee a restorer of *thy* life, and a nourisher of thine old age: for thy daughter in law, which loveth thee, which is better to thee than seven sons, hath borne him.

And Naomi took the child, and laid it in her bosom, and became nurse unto it. unto it. And the women her neighbours gave it a name, saying, There is a son born to Naomi; and they called his name Obed: he *is* the father of Jesse, the father of David.

RUTH 4:9-17

*Related texts:* GENESIS 29:31–30:4; 38; MICAH 5:2; MATTHEW 1:1-6

# I am: *The Bread of Life*

**THE ONE
MINUTE
BIBLE**

The people said therefore unto Jesus, What sign showest thou then, that we may see, and believe thee? What dost thou work? Our fathers did eat manna in the desert; as it is written, He gave them bread from heaven to eat.

Then Jesus said unto them, Verily, verily, I say unto you, Moses gave you not that bread from heaven; but my Father giveth you the true bread from heaven. For the bread of God is he which cometh down from heaven, and giveth life unto the world.

Then said they unto him, Lord, evermore give us this bread.

And Jesus said unto them, I am the bread of life: he that cometh to me shall never hunger; and he that believeth on me shall never thirst. But I said unto you, That ye also have seen me, and believe not. All that the Father giveth me shall come to me; and him that cometh to me I will in no wise cast out. For I came down from heaven, not to do mine own will, but the will of him that sent me. And this is the Father's will which hath sent me, that of all which he hath given me I should lose nothing, but should raise it up again at the last day. And this is the will of him that sent me, that every one which seeth the Son, and believeth on him, may have everlasting life: and I will raise him up at the last day.

JOHN 6:30-40

***Related texts:*** DEUTERONOMY 8:2; PROVERBS 30:7-9; JOHN 6:25-59; 1 CORINTHIANS 10:16-17; REVELATION 2:17

# I am: *The Light of the World*

Then spake Jesus again unto them, saying, I am the light of the world: he that followeth me shall not walk in darkness, but shall have the light of life.

And as *Jesus* passed by, he saw a man which was blind from *his* birth. And his disciples asked him, saying, Master, who did sin, this man, or his parents, that he was born blind?

Jesus answered, Neither hath this man sinned, nor his parents: but that the works of God should be made manifest in him. I must work the works of him that sent me, while it is day: the night cometh, when no man can work. As long as I am in the world, I am the light of the world.

When he had thus spoken, he spat on the ground, and made clay of the spittle, and he anointed the eyes of the blind man with the clay, and said unto him, Go, wash in the pool of Siloam, (which is by interpretation, Sent.) He went his way therefore, and washed, and came seeing.

In him was life; and the life was the light of men. And the light shineth in darkness; and the darkness comprehended it not.

JOHN 8:12; 9:1-7; 1:4-5

**THE ONE MINUTE BIBLE**

*Related texts:* PSALM 27:1; JOHN 1:1-14; 3:19-22; 12:44-46; 1 JOHN 1:1-7; REVELATION 21:2-27

# I am: *The Door for the Sheep*

**THE ONE
MINUTE
BIBLE**

[Jesus said,] Verily, verily, I say unto you, He that entereth not by the door into the sheepfold, but climbeth up some other way, the same is a thief and a robber. But he that entereth in by the door is the shepherd of the sheep. To him the porter openeth; and the sheep hear his voice: and he calleth his own sheep by name, and leadeth them out. And when he putteth forth his own sheep, he goeth before them, and the sheep follow him: for they know his voice. And a stranger will they not follow, but will flee from him: for they know not the voice of strangers. This parable spake Jesus unto them: but they understood not what things they were which he spake unto them.

Then said Jesus unto them again, Verily, verily, I say unto you, I am the door of the sheep. All that ever came before me are thieves and robbers: but the sheep did not hear them. I am the door: by me if any man enter in, he shall be saved, and shall go in and out, and find pasture. The thief cometh not, but for to steal, and to kill, and to destroy: I am come that they might have life, and that they might have *it* more abundantly.

JOHN 10:1-10

***Related texts:*** PSALM 118:17-21; MATTHEW 7:13-14; 25:1-13; LUKE 13:23-29; JOHN 14

# I am: *The Good Shepherd*

**THE ONE MINUTE BIBLE**

[Jesus said,] I am the good shepherd: the good shepherd giveth his life for the sheep. But he that is an hireling, and not the shepherd, whose own the sheep are not, seeth the wolf coming, and leaveth the sheep, and fleeth: and the wolf catcheth them, and scattereth the sheep. The hireling fleeth, because he is an hireling, and careth not for the sheep.

I am the good shepherd, and know my *sheep*, and am known of mine. As the Father knoweth me, even so know I the Father: and I lay down my life for the sheep. And other sheep I have, which are not of this fold: them also I must bring, and they shall hear my voice; and there shall be one fold, *and* one shepherd. Therefore doth my Father love me, because I lay down my life, that I might take it again. No man taketh it from me, but I lay it down of myself. I have power to lay it down, and I have power to take it again. This commandment have I received of my Father.

[Jesus,] who his own self bare our sins in his own body on the tree, that we, being dead to sins, should live unto righteousness: by whose stripes ye were healed. For ye were as sheep going astray; but are now returned unto the Shepherd and Bishop of your souls.

JOHN 10:11-18; 1 PETER 2:24-25

***Related texts:*** PSALM 23; ISAIAH 40:10-11; ZECHARIAH 11:4-17; MATTHEW 25:31-46; LUKE 15:3-7; HEBREWS 13:20-21

**THE ONE MINUTE BIBLE**

# I am: *The Resurrection and the Life*

Now a certain *man* was sick, *named* Lazarus, of Bethany, the town of Mary and her sister Martha.

When Jesus heard *that*, he said, This sickness is not unto death, but for the glory of God, that the Son of God might be glorified thereby.

Then when Jesus came, he found that he had *lain* in the grave four days already.

Then said Martha unto Jesus, Lord, if thou hadst been here, my brother had not died. But I know, that even now, whatsoever thou wilt ask of God, God will give *it* thee.

Jesus saith unto her, Thy brother shall rise again.

Martha saith unto him, I know that he shall rise again in the resurrection at the last day.

Jesus said unto her, I am the resurrection, and the life: he that believeth in me, though he were dead, yet shall he live: and whosoever liveth and believeth in me shall never die. Believest thou this?

She saith unto him, Yea, Lord: I believe that thou art the Christ, the Son of God, which should come into the world.

And when he thus had spoken, he cried with a loud voice, Lazarus, come forth. And he that was dead came forth, bound hand and foot with graveclothes: and his face was bound about with a napkin.

Jesus saith unto them, Loose him, and let him go.

JOHN 11:1, 4, 17, 21-27, 43-44

---

***Related texts:*** DEUTERONOMY 32:39; JOHN 5:19-26; ROMANS 5–6; 2 TIMOTHY 1:8-10; 1 JOHN 1:1-3

# I am: *The Way and the Truth and the Life*

**THE ONE MINUTE BIBLE**

[Jesus said,] Let not your heart be troubled: ye believe in God, believe also in me. In my Father's house are many mansions: if *it were* not *so*, I would have told you. I go to prepare a place for you. And if I go and prepare a place for you, I will come again, and receive you unto myself; that where I am, *there* ye may be also. And whither I go ye know, and the way ye know.

Thomas saith unto him, Lord, we know not whither thou goest; and how can we know the way?

Jesus saith unto him, I am the way, the truth, and the life: no man cometh unto the Father, but by me. If ye had known me, ye should have known my Father also: and from henceforth ye know him, and have seen him.

Philip saith unto him, Lord, show us the Father, and it sufficeth us.

Jesus saith unto him, Have I been so long time with you, and yet hast thou not known me, Philip? He that hath seen me hath seen the Father.

Neither is there salvation in any other: for there is none other name under heaven given among men, whereby we must be saved.

JOHN 14:1-9a; ACTS 4:12

*Related texts:* PSALM 96; JOHN 1:1-18; 3:13-16; HEBREWS 10:19-22

# I am: *The True Vine*

**THE ONE
MINUTE
BIBLE**

[Jesus said,] I am the true vine, and my Father is the husbandman. Every branch in me that beareth not fruit he taketh away: and every *branch* that beareth fruit, he purgeth it, that it may bring forth more fruit. Now ye are clean through the word which I have spoken unto you. Abide in me, and I in you. As the branch cannot bear fruit of itself, except it abide in the vine; no more can ye, except ye abide in me.

I am the vine, ye *are* the branches: he that abideth in me, and I in him, the same bringeth forth much fruit: for without me ye can do nothing. If a man abide not in me, he is cast forth as a branch, and is withered; and men gather them, and cast *them* into the fire, and they are burned. If ye abide in me, and my words abide in you, ye shall ask what ye will, and it shall be done unto you. Herein is my Father glorified, that ye bear much fruit; so shall ye be my disciples.

As the Father hath loved me, so have I loved you: continue ye in my love. If ye keep my commandments, ye shall abide in my love; even as I have kept my Father's commandments, and abide in his love. These things have I spoken unto you, that my joy might remain in you, and *that* your joy might be full.

JOHN 15:1-11

---

***Related texts:*** PSALM 80:8-19; ISAIAH 5:1-7; 27:2-6; LUKE 6:43-45; GALATIANS 5:22-23; COLOSSIANS 1:3-12

## *Hannah Prays for a Son*

**THE ONE
MINUTE
BIBLE**

Now there was a certain man of Ramathaim-zophim, of mount Ephraim, and his name *was* Elkanah, the son of Jeroham, the son of Elihu, the son of Tohu, the son of Zuph, an Ephrathite: and he had two wives; the name of the one *was* Hannah, and the name of the other Peninnah: and Peninnah had children, but Hannah had no children.

And this man went up out of his city yearly to worship and to sacrifice unto the LORD of hosts in Shiloh. And the two sons of Eli, Hophni and Phinehas, the priests of the LORD, *were* there. And when the time was that Elkanah offered, he gave to Peninnah his wife, and to all her sons and her daughters, portions: but unto Hannah he gave a worthy portion; for he loved Hannah: but the LORD had shut up her womb. And her adversary also provoked her sore, for to make her fret, because the LORD had shut up her womb.

And Hannah *was* in bitterness of soul, and prayed unto the LORD, and wept sore. And she vowed a vow, and said, O LORD of hosts, if thou wilt indeed look on the affliction of thine handmaid, and remember me, and not forget thine handmaid, but wilt give unto thine handmaid a man child, then I will give him unto the LORD all the days of his life, and there shall no razor come upon his head.

1 SAMUEL 1:1-6, 10-11

***Related texts:*** GENESIS 11:29-30; 25:21; 29:31; PSALM 113:9; ISAIAH 54:1; LUKE 1:4-22; 23:28-30; HEBREWS 11:11

## Samuel: Hannah's Firstborn

**THE ONE
MINUTE
BIBLE**

And they rose up in the morning early, and worshipped before the LORD, and returned, and came to their house to Ramah: and Elkanah knew Hannah his wife; and the LORD remembered her. Wherefore it came to pass, when the time was come about after Hannah had conceived, that she bare a son, and called his name Samuel, *saying*, Because I have asked him of the LORD.

And the man Elkanah, and all his house, went up to offer unto the LORD the yearly sacrifice, and his vow. But Hannah went not up; for she said unto her husband, *I will not go up* until the child be weaned, and *then* I will bring him, that he may appear before the LORD, and there abide for ever.

And when she had weaned him, she took him up with her, with three bullocks, and one ephah of flour, and a bottle of wine, and brought him unto the house of the LORD in Shiloh: and the child *was* young. And they slew a bullock, and brought the child to Eli. And she said, Oh my lord, *as* thy soul liveth, my lord, I *am* the woman that stood by thee here, praying unto the LORD. For this child I prayed; and the LORD hath given me my petition which I asked of him: therefore also I have lent him to the LORD; as long as he liveth he shall be lent to the LORD. And he worshipped the LORD there.

1 SAMUEL 1:19-22, 24-28

---

*Related texts:* GENESIS 8:1; 19:29; 30:22; EXODUS 2:24;
LUKE 1:23-45; ACTS 10:25-31; REVELATION 16:19; 18:5

## Samuel: Prophet and Judge

THE ONE
MINUTE
BIBLE

Now the sons of Eli *were* sons of Belial; they knew not the LORD.

But Samuel ministered before the LORD, *being* a child, girded with a linen ephod. Moreover his mother made him a little coat, and brought *it* to him from year to year, when she came up with her husband to offer the yearly sacrifice. And Eli blessed Elkanah and his wife, and said, The LORD give thee seed of this woman for the loan which is lent to the LORD. And they went unto their own home. And the LORD visited Hannah, so that she conceived, and bare three sons and two daughters. And the child Samuel grew before the LORD.

And Samuel grew, and the LORD was with him, and did let none of his words fall to the ground. And all Israel from Dan even to Beer-sheba knew that Samuel *was* established *to be* a prophet of the LORD. And the LORD appeared again in Shiloh: for the LORD revealed himself to Samuel in Shiloh by the word of the LORD.

And Samuel judged Israel all the days of his life. And he went from year to year in circuit to Beth-el, and Gilgal, and Mizpeh, and judged Israel in all those places. And his return *was* to Ramah; for there *was* his house; and there he judged Israel; and there he built an altar unto the LORD.

1 SAMUEL 2:12, 18-21; 3:19-21; 7:15-17

---

***Related texts:*** GENESIS 4:25-26; DEUTERONOMY 18:15-19; JOSHUA 21:45; LUKE 1:13-17

*Sin will keep you from this Book.*
*This Book will keep you from sin.*
**Dwight L. Moody (1837-1899)**
AMERICAN EVANGELIST

*The Bible is the greatest benefit which*
*the human race has ever experienced.*
*A single line in the Bible has consoled*
*me more than all the books I ever*
*read besides.*
**Immanuel Kant (1724-1804)**
GERMAN PHILOSOPHER

*The Bible is the one Book to which*
*any thoughtful man may go with*
*any honest question of life or destiny*
*and find the answer of God by*
*honest searching.*
**John Ruskin (1819-1900)**
ENGLISH AUTHOR, REFORMER

## Israel Asks for a King

And it came to pass, when Samuel was old, that he made his sons judges over Israel. And his sons walked not in his ways, but turned aside after lucre, and took bribes, and perverted judgment.

Then all the elders of Israel gathered themselves together, and came to Samuel unto Ramah, and said unto him, Behold, thou art old, and thy sons walk not in thy ways: now make us a king to judge us like all the nations.

But the thing displeased Samuel, when they said, Give us a king to judge us. And Samuel prayed unto the LORD. And the LORD said unto Samuel, Hearken unto the voice of the people in all that they say unto thee: for they have not rejected thee, but they have rejected me, that I should not reign over them. According to all the works which they have done since the day that I brought them up out of Egypt even unto this day, wherewith they have forsaken me, and served other gods, so do they also unto thee. Now therefore hearken unto their voice: howbeit yet protest solemnly unto them, and show them the manner of the king that shall reign over them.

And Samuel told all the words of the LORD unto the people that asked of him a king.

Nevertheless the people refused to obey the voice of Samuel; and they said, Nay; but we will have a king over us; that we also may be like all the nations; and that our king may judge us, and go out before us, and fight our battles.

And Samuel heard all the words of the people, and he rehearsed them in the ears of the LORD. And the LORD said to Samuel, Hearken unto their voice, and make them a king.

1 SAMUEL 8:1, 3-10, 19-22a

*Related texts:* DEUTERONOMY 17:14-20; 1 SAMUEL 8:11-18; ISAIAH 9:6; JEREMIAH 10:1-10; 1 TIMOTHY 1:17

## Saul: The First King of Israel

**THE ONE
MINUTE
BIBLE**

And Samuel called the people together unto the LORD to Mizpeh; and said unto the children of Israel, Thus saith the LORD God of Israel, I brought up Israel out of Egypt, and delivered you out of the hand of the Egyptians, and out of the hand of all kingdoms, *and* of them that oppressed you: and ye have this day rejected your God, who himself saved you out of all your adversities and your tribulations; and ye have said unto him, *Nay*, but set a king over us. Now therefore present yourselves before the LORD by your tribes, and by your thousands.

And when Samuel had caused all the tribes of Israel to come near, the tribe of Benjamin was taken. When he had caused the tribe of Benjamin to come near by their families, the family of Matri was taken, and Saul the son of Kish was taken: and when they sought him, he could not be found. Therefore they inquired of the LORD further, if the man should yet come thither. And the LORD answered, Behold, he hath hid himself among the stuff.

And they ran and fetched him thence: and when he stood among the people, he was higher than any of the people from his shoulders and upward. And Samuel said to all the people, See ye him whom the LORD hath chosen, that *there is* none like him among all the people?

And all the people shouted, and said, God save the king.

Then Samuel told the people the manner of the kingdom, and wrote *it* in a book, and laid *it* up before the LORD. And Samuel sent all the people away, every man to his house.

1 SAMUEL 10:17-25

***Related texts:*** DEUTERONOMY 17:14-20; 1 SAMUEL 9:1–10:16; 11–14; JOHN 12:12-15

## *The Lord Rejects Saul as King*

Samuel also said unto Saul, The Lord sent me to anoint thee *to be* king over his people, over Israel: now therefore hearken thou unto the voice of the words of the Lord. Thus saith the Lord of hosts, I remember *that* which Amalek did to Israel, how he laid *wait* for him in the way, when he came up from Egypt. Now go and smite Amalek, and utterly destroy all that they have.

And Saul smote the Amalekites from Havilah *until* thou comest to Shur, that *is* over against Egypt. But Saul and the people spared Agag, and the best of the sheep, and of the oxen, and of the fatlings, and the lambs, and all *that was* good, and would not utterly destroy them: but every thing *that was* vile and refuse, that they destroyed utterly.

Then came the word of the Lord unto Samuel, saying, It repenteth me that I have set up Saul *to be* king: for he is turned back from following me, and hath not performed my commandments.

And Samuel came to Saul: and Saul said unto him, Blessed *be* thou of the Lord: I have performed the commandment of the Lord.

And Samuel said,

Hath the Lord *as great* delight in burnt offerings
   and sacrifices,
   as in obeying the voice of the Lord?
Behold, to obey *is* better than sacrifice,
   *and* to hearken than the fat of rams.
For rebellion *is as* the sin of witchcraft,
   and stubbornness *is as* iniquity and idolatry.
Because thou hast rejected the word of the Lord,
   he hath also rejected thee from *being* king.

1 Samuel 15:1-3a, 7, 9-11a, 13, 22-23

**THE ONE
MINUTE
BIBLE**

*Related texts:* Exodus 17:8-16; Deuteronomy 25:17-19; Micah 6:6-8; Luke 16:10-13

## *Samuel Anoints David as King*

**THE ONE
MINUTE
BIBLE**

And the LORD said unto Samuel, How long wilt thou mourn for Saul, seeing I have rejected him from reigning over Israel? Fill thine horn with oil, and go, I will send thee to Jesse the Beth-lehemite: for I have provided me a king among his sons.

And it came to pass, when they were come, that he looked on Eliab, and said, Surely the LORD's anointed *is* before him.

But the LORD said unto Samuel, Look not on his countenance, or on the height of his stature; because I have refused him: for *the LORD seeth* not as man seeth; for man looketh on the outward appearance, but the LORD looketh on the heart.

Again, Jesse made seven of his sons to pass before Samuel. And Samuel said unto Jesse, The LORD hath not chosen these. And Samuel said unto Jesse, Are here all *thy* children?

And he said, There remaineth yet the youngest, and, behold, he keepeth the sheep.

And Samuel said unto Jesse, Send and fetch him: for we will not sit down till he come hither.

And he sent, and brought him in. Now he *was* ruddy, *and* withal of a beautiful countenance, and goodly to look to.

And the LORD said, Arise, anoint him: for this *is* he.

Then Samuel took the horn of oil, and anointed him in the midst of his brethren: and the spirit of the LORD came upon David from that day forward.

1 SAMUEL 16:1, 6-7, 10-13a

---

***Related texts:*** PSALM 78:70-72; MATTHEW 5:8; 12:33-35; LUKE 6:43-45;
ACTS 13:21-23

# Goliath Challenges the Armies of Israel

Now the Philistines gathered together their armies to battle, and were gathered together at Shochoh, which *belongeth* to Judah, and pitched between Shochoh and Azekah, in Ephes-dammim. And Saul and the men of Israel were gathered together, and pitched by the valley of Elah, and set the battle in array against the Philistines. And the Philistines stood on a mountain on the one side, and Israel stood on a mountain on the other side: and *there was* a valley between them.

And there went out a champion out of the camp of the Philistines, named Goliath, of Gath, whose height *was* six cubits and a span. And *he had* an helmet of brass upon his head, and he *was* armed with a coat of mail; and the weight of the coat *was* five thousand shekels of brass. And *he had* greaves of brass upon his legs, and a target of brass between his shoulders. And the staff of his spear *was* like a weaver's beam; and his spear's head *weighed* six hundred shekels of iron: and one bearing a shield went before him.

And Goliath stood and cried unto the armies of Israel, and said unto them, Why are ye come out to set *your* battle in array? Am not I a Philistine, and ye servants to Saul? Choose you a man for you, and let him come down to me. If he be able to fight with me, and to kill me, then will we be your servants: but if I prevail against him, and kill him, then shall ye be our servants, and serve us. And the Philistine said, I defy the armies of Israel this day; give me a man, that we may fight together. When Saul and all Israel heard those words of the Philistine, they were dismayed, and greatly afraid.

1 SAMUEL 17:1-11

*Related texts:* NUMBERS 13:26-33; DEUTERONOMY 11:22-25; PSALM 15; PROVERBS 14:27; 15:33; 29:25

## *David Accepts Goliath's Challenge*

**THE ONE
MINUTE
BIBLE**

And David said to Saul, Let no man's heart fail because of him; thy servant will go and fight with this Philistine.

And Saul said to David, Thou art not able to go against this Philistine to fight with him: for thou *art* but a youth, and he a man of war from his youth.

And David said unto Saul, Thy servant kept his father's sheep, and there came a lion, and a bear, and took a lamb out of the flock: and I went out after him, and smote him, and delivered *it* out of his mouth: and when he arose against me, I caught *him* by his beard, and smote him, and slew him. Thy servant slew both the lion and the bear: and this uncircumcised Philistine shall be as one of them, seeing he hath defied the armies of the living God.

David said moreover, The LORD that delivered me out of the paw of the lion, and out of the paw of the bear, he will deliver me out of the hand of this Philistine.

And Saul said unto David, Go, and the LORD be with thee.

And he took his staff in his hand, and chose him five smooth stones out of the brook, and put them in a shepherd's bag which he had, even in a scrip; and his sling was in his hand: and he drew near to the Philistine.

1 SAMUEL 17:32-37, 40

*Related texts:* PSALMS 31:11-18; 97:10; 144; EPHESIANS 6:10-18; 1 TIMOTHY 4:12

# David Kills Goliath

And the Philistine came on and drew near unto David; and the man that bare the shield *went* before him. And when the Philistine looked about, and saw David, he disdained him: for he was *but* a youth, and ruddy, and of a fair countenance. And the Philistine said unto David, *Am* I a dog, that thou comest to me with staves? And the Philistine cursed David by his gods.

Then said David to the Philistine, Thou comest to me with a sword, and with a spear, and with a shield: but I come to thee in the name of the LORD of hosts, the God of the armies of Israel, whom thou hast defied. This day will the LORD deliver thee into mine hand; and I will smite thee, and take thine head from thee; and I will give the carcases of the host of the Philistines this day unto the fowls of the air, and to the wild beasts of the earth; that all the earth may know that there is a God in Israel. And all this assembly shall know that the LORD saveth not with sword and spear: for the battle *is* the LORD's, and he will give you into our hands.

And it came to pass, when the Philistine arose, and came and drew nigh to meet David, that David hasted, and ran toward the army to meet the Philistine. And David put his hand in his bag, and took thence a stone, and slang *it*, and smote the Philistine in his forehead, that the stone sunk into his forehead; and he fell upon his face to the earth.

So David prevailed over the Philistine with a sling and with a stone, and smote the Philistine, and slew him; but *there was* no sword in the hand of David.

1 SAMUEL 17:41-43, 45-50

**THE ONE MINUTE BIBLE**

---

*Related texts:* 2 SAMUEL 21:15-22; PSALM 27; HEBREWS 11:32-34

## Saul Becomes Jealous of David

**THE ONE
MINUTE
BIBLE**

And it came to pass, when he had made an end of speaking unto Saul, that the soul of Jonathan was knit with the soul of David, and Jonathan loved him as his own soul. And Saul took him that day, and would let him go no more home to his father's house. Then Jonathan and David made a covenant, because he loved him as his own soul. And Jonathan stripped himself of the robe that *was* upon him, and gave it to David, and his garments, even to his sword, and to his bow, and to his girdle.

And David went out whithersoever Saul sent him, *and* behaved himself wisely: and Saul set him over the men of war, and he was accepted in the sight of all the people, and also in the sight of Saul's servants.

And it came to pass as they came, when David was returned from the slaughter of the Philistine, that the women came out of all cities of Israel, singing and dancing, to meet king Saul, with tabrets, with joy, and with instruments of music. And the women answered *one another* as they played, and said,

Saul hath slain his thousands,
    and David his ten thousands.

And Saul was very wroth, and the saying displeased him; and he said, They have ascribed unto David ten thousands, and to me they have ascribed *but* thousands: and *what* can he have more but the kingdom? And Saul eyed David from that day and forward.

1 Samuel 18:1-9

---

***Related texts:*** Proverbs 27:4; Acts 5:12-19; 7:9-10; Romans 13:12-14; 2 Corinthians 11:2; Galatians 5:19-20

## Saul Tries to Kill David

And Saul spake to Jonathan his son, and to all his servants, that they should kill David. But Jonathan Saul's son delighted much in David: and Jonathan told David, saying, Saul my father seeketh to kill thee: now therefore, I pray thee, take heed to thyself until the morning, and abide in a secret *place*, and hide thyself: and I will go out and stand beside my father in the field where thou *art*, and I will commune with my father of thee; and what I see, that I will tell thee.

And Jonathan spake good of David unto Saul his father, and said unto him, Let not the king sin against his servant, against David; because he hath not sinned against thee, and because his works *have been* to thee-ward very good: for he did put his life in his hand, and slew the Philistine, and the LORD wrought a great salvation for all Israel: thou sawest *it*, and didst rejoice: wherefore then wilt thou sin against innocent blood, to slay David without a cause?

And Saul hearkened unto the voice of Jonathan: and Saul sware, *As* the LORD liveth, he shall not be slain.

And Jonathan called David, and Jonathan showed him all those things. And Jonathan brought David to Saul, and he was in his presence, as in times past.

And the evil spirit from the LORD was upon Saul, as he sat in his house with his javelin in his hand: and David played with *his* hand. And Saul sought to smite David even to the wall with the javelin; but he slipped away out of Saul's presence, and he smote the javelin into the wall: and David fled, and escaped that night.

1 SAMUEL 19:1-7, 9-10

---

*Related texts:* 1 SAMUEL 19–30; PSALMS 52; 54; 57; 59; JAMES 1:13-15

**THE ONE**
**MINUTE**
**BIBLE**

## The Death of Saul and His Sons

Now the Philistines fought against Israel; and the men of Israel fled from before the Philistines, and fell down slain in mount Gilboa. And the Philistines followed hard after Saul, and after his sons; and the Philistines slew Jonathan, and Abinadab, and Malchi-shua, the sons of Saul. And the battle went sore against Saul, and the archers hit him, and he was wounded of the archers.

Then said Saul to his armourbearer, Draw thy sword, and thrust me through therewith; lest these uncircumcised come and abuse me.

But his armourbearer would not; for he was sore afraid. So Saul took a sword, and fell upon it. And when his armourbearer saw that Saul was dead, he fell likewise on the sword, and died. So Saul died, and his three sons, and all his house died together.

And when all the men of Israel that *were* in the valley saw that they fled, and that Saul and his sons were dead, then they forsook their cities, and fled: and the Philistines came and dwelt in them.

So Saul died for his transgression which he committed against the Lord, *even* against the word of the Lord, which he kept not, and also for asking *counsel* of *one that had* a familiar spirit, to inquire *of it*; and inquired not of the Lord: therefore he slew him, and turned the kingdom unto David the son of Jesse.

1 Chronicles 10:1-7, 13-14

---

***Related texts:*** 1 Samuel 28; 30–31; 2 Samuel 1; 16:15–17:23; Matthew 27:1-5; Acts 16:22-28

242

## *The* LORD *Makes a Covenant With David*

**THE ONE
MINUTE
BIBLE**

And it came to pass, when the king sat in his house, and the LORD had given him rest round about from all his enemies; that the king said unto Nathan the prophet, See now, I dwell in an house of cedar, but the ark of God dwelleth within curtains.

And Nathan said to the king, Go, do all that *is* in thine heart; for the LORD *is* with thee.

And it came to pass that night, that the word of the LORD came unto Nathan, saying,

Now therefore so shalt thou say unto my servant David, Thus saith the LORD of hosts, I took thee from the sheepcote, from following the sheep, to be ruler over my people, over Israel: and I was with thee whithersoever thou wentest, and have cut off all thine enemies out of thy sight, and have made thee a great name, like unto the name of the great *men* that *are* in the earth.

Also the LORD telleth thee that he will make thee an house. And when thy days be fulfilled, and thou shalt sleep with thy fathers, I will set up thy seed after thee, which shall proceed out of thy bowels, and I will establish his kingdom. He shall build an house for my name, and I will stablish the throne of his kingdom for ever. I will be his father, and he shall be my son. If he commit iniquity, I will chasten him with the rod of men, and with the stripes of the children of men: but my mercy shall not depart away from him, as I took *it* from Saul, whom I put away before thee. And thine house and thy kingdom shall be established for ever before thee: thy throne shall be established for ever.

2 SAMUEL 7:1-4, 8-9, 11b-16

***Related texts:*** 1 CHRONICLES 17; PSALMS 2; 89; JEREMIAH 33:14-26; ROMANS 1:1-4

# The LORD Is My Shepherd

**THE ONE
MINUTE
BIBLE**

A psalm of David

The LORD *is* my shepherd; I shall not want.
 He maketh me to lie down in green pastures:
he leadeth me beside the still waters.
 He restoreth my soul:
he leadeth me in the paths of righteousness
 for his name's sake.
Yea, though I walk
 through the valley of the shadow of death,
I will fear no evil:
 for thou *art* with me;
thy rod and thy staff
 they comfort me.

Thou preparest a table before me
 in the presence of mine enemies:
thou anointest my head with oil;
 my cup runneth over.
Surely goodness and mercy shall follow me
 all the days of my life:
and I will dwell in the house of the LORD for ever.


[Jesus said,] I am the good shepherd: the good
shepherd giveth his life for the sheep.

PSALM 23; JOHN 10:11

---

***Related texts:*** ISAIAH 40:10-11; MICAH 5:2-5; HEBREWS 13:20-21;
1 PETER 2:21-25; REVELATION 7:15-17

# David Commits Adultery with Bathsheba

And it came to pass, after the year was expired, at the time when kings go forth *to battle*, that David sent Joab, and his servants with him, and all Israel; and they destroyed the children of Ammon, and besieged Rabbah. But David tarried still at Jerusalem.

And it came to pass in an eveningtide, that David arose from off his bed, and walked upon the roof of the king's house: and from the roof he saw a woman washing herself; and the woman *was* very beautiful to look upon. And David sent and inquired after the woman. And *one* said, *Is* not this Bath-sheba, the daughter of Eliam, the wife of Uriah the Hittite? And David sent messengers, and took her; and she came in unto him, and he lay with her; for she was purified from her uncleanness: and she returned unto her house. And the woman conceived, and sent and told David, and said, I *am* with child.

And David sent to Joab, *saying*, Send me Uriah the Hittite. And Joab sent Uriah to David. And when Uriah was come unto him, David demanded *of him* how Joab did, and how the people did, and how the war prospered. And David said to Uriah, Go down to thy house, and wash thy feet. And Uriah departed out of the king's house, and there followed him a mess *of meat* from the king. But Uriah slept at the door of the king's house with all the servants of his lord, and went not down to his house.

2 Samuel 11:1-9

*Related texts:* Deuteronomy 5:18; Job 31:1; Psalm 119:9-16; Proverbs 5–6; 1 Corinthians 6:9-11

245

# David Arranges Uriah's Death

**THE ONE
MINUTE
BIBLE**

And it came to pass in the morning, that David wrote a letter to Joab, and sent *it* by the hand of Uriah. And he wrote in the letter, saying, Set ye Uriah in the forefront of the hottest battle, and retire ye from him, that he may be smitten, and die.

And it came to pass, when Joab observed the city, that he assigned Uriah unto a place where he knew that valiant men *were*. And the men of the city went out, and fought with Joab: and there fell *some* of the people of the servants of David; and Uriah the Hittite died also.

And when the wife of Uriah heard that Uriah her husband was dead, she mourned for her husband. And when the mourning was past, David sent and fetched her to his house, and she became his wife, and bare him a son. But the thing that David had done displeased the LORD.

And David said unto Nathan, I have sinned against the LORD.

And Nathan said unto David, The LORD also hath put away thy sin; thou shalt not die. Howbeit, because by this deed thou hast given great occasion to the enemies of the LORD to blaspheme, the child also *that is* born unto thee shall surely die.

For the wages of sin *is* death; but the gift of God is eternal life through Jesus Christ our Lord.

2 SAMUEL 11:14-17, 26-27; 12:13-14; ROMANS 6:23

---

***Related texts:*** NUMBERS 32:23; 2 SAMUEL 12:15-25; PROVERBS 26:27; MATTHEW 1:1-6; HEBREWS 13:4

## *David's Prayer of Repentance*

To the chief Musician, A Psalm of David, when Nathan the prophet came unto him, after he had gone in to Bath-sheba.

Have mercy upon me, O God,
    according to thy lovingkindness:
according unto the multitude of thy tender mercies
    blot out my transgressions.
Wash me thoroughly from mine iniquity,
    and cleanse me from my sin.
For I acknowledge my transgressions:
    and my sin *is* ever before me.
Against thee, thee only, have I sinned,
    and done *this* evil in thy sight:
that thou mightest be justified when thou speakest,
    *and* be clear when thou judgest.
Behold, I was shapen in iniquity,
    and in sin did my mother conceive me.
Behold, thou desirest truth in the inward parts:
    and in the hidden *part* thou shalt make me to know
        wisdom.
Purge me with hyssop, and I shall be clean:
    wash me, and I shall be whiter than snow.
Make me to hear joy and gladness;
    *that* the bones *which* thou hast broken may rejoice.
Hide thy face from my sins,
    and blot out all mine iniquities.
Create in me a clean heart, O God;
    and renew a right spirit within me.
Cast me not away from thy presence;
    and take not thy holy spirit from me.
Restore unto me the joy of thy salvation;
    and uphold me *with thy* free spirit.
*Then* will I teach transgressors thy ways;
    and sinners shall be converted unto thee.

PSALM 51:1-13

*Related texts:* 2 SAMUEL 12; PSALM 32; ISAIAH 40:28-31; HABAKKUK 3:2;
TITUS 3:3-7

## David Appoints Solomon as King

**THE ONE
MINUTE
BIBLE**

Now the days of David drew nigh that he should die; and he charged Solomon his son, saying,

I go the way of all the earth: be thou strong therefore, and show thyself a man; and keep the charge of the Lord thy God, to walk in his ways, to keep his statutes, and his commandments, and his judgments, and his testimonies, as it is written in the law of Moses, that thou mayest prosper in all that thou doest, and whithersoever thou turnest thyself: that the Lord may continue his word which he spake concerning me, saying, If thy children take heed to their way, to walk before me in truth with all their heart and with all their soul, there shall not fail thee (said he) a man on the throne of Israel.

Then Solomon sat on the throne of the Lord as king instead of David his father, and prospered; and all Israel obeyed him. And all the princes, and the mighty men, and all the sons likewise of king David, submitted themselves unto Solomon the king.

And the Lord magnified Solomon exceedingly in the sight of all Israel, and bestowed upon him *such* royal majesty as had not been on any king before him in Israel.

Trust in the Lord with all thine heart;
  and lean not unto thine own understanding.
In all thy ways acknowledge him,
  and he shall direct thy paths.

1 Kings 2:1-4; 1 Chronicles 29:23-25; Proverbs 3:5-6

*Related texts:* 2 Samuel 7; 1 Kings 1; 1 Chronicles 17; 23–29; Matthew 1:1-6; Luke 12:22-31

248

## Solomon Asks for Wisdom

In Gibeon the LORD appeared to Solomon in a dream by night: and God said, Ask what I shall give thee.

[Solomon answered,] And now, O LORD my God, thou hast made thy servant king instead of David my father: and I *am but* a little child: I know not *how* to go out or come in. And thy servant *is* in the midst of thy people which thou hast chosen, a great people, that cannot be numbered nor counted for multitude. Give therefore thy servant an understanding heart to judge thy people, that I may discern between good and bad: for who is able to judge this thy so great a people?

And the speech pleased the Lord, that Solomon had asked this thing. And God said unto him, Because thou hast asked this thing, and hast not asked for thyself long life; neither hast asked riches for thyself, nor hast asked the life of thine enemies; but hast asked for thyself understanding to discern judgment; behold, I have done according to thy words: lo, I have given thee a wise and an understanding heart; so that there was none like thee before thee, neither after thee shall any arise like unto thee.

And I have also given thee that which thou hast not asked, both riches, and honour: so that there shall not be any among the kings like unto thee all thy days. And if thou wilt walk in my ways, to keep my statutes and my commandments, as thy father David did walk, then I will lengthen thy days.

1 KINGS 3:5, 7-14

**THE ONE MINUTE BIBLE**

---

***Related texts:*** 1 KINGS 3:16-28; 2 CHRONICLES 1:1-13; PROVERBS 1–4; 8:10-21; JAMES 1:5-8

# The Wisdom of Solomon

**THE ONE
MINUTE
BIBLE**

Judah and Israel *were* many, as the sand which *is* by the sea in multitude, eating and drinking, and making merry. And Solomon reigned over all kingdoms from the river unto the land of the Philistines, and unto the border of Egypt: they brought presents, and served Solomon all the days of his life.

And God gave Solomon wisdom and understanding exceeding much, and largeness of heart, even as the sand that *is* on the sea shore. And Solomon's wisdom excelled the wisdom of all the children of the east country, and all the wisdom of Egypt. For he was wiser than all men; than Ethan the Ezrahite, and Heman, and Chalcol, and Darda, the sons of Mahol: and his fame was in all nations round about.

And he spake three thousand proverbs: and his songs were a thousand and five. And he spake of trees, from the cedar tree that *is* in Lebanon even unto the hyssop that springeth out of the wall: he spake also of beasts, and of fowl, and of creeping things, and of fishes. And there came of all people to hear the wisdom of Solomon, from all kings of the earth, which had heard of his wisdom.

1 Kings 4:20-21, 29-34

*Related texts:* 1 Kings 10:1-13; Psalm 72; Proverbs 13:10; 16:16; 23:23; Matthew 12:38-42

## The Proverbs of Solomon

The proverbs of Solomon the son of David, king of Israel;

> To know wisdom and instruction;
>> to perceive the words of understanding;
> to receive the instruction of wisdom, justice,
>> and judgment, and equity;
> to give subtlety to the simple,
>> to the young man knowledge and discretion.
> A wise *man* will hear, and will increase learning;
>> and a man of understanding shall attain unto wise
>>> counsels:
> to understand a proverb, and the interpretation;
>> the words of the wise, and their dark sayings.

> The fear of the LORD *is* the beginning of knowledge:
>> *but* fools despise wisdom and instruction.

And when the people were gathered thick together, Jesus began to say, This is an evil generation: they seek a sign; and there shall no sign be given it, but the sign of Jonas the prophet. For as Jonas was a sign unto the Ninevites, so shall also the Son of man be to this generation. The queen of the south shall rise up in the judgment with the men of this generation, and condemn them: for she came from the utmost parts of the earth to hear the wisdom of Solomon; and, behold, a greater than Solomon *is* here.

PROVERBS 1:1-7; LUKE 11:29-31

*Related texts:* 2 CHRONICLES 9:1-12; PROVERBS 10:1; 25:1;
SONG OF SONGS 1–8; JONAH 3; 1 CORINTHIANS 12:1-11

# Parables of Jesus: *The Sower*

**THE ONE
MINUTE
BIBLE**

And when much people were gathered together, and were come to Jesus out of every city, he spake by a parable: A sower went out to sow his seed: and as he sowed, some fell by the way side; and it was trodden down, and the fowls of the air devoured it. And some fell upon a rock; and as soon as it was sprung up, it withered away, because it lacked moisture. And some fell among thorns; and the thorns sprang up with it, and choked it. And other fell on good ground, and sprang up, and bare fruit an hundredfold.

And when he had said these things, he cried, He that hath ears to hear, let him hear.

And his disciples asked him, saying, What might this parable be?

And he said, Unto you it is given to know the mysteries of the kingdom of God: but to others in parables;

> that seeing they might not see,
>> and hearing they might not understand.

Hear this, all ye people;
> give ear, all *ye* inhabitants of the world:
both high and low,
> rich and poor, together.
My mouth shall speak of wisdom;
> and the meditation of my heart *shall be*
>> of understanding.
I will incline mine ear to a parable:
> I will open dark saying upon the harp.

LUKE 8:4-10; PSALM 49:1-4

*Related texts:* PSALM 126; PROVERBS 11:18-21; ISAIAH 6:8-13; HOSEA 10:12-13; MATTHEW 13:1-17; MARK 4:1-12

252

# Parables of Jesus: *The Sower Explained*

**THE ONE
MINUTE
BIBLE**

Now the parable is this: The seed is the word of God. Those by the way side are they that hear; then cometh the devil, and taketh away the word out of their hearts, lest they should believe and be saved. They on the rock *are* they, which, when they hear, receive the word with joy; and these have no root, which for a while believe, and in time of temptation fall away. And that which fell among thorns are they, which, when they have heard, go forth, and are choked with cares and riches and pleasures of *this* life, and bring no fruit to perfection. But that on the good ground are they, which in an honest and good heart, having heard the word, keep *it*, and bring forth fruit with patience.

No man, when he hath lighted a candle, covereth it with a vessel, or putteth *it* under a bed; but setteth *it* on a candlestick, that they which enter in may see the light. For nothing is secret, that shall not be made manifest; neither *any thing* hid, that shall not be known and come abroad. Take heed therefore how ye hear: for whosoever hath, to him shall be given; and whosoever hath not, from him shall be taken even that which he seemeth to have.

LUKE 8:11-18

---

***Related texts:*** PROVERBS 11:30; MATTHEW 13:18-23; MARK 4:13-25; JOHN 15:1-17; GALATIANS 6:7-10

# Parables of Jesus: *The Kingdom*

**THE ONE
MINUTE
BIBLE**

Another parable put Jesus forth unto them, saying, The kingdom of heaven is like to a grain of mustard seed, which a man took, and sowed in his field: which indeed is the least of all seeds: but when it is grown, it is the greatest among herbs, and becometh a tree, so that the birds of the air come and lodge in the branches thereof.

Another parable spake he unto them; The kingdom of heaven is like unto leaven, which a woman took, and hid in three measures of meal, till the whole was leavened.

Again, the kingdom of heaven is like unto treasure hid in a field; the which when a man hath found, he hideth, and for joy thereof goeth and selleth all that he hath, and buyeth that field.

Again, the kingdom of heaven is like unto a merchant man, seeking goodly pearls: who, when he had found one pearl of great price, went and sold all that he had, and bought it.

Again, the kingdom of heaven is like unto a net, that was cast into the sea, and gathered of every kind: which, when it was full, they drew to shore, and sat down, and gathered the good into vessels, but cast the bad away. So shall it be at the end of the world: the angels shall come forth, and sever the wicked from among the just, and shall cast them into the furnace of fire: there shall be wailing and gnashing of teeth.

MATTHEW 13:31-33, 44-50

*Related texts:* PSALM 45:6; MARK 1:1-15; 4:30-32; LUKE 13:18-19

# Parables of Jesus: *Lost and Found*

Then drew near unto him all the publicans and sinners for to hear him. And the Pharisees and scribes murmured, saying, This man receiveth sinners, and eateth with them.

And Jesus spake this parable unto them, saying, What man of you, having an hundred sheep, if he lose one of them, doth not leave the ninety and nine in the wilderness, and go after that which is lost, until he find it? And when he hath found *it*, he layeth *it* on his shoulders, rejoicing. And when he cometh home, he calleth together *his* friends and neighbours, saying unto them, Rejoice with me; for I have found my sheep which was lost. I say unto you, that likewise joy shall be in heaven over one sinner that repenteth, more than over ninety and nine just persons, which need no repentance.

Either what woman having ten pieces of silver, if she lose one piece, doth not light a candle, and sweep the house, and seek diligently till she find *it*? And when she hath found *it*, she calleth *her* friends and *her* neighbours together, saying, Rejoice with me; for I have found the piece which I had lost. Likewise, I say unto you, there is joy in the presence of the angels of God over one sinner that repenteth.

Luke 15:1-10

**THE ONE MINUTE BIBLE**

*Related texts:* Psalm 119:169-176; Matthew 18:12-14; Luke 9:22-26; 19:1-10

# Parables of Jesus: *The Prodigal Son, Part 1*

**THE ONE
MINUTE
BIBLE**

And Jesus said, A certain man had two sons: and the younger of them said to *his* father, Father, give me the portion of goods that falleth *to me*. And he divided unto them *his* living.

And not many days after the younger son gathered all together, and took his journey into a far country, and there wasted his substance with riotous living. And when he had spent all, there arose a mighty famine in that land; and he began to be in want. And he went and joined himself to a citizen of that country; and he sent him into his fields to feed swine. And he would fain have filled his belly with the husks that the swine did eat: and no man gave unto him.

And when he came to himself, he said, How many hired servants of my father's have bread enough and to spare, and I perish with hunger! I will arise and go to my father, and will say unto him, Father, I have sinned against heaven, and before thee, and am no more worthy to be called thy son: make me as one of thy hired servants. And he arose, and came to his father.

But when he was yet a great way off, his father saw him, and had compassion, and ran, and fell on his neck, and kissed him.

And the son said unto him, Father, I have sinned against heaven, and in thy sight, and am no more worthy to be called thy son.

Luke 15:11-21

---

***Related texts:*** 2 Chronicles 7:13-14; Proverbs 17:6, 21; Hosea 6:1-3; Acts 3:19-20

# Parables of Jesus: *The Prodigal Son, Part 2*

**THE ONE
MINUTE
BIBLE**

But the father said to his servants, Bring forth the best robe, and put *it* on him; and put a ring on his hand, and shoes on *his* feet: and bring hither the fatted calf, and kill *it*; and let us eat, and be merry: for this my son was dead, and is alive again; he was lost, and is found. And they began to be merry.

Now his elder son was in the field: and as he came and drew nigh to the house, he heard music and dancing. And he called one of the servants, and asked what these things meant. And he said unto him, Thy brother is come; and thy father hath killed the fatted calf, because he hath received him safe and sound.

And he was angry, and would not go in: therefore came his father out, and entreated him. And he answering said to *his* father, Lo, these many years do I serve thee, neither transgressed I at any time thy commandment: and yet thou never gavest me a kid, that I might make merry with my friends: but as soon as this thy son was come, which hath devoured thy living with harlots, thou hast killed for him the fatted calf.

And he said unto him, Son, thou art ever with me, and all that I have is thine. It was meet that we should make merry, and be glad: for this thy brother was dead, and is alive again; and was lost, and is found.

LUKE 15:22-32

*Related texts:* ISAIAH 55:6-7; MATTHEW 18:12-14; COLOSSIANS 1:1-14; 1 PETER 2:24-25

## Solomon Builds the Temple

**THE ONE
MINUTE
BIBLE**

And Hiram king of Tyre sent his servants unto Solomon; for he had heard that they had anointed him king in the room of his father: for Hiram was ever a lover of David. And Solomon sent to Hiram, saying,

Thou knowest how that David my father could not build an house unto the name of the LORD his God for the wars which were about him on every side, until the LORD put them under the soles of his feet. But now the LORD my God hath given me rest on every side, *so that there is* neither adversary nor evil occurrent. And, behold, I purpose to build an house unto the name of the LORD my God, as the LORD spake unto David my father, saying, Thy son, whom I will set upon thy throne in thy room, he shall build an house unto my name.

Now therefore command thou that they hew me cedar trees out of Lebanon; and my servants shall be with thy servants: and unto thee will I give hire for thy servants according to all that thou shalt appoint: for thou knowest that *there is* not among us any that can skill to hew timber like unto the Sidonians.

And it came to pass, when Hiram heard the words of Solomon, that he rejoiced greatly, and said, Blessed *be* the LORD this day, which hath given unto David a wise son over this great people.

1 KINGS 5:1-7

---

***Related texts:*** 1 KINGS 5–9; 2 CHRONICLES 2–8; PSALM 127; MATTHEW 12:1-6; JOHN 2:13-21; EPHESIANS 2:11-22

## The Wisdom of the Preacher

I the Preacher was king over Israel in Jerusalem. And I gave my heart to seek and search out by wisdom concerning all *things* that are done under heaven: this sore travail hath God given to the sons of man to be exercised therewith. I have seen all the works that are done under the sun; and, behold, all *is* vanity and vexation of spirit.

To every *thing there is* a season,
> and a time to every purpose under the heaven:

> a time to be born, and a time to die;
> a time to plant, and a time to pluck up *that which is* planted;
> a time to kill, and a time to heal;
> a time to break down, and a time to build up;
> a time to weep, and a time to laugh;
> a time to mourn, and a time to dance;
> a time to cast away stones, and a time to gather stones together;
> a time to embrace, and a time to refrain from embracing;
> a time to get, and a time to lose;
> a time to keep, and a time to cast away;
> a time to rend, and a time to sew;
> a time to keep silence, and a time to speak;
> a time to love, and a time to hate;
> a time of war, and a time of peace.

ECCLESIASTES 1:12-14; 3:1-8

*Related texts:* ECCLESIASTES 1:1-11; GALATIANS 4:4-5; 6:8-9; 1 TIMOTHY 2:3-6; 1 PETER 5:5-6

# The Preacher's Proverbs and Conclusion

**THE ONE
MINUTE
BIBLE**

Two *are* better than one;
>because they have a good reward for their labour.

For if they fall,
>the one will lift up his fellow:

but woe to him *that is* alone when he falleth;
>for *he hath* not another to help him up.

Again, if two lie together, then they have heat:
>but how can one be warm *alone*?

And if one prevail against him,
>two shall withstand him;

and a threefold cord is not quickly broken.

And moreover, because the preacher was wise, he still taught the people knowledge; yea, he gave good heed, and sought out, *and* set in order many proverbs. The preacher sought to find out acceptable words: and *that* which was written *was* upright, *even* words of truth.

The words of the wise *are* as goads, and as nails fastened *by* the masters of assemblies, *which* are given from one shepherd.

And further, by these, my son, be admonished: of making many books *there is* no end; and much study *is* a weariness of the flesh.

Let us hear
>the conclusion of the whole matter:

Fear God, and keep his commandments:
>for this *is* the whole *duty* of man.

For God shall bring every work into judgment,
>with every secret thing,
>>whether *it be* good, or whether *it be* evil.

ECCLESIASTES 4:9-12; 12:9-14

---

*Related texts:* 1 SAMUEL 20:24-42; PSALM 37; PROVERBS 17:17; 27:6, 10; 1 CORINTHIANS 4:5; REVELATION 20:11-15

## The Sins of Solomon

But king Solomon loved many strange women, together with the daughter of Pharaoh, women of the Moabites, Ammonites, Edomites, Zidonians, *and* Hittites; of the nations *concerning* which the LORD said unto the children of Israel, Ye shall not go in to them, neither shall they come in unto you: *for* surely they will turn away your heart after their gods: Solomon clave unto these in love. For it came to pass, when Solomon was old, *that* his wives turned away his heart after other gods: and his heart was not perfect with the LORD his God, as *was* the heart of David his father.

And the LORD was angry with Solomon, because his heart was turned from the LORD God of Israel, which had appeared unto him twice, and had commanded him concerning this thing, that he should not go after other gods: but he kept not that which the LORD commanded.

Wherefore the LORD said unto Solomon, Forasmuch as this is done of thee, and thou hast not kept my covenant and my statutes, which I have commanded thee, I will surely rend the kingdom from thee, and will give it to thy servant. Notwithstanding in thy days I will not do it for David thy father's sake: *but* I will rend it out of the hand of thy son. Howbeit I will not rend away all the kingdom; *but* will give one tribe to thy son for David my servant's sake, and for Jerusalem's sake which I have chosen.

1 KINGS 11:1-2, 4, 9-13

***Related texts:*** DEUTERONOMY 7; EZRA 9–10; NEHEMIAH 13:23-27; 1 CORINTHIANS 7:39; 2 CORINTHIANS 6:14-16

## The Kingdom Divides

**THE ONE
MINUTE
BIBLE**

And the time that Solomon reigned in Jerusalem over all Israel *was* forty years. And Solomon slept with his fathers, and was buried in the city of David his father: and Rehoboam his son reigned in his stead.

And Rehoboam went to Shechem: for all Israel were come to Shechem to make him king. And Jeroboam and all the congregation of Israel came, and spake unto Rehoboam, saying, Thy father made our yoke grievous: now therefore make thou the grievous service of thy father, and his heavy yoke which he put upon us, lighter, and we will serve thee.

And he said unto them, Depart yet *for* three days, then come again to me. And the people departed.

And the king answered the people roughly, and forsook the old men's counsel that they gave him; and spake to them after the counsel of the young men, saying, My father made your yoke heavy, and I will add to your yoke: my father *also* chastised you with whips, but I will chastise you with scorpions.

So when all Israel saw that the king hearkened not unto them, the people answered the king, saying,

What portion have we in David?

neither *have we* inheritance in the son of Jesse:
to your tents, O Israel:

now see to thine own house, David.

So Israel departed unto their tents.

And it came to pass, when all Israel heard that Jeroboam was come again, that they sent and called him unto the congregation, and made him king over all Israel: there was none that followed the house of David, but the tribe of Judah only.

1 KINGS 11:42-43; 12:1, 3b-5, 13-14, 16, 20

---

***Related texts:*** 1 KINGS 11:26-40; 2 CHRONICLES 9:29–10:19; PROVERBS 15:1

## The Sins of Jeroboam

Then Jeroboam built Shechem in mount Ephraim, and dwelt therein; and went out from thence, and built Penuel.

And Jeroboam said in his heart, Now shall the kingdom return to the house of David: if this people go up to do sacrifice in the house of the LORD at Jerusalem, then shall the heart of this people turn again unto their lord, *even* unto Rehoboam king of Judah, and they shall kill me, and go again to Rehoboam king of Judah.

Whereupon the king took counsel, and made two calves *of* gold, and said unto them, It is too much for you to go up to Jerusalem: behold thy gods, O Israel, which brought thee up out of the land of Egypt. And he set the one in Beth-el, and the other put he in Dan. And this thing became a sin: for the people went *to worship* before the one, *even* unto Dan.

And he made an house of high places, and made priests of the lowest of the people, which were not of the sons of Levi.

And this thing became sin unto the house of Jeroboam, even to cut *it* off, and to destroy *it* from off the face of the earth.

1 KINGS 12:25-31; 13:34

*When you read God's word, you must*
*constantly be saying to yourself,*
*"It is talking to me, and about me."*
**Soren Kierkegaard (1813-1855)**
DANISH PHILOSOPHER

*I must confess to you that the majesty*
*of the Scriptures astonishes me...*
*if it had been the invention of men,*
*the inventors would be greater than*
*the greatest heroes.*
**Jean Jacques Rousseau (1712-1778)**
FRENCH PHILOSOPHER

*After more than sixty years of almost*
*daily reading of the Bible, I never*
*fail to find it always new and marvellously*
*in tune with the changing needs of every day.*
**Cecil B. DeMille (1881-1959)**
AMERICAN MOVIE PRODUCER

## Elijah Confronts King Ahab

**THE ONE
MINUTE
BIBLE**

And in the thirty and eighth year of Asa king of Judah began Ahab the son of Omri to reign over Israel: and Ahab the son of Omri reigned over Israel in Samaria twenty and two years. And Ahab the son of Omri did evil in the sight of the LORD above all that *were* before him. And it came to pass, as if it had been a light thing for him to walk in the sins of Jeroboam the son of Nebat, that he took to wife Jezebel the daughter of Ethbaal king of the Zidonians, and went and served Baal, and worshipped him. And he reared up an altar for Baal in the house of Baal, which he had built in Samaria. And Ahab made a grove; and Ahab did more to provoke the LORD God of Israel to anger than all the kings of Israel that were before him.

And Elijah the Tishbite, *who was* of the inhabitants of Gilead, said unto Ahab, *As* the LORD God of Israel liveth, before whom I stand, there shall not be dew nor rain these years, but according to my word.

And the word of the LORD came unto him, saying, Get thee hence, and turn thee eastward, and hide thyself by the brook Cherith, that *is* before Jordan. And it shall be, *that* thou shalt drink of the brook; and I have commanded the ravens to feed thee there. So he went and did according unto the word of the LORD.

If I shut up heaven that there be no rain, or if I command the locusts to devour the land, or if I send pestilence among my people; if my people, which are called by my name, shall humble themselves, and pray, and seek my face, and turn from their wicked ways; then will I hear from heaven, and will forgive their sin, and will heal their land.

1 KINGS 16:29-33; 17:1-5a; 2 CHRONICLES 7:13-14

*Related texts:* DEUTERONOMY 11:16-17; MARK 6:14-15; LUKE 1:11-17; 9:7-8; JAMES 5:17-18

**THE ONE
MINUTE
BIBLE**

## Elijah Challenges the Prophets of Baal

And it came to pass *after* many days, that the word of the LORD came to Elijah in the third year, saying, Go, show thyself unto Ahab; and I will send rain upon the earth.

And it came to pass, when Ahab saw Elijah, that Ahab said unto him, *Art* thou he that troubleth Israel?

And he answered, I have not troubled Israel; but thou, and thy father's house, in that ye have forsaken the commandments of the LORD, and thou hast followed Baalim. Now therefore send, *and* gather to me all Israel unto mount Carmel, and the prophets of Baal four hundred and fifty, and the prophets of the groves four hundred, which eat at Jezebel's table.

So Ahab sent unto all the children of Israel, and gathered the prophets together unto mount Carmel. And Elijah came unto all the people, and said, How long halt ye between two opinions? If the LORD *be* God, follow him: but if Baal, *then* follow him.

And the people answered him not a word.

Then said Elijah unto the people, I, *even* I only, remain a prophet of the LORD; but Baal's prophets *are* four hundred and fifty men. Let them therefore give us two bullocks; and let them choose one bullock for themselves, and cut it in pieces, and lay *it* on wood, and put no fire *under*: and I will dress the other bullock, and lay *it* on wood, and put no fire *under*: and call ye on the name of your gods, and I will call on the name of the LORD: and the God that answereth by fire, let him be God.

And all the people answered and said, It is well spoken.

1 KINGS 18:1, 17-24

---

*Related texts:* DEUTERONOMY 12:28-31; 32:36-39; MARK 8:27-29; LUKE 9:28-36; JAMES 5:14-18

## *The LORD Defeats Baal*

And Elijah said unto the prophets of Baal, Choose you one bullock for yourselves, and dress *it* first; for ye *are* many; and call on the name of your gods, but put no fire *under*.

And they took the bullock which was given them, and they dressed *it*, and called on the name of Baal from morning even until noon, saying, O Baal, hear us. But *there was* no voice, nor any that answered. And they leaped upon the altar which was made.

And it came to pass, when midday was past, and they prophesied until the *time* of the offering of the *evening* sacrifice, that *there was* neither voice, nor any to answer, nor any that regarded.

And it came to pass at *the time of* the offering of the *evening* sacrifice, that Elijah the prophet came near, and said, LORD God of Abraham, Isaac, and of Israel, let it be known this day that thou *art* God in Israel, and *that* I *am* thy servant, and *that* I have done all these things at thy word. Hear me, O LORD, hear me, that this people may know that thou *art* the LORD God, and *that* thou hast turned their heart back again.

Then the fire of the LORD fell, and consumed the burnt sacrifice, and the wood, and the stones, and the dust, and licked up the water that *was* in the trench.

And when all the people saw *it*, they fell on their faces: and they said, The LORD, he *is* the God; the LORD, he *is* the God.

And Elijah said unto them, Take the prophets of Baal; let not one of them escape. And they took them: and Elijah brought them down to the brook Kishon, and slew them there.

1 KINGS 18:25-26, 29, 36-40

*Related texts:* DEUTERONOMY 13; 17:2-5; 18:18-22; 1 KINGS 21-22; 2 KINGS 9:30-10:28; PHILIPPIANS 2:5-11

**THE ONE
MINUTE
BIBLE**

## Jonah Disobeys the Lord

Now the word of the Lord came unto Jonah the son of Amittai, saying, Arise, go to Nineveh, that great city, and cry against it; for their wickedness is come up before me.

But Jonah rose up to flee unto Tarshish from the presence of the Lord, and went down to Joppa; and he found a ship going to Tarshish: so he paid the fare thereof, and went down into it, to go with them unto Tarshish from the presence of the Lord.

But the Lord sent out a great wind into the sea, and there was a mighty tempest in the sea, so that the ship was like to be broken. Then the mariners were afraid, and cried every man unto his god.

And they said every one to his fellow, Come, and let us cast lots, that we may know for whose cause this evil *is* upon us. So they cast lots, and the lot fell upon Jonah.

Then said they unto him, What shall we do unto thee, that the sea may be calm unto us? For the sea wrought, and was tempestuous.

And he said unto them, Take me up, and cast me forth into the sea; so shall the sea be calm unto you: for I know that for my sake this great tempest *is* upon you.

So they took up Jonah, and cast him forth into the sea: and the sea ceased from her raging. Then the men feared the Lord exceedingly, and offered a sacrifice unto the Lord, and made vows.

Now the Lord had prepared a great fish to swallow up Jonah. And Jonah was in the belly of the fish three days and three nights.

JONAH 1:1-5a, 7, 11-12, 15-17

---

*Related texts:* 2 KINGS 14:25; MATTHEW 12:38-41; 16:1-4; LUKE 11:29-32

## *Jonah Prays from the Belly of a Fish*

THE ONE
M I N U T E
B I B L E

Then Jonah prayed unto the LORD his God out of the fish's belly, and said,

I cried by reason of mine affliction unto the LORD,
  and he heard me;
out of the belly of hell cried I,
  *and* thou heardest my voice.
For thou hadst cast me into the deep,
  in the midst of the seas;
and the floods compassed me about:
  all thy billows and thy waves passed over me.
Then I said, I am cast out of thy sight;
  yet I will look again toward thy holy temple.
The waters compassed me about, *even* to the soul:
  the depth closed me round about,
  the weeds were wrapped about my head.
I went down to the bottoms of the mountains;
  the earth with her bars *was* about me for ever:
yet hast thou brought up my life from corruption,
  O LORD my God.
When my soul fainted within me
  I remembered the LORD:
and my prayer came in unto thee,
  into thine holy temple.
They that observe lying vanities
  forsake their own mercy.
But I will sacrifice unto thee
  with the voice of thanksgiving;
I will pay *that* that I have vowed.
  Salvation *is* of the LORD.

And the LORD spake unto the fish, and it vomited out Jonah upon the dry *land*.

JONAH 2

---

*Related texts:* 2 KINGS 17:13-15; PSALMS 42; 69; ISAIAH 44:9-20;
ACTS 27

# The LORD Relents from Sending Disaster

**THE ONE**
**MINUTE**
**BIBLE**

And the word of the LORD came unto Jonah the second time, saying, Arise, go unto Nineveh, that great city, and preach unto it the preaching that I bid thee.

So Jonah arose, and went unto Nineveh, according to the word of the LORD. Now Nineveh was an exceeding great city of three days' journey. And Jonah began to enter into the city a day's journey, and he cried, and said, Yet forty days, and Nineveh shall be overthrown. So the people of Nineveh believed God, and proclaimed a fast, and put on sackcloth, from the greatest of them even to the least of them.

For word came unto the king of Nineveh, and he arose from his throne, and he laid his robe from him, and covered *him* with sackcloth, and sat in ashes. And he caused *it* to be proclaimed and published through Nineveh by the decree of the king and his nobles, saying,

Let neither man nor beast, herd nor flock, taste any thing: let them not feed, nor drink water: but let man and beast be covered with sackcloth, and cry mightily unto God: yea, let them turn every one from his evil way, and from the violence that *is* in their hands. Who can tell *if* God will turn and repent, and turn away from his fierce anger, that we perish not?

And God saw their works, that they turned from their evil way; and God repented of the evil, that he had said that he would do unto them; and he did *it* not.

JONAH 3

---

***Related texts:*** EXODUS 32:1-14; JEREMIAH 18:1-11; JOEL 2:12-14; LUKE 11:29-32

## *Joel Calls Israel to Repent*

Therefore also now, saith the LORD,
    turn ye *even* to me with all your heart,
    and with fasting, and with weeping, and with
        mourning:
and rend your heart,
    and not your garments,
and turn unto the LORD your God:
    for he *is* gracious and merciful,
slow to anger, and of great kindness,
    and repenteth him of the evil.
Who knoweth *if* he will return and repent,
    and leave a blessing behind him;
*even* a meat offering and a drink offering
    unto the LORD your God?
Blow the trumpet in Zion,
    sanctify a fast, call a solemn assembly:
gather the people,
    sanctify the congregation,
assemble the elders,
    gather the children,
    and those that suck the breasts:
let the bridegroom go forth of his chamber,
    and the bride out of her closet.
Let the priests, the ministers of the LORD,
    weep between the porch and the altar,
and let them say, Spare thy people, O LORD,
    and give not thine heritage to reproach,
    that the heathen should rule over them:
wherefore should they say among the people,
    Where *is* their God?
Then will the LORD be jealous for his land,
    and pity his people.

JOEL 2:12-18

*Related texts:* EXODUS 34:1-7; DEUTERONOMY 10:16; JONAH 3;
JAMES 4:6-8

**THE ONE**
**MINUTE**
**BIBLE**

## Amos: Judgment and Hope

Behold, the eyes of the Lord G<small>OD</small>
    *are* upon the sinful kingdom,
and I will destroy it
    from off the face of the earth;
saving that I will not utterly destroy
    the house of Jacob,

saith the L<small>ORD</small>.

All the sinners of my people
    shall die by the sword,
    which say, The evil shall not overtake nor prevent us.
In that day will I raise up
    the tabernacle of David that is fallen,
and close up the breaches thereof;
    and I will raise up his ruins,
    and I will build it as in the days of old:
that they may possess the remnant of Edom,
    and of all the heathen, which are called by my name,
saith the L<small>ORD</small> that doeth this.

Behold, the days come, saith the L<small>ORD</small>,

that the plowman shall overtake the reaper,
    and the treader of grapes him that soweth seed;
and the mountains shall drop sweet wine,
    and all the hills shall melt.
And I will bring again the captivity of my people of Israel,
    and they shall build the waste cities, and inhabit *them*;
and they shall plant vineyards, and drink the wine thereof;
    they shall also make gardens, and eat the fruit of them.
And I will plant them upon their land,
    and they shall no more be pulled up
    out of their land which I have given them,
saith the L<small>ORD</small> thy God.

A<small>MOS</small> 9:8, 10-15

*Related texts:* 2 S<small>AMUEL</small> 7; I<small>SAIAH</small> 55; A<small>CTS</small> 15:1-21; R<small>OMANS</small> 9–11

## *Hosea: The LORD's Anger and Compassion*

When Israel *was* a child, then I loved him,
   and called my son out of Egypt.
*As* they called them,
   so they went from them:
they sacrificed unto Baalim,
   and burned incense to graven images.
I taught Ephraim also to go,
   taking them by their arms;
but they knew not
   that I healed them.
I drew them with cords of a man,
   with bands of love:
and I was to them as they that take off the yoke
     on their jaws,
   and I laid meat unto them.
He shall not return into the land of Egypt,
   but the Assyrian shall be his king,
   because they refused to return.
How shall I give thee up, Ephraim?
   *How* shall I deliver thee, Israel?
How shall I make thee as Admah?
   *How* shall I set thee as Zeboim?
Mine heart is turned within me,
   my repentings are kindled together.
I will not execute the fierceness of mine anger,
   I will not return to destroy Ephraim:
for I *am* God, and not man;
   the Holy One in the midst of thee:
   and I will not enter into the city.
They shall walk after the LORD:
   he shall roar like a lion:
when he shall roar,
   then the children shall tremble from the west.
They shall tremble as a bird out of Egypt,
   and as a dove out of the land of Assyria:
and I will place them in their houses, saith the LORD.

HOSEA 11:1-5, 8-11

*Related texts:* GENESIS 19:1-29; DEUTERONOMY 29:18-23;
ZECHARIAH 10:6-12; 2 PETER 3:8-15

## Isaiah Sees the Lord

**THE ONE
MINUTE
BIBLE**

   In the year that king Uzziah died I saw also the Lord sitting upon a throne, high and lifted up, and his train filled the temple. Above it stood the seraphims: each one had six wings; with twain he covered his face, and with twain he covered his feet, and with twain he did fly. And one cried unto another, and said,

   Holy, holy, holy, *is* the LORD of hosts:
      the whole earth *is* full of his glory.
And the posts of the door moved at the voice of him that cried, and the house was filled with smoke.

   Then said I, Woe *is* me! For I am undone; because I *am* a man of unclean lips, and I dwell in the midst of a people of unclean lips: for mine eyes have seen the King, the LORD of hosts.

   Then flew one of the seraphims unto me, having a live coal in his hand, *which* he had taken with the tongs from off the altar: and he laid *it* upon my mouth, and said, Lo, this hath touched thy lips; and thine iniquity is taken away, and thy sin purged.

   Also I heard the voice of the Lord, saying, Whom shall I send, and who will go for us?

   Then said I, Here *am* I; send me.

   And he said, Go, and tell this people,
Hear ye indeed, but understand not;
      and see ye indeed, but perceive not.
Make the heart of this people fat,
      and make their ears heavy,
      and shut their eyes;
lest they see with their eyes,
      and hear with their ears,
      and understand with their heart,
and convert, and be healed.

ISAIAH 6:1-10

***Related texts:*** EXODUS 3:1-6; 33:15-23; JOB 19:25-27; MATTHEW 5:8; 13:10-17; JOHN 12:37-41; REVELATION 4

## Micah: The Sins of Israel

The word of the L ORD that came to Micah the Morasthite in the days of Jotham, Ahaz, *and* Hezekiah, kings of Judah, which he saw concerning Samaria and Jerusalem.

Hear, all ye people;
  hearken, O earth, and all that therein is:
and let the Lord G OD be witness against you,
  the Lord from his holy temple.
For, behold, the L ORD cometh forth out of his place,
  and will come down, and tread upon the high places
    of the earth.
And the mountains shall be molten under him,
  and the valleys shall be cleft,
as wax before the fire,
  *and* as the waters *that are* poured down a steep place.
For the transgression of Jacob *is* all this,
  and for the sins of the house of Israel.
What *is* the transgression of Jacob?
  *Is it* not Samaria?
And what *are* the high places of Judah?
  *Are they* not Jerusalem?
Therefore I will make Samaria as an heap of the field,
  *and* as plantings of a vineyard:
and I will pour down the stones thereof into the valley,
  and I will discover the foundations thereof.
And all the graven images thereof shall be beaten
    to pieces,
  and all the hires thereof shall be burned with the fire,
  and all the idols thereof will I lay desolate:
for she gathered *it* of the hire of an harlot,
  and they shall return to the hire of an harlot.

M ICAH 1:1-7

**THE ONE
MINUTE
BIBLE**

*Related texts:* D EUTERONOMY 5:6-10; J UDGES 10:11-16;
P SALMS 68:1-3; 97; J EREMIAH 26; A CTS 1:1-8

**THE ONE
MINUTE
BIBLE**

## *Israel Goes into Exile*

In the ninth year of Hoshea the king of Assyria took Samaria, and carried Israel away into Assyria, and placed them in Halah and in Habor *by* the river of Gozan, and in the cities of the Medes.

For *so* it was, that the children of Israel had sinned against the LORD their God, which had brought them up out of the land of Egypt, from under the hand of Pharaoh king of Egypt, and had feared other gods, and walked in the statutes of the heathen, whom the LORD cast out from before the children of Israel, and of the kings of Israel, which they had made. And the children of Israel did secretly *those* things that *were* not right against the LORD their God, and they built them high places in all their cities, from the tower of the watchmen to the fenced city. And they set them up images and groves in every high hill, and under every green tree: and there they burnt incense in all the high places, as *did* the heathen whom the LORD carried away before them; and wrought wicked things to provoke the LORD to anger; for they served idols, whereof the LORD had said unto them, Ye shall not do this thing.

Yet the LORD testified against Israel, and against Judah, by all the prophets, *and by* all the seers, saying, Turn ye from your evil ways, and keep my commandments *and* my statutes, according to all the law which I commanded your fathers, and which I sent to you by my servants the prophets.

Notwithstanding they would not hear, but hardened their necks, like to the neck of their fathers, that did not believe in the LORD their God.

2 KINGS 17:6-14

---

***Related texts:*** DEUTERONOMY 28:14-68; 2 KINGS 15:16-20; ACTS 7:51-53

## Good King Hezekiah

Now it came to pass in the third year of Hoshea son
of Elah king of Israel, *that* Hezekiah the son of Ahaz
king of Judah began to reign. Twenty and five years old
was he when he began to reign; and he reigned twenty
and nine years in Jerusalem. His mother's name also
*was* Abi, the daughter of Zachariah. And he did *that
which was* right in the sight of the LORD, according to all
that David his father did. He removed the high places,
and brake the images, and cut down the groves, and
brake in pieces the brazen serpent that Moses had
made: for unto those days the children of Israel did burn
incense to it: and he called it Nehushtan.

He trusted in the LORD God of Israel; so that after him
was none like him among all the kings of Judah, nor
*any* that were before him. For he clave to the LORD, *and*
departed not from following him, but kept his
commandments, which the LORD commanded Moses.
And the LORD was with him; *and* he prospered
whithersoever he went forth: and he rebelled against
the king of Assyria, and served him not. He smote the
Philistines, *even* unto Gaza, and the borders thereof,
from the tower of the watchmen to the fenced city.

And it came to pass in the fourth year of king
Hezekiah, which *was* the seventh year of Hoshea son of
Elah king of Israel, *that* Shalmaneser king of Assyria
came up against Samaria, and besieged it. And at the
end of three years they took it: *even* in the sixth year of
Hezekiah, that is the ninth year of Hoshea king of
Israel, Samaria was taken.

2 KINGS 18:1-10

---

*Related texts:* NUMBERS 21:1-9; DEUTERONOMY 28:1-14;
2 CHRONICLES 29–31; PROVERBS 25:1; MATTHEW 1:1-10

# The LORD Delivers Judah from Assyria

**THE ONE
MINUTE
BIBLE**

Now in the fourteenth year of king Hezekiah did Sennacherib king of Assyria come up against all the fenced cities of Judah, and took them.

And Hezekiah prayed before the LORD, and said, O LORD God of Israel, which dwellest *between* the cherubims, thou art the God, *even* thou alone, of all the kingdoms of the earth; thou hast made heaven and earth. LORD, bow down thine ear, and hear: open, LORD, thine eyes, and see: and hear the words of Sennacherib, which hath sent him to reproach the living God. Of a truth, LORD, the kings of Assyria have destroyed the nations and their lands, and have cast their gods into the fire: for they *were* no gods, but the work of men's hands, wood and stone: therefore they have destroyed them. Now therefore, O LORD our God, I beseech thee, save thou us out of his hand, that all the kingdoms of the earth may know that thou *art* the LORD God, *even* thou only.

Then Isaiah the son of Amoz sent to Hezekiah, saying, Thus saith the LORD God of Israel, *That* which thou hast prayed to me against Sennacherib king of Assyria I have heard.

And it came to pass that night, that the angel of the LORD went out, and smote in the camp of the Assyrians an hundred fourscore and five thousand: and when they arose early in the morning, behold, they *were* all dead corpses. So Sennacherib king of Assyria departed, and went and returned, and dwelt at Nineveh.

2 KINGS 18:13; 19:15-20, 35-36

---

***Related texts:*** 2 KINGS 19–20; 2 CHRONICLES 32; ISAIAH 36–39; ACTS 12

## Nahum: God's Vengeance on Assyria

God *is* jealous, and the LORD revengeth;
  the LORD revengeth, and *is* furious;
the LORD will take vengeance on his adversaries,
  and he reserveth *wrath* for his enemies.
The LORD *is* slow to anger, and great in power,
  and will not at all acquit *the wicked*:
the LORD *hath* his way in the whirlwind and in the storm,
  and the clouds *are* the dust of his feet.
Who can stand before his indignation?
  And who can abide in the fierceness of his anger?
His fury is poured out like fire,
  and the rocks are thrown down by him.
The LORD *is* good,
  a strong hold in the day of trouble;
  and he knoweth them that trust in him.
But with an overrunning flood
  he will make an utter end of the place thereof,
  and darkness shall pursue his enemies.
What do ye imagine against the LORD?
  He will make an utter end:
  affliction shall not rise up the second time.

Thy shepherds slumber, O king of Assyria:
  thy nobles shall dwell *in* the dust:
thy people is scattered upon the mountains,
  and no man gathereth *them*.
*There is* no healing of thy bruise;
  thy wound is grievous:
all that hear the bruit of thee
  shall clap the hands over thee:
for upon whom
  hath not thy wickedness passed continually?

NAHUM 1:2-3, 6-9; 3:18-19

**THE ONE MINUTE BIBLE**

*Related texts:* EXODUS 34:1-7; JONAH; JOHN 3:31-36; ROMANS 1:18-19;
EPHESIANS 5:5-6

281

# Zephaniah: Jerusalem's Correction

**THE ONE
MINUTE
BIBLE**

Woe to her that is filthy and polluted,
    to the oppressing city!
She obeyed not the voice;
    she received not correction;
she trusted not in the LORD;
    she drew not near to her God.
Her princes within her *are* roaring lions;
    her judges *are* evening wolves;
    they gnaw not the bones till the morrow.
Her prophets *are* light
    *and* treacherous persons:
her priests have polluted the sanctuary,
    they have done violence to the law.
The just LORD *is* in the midst thereof;
    he will not do iniquity:
every morning doth he bring his judgment to light,
    he faileth not;
    but the unjust knoweth no shame.
Sing, O daughter of Zion;
    shout, O Israel;
be glad and rejoice with all the heart,
    O daughter of Jerusalem.
The LORD hath taken away thy judgments,
    he hath cast out thine enemy:
the king of Israel, *even* the LORD, *is* in the midst of thee:
    thou shalt not see evil any more.
In that day it shall be said to Jerusalem, Fear thou not:
    *and to* Zion, Let not thine hands be slack.
The LORD thy God in the midst of thee *is* mighty;
    he will save,
he will rejoice over thee with joy;
    he will rest in his love,
    he will joy over thee with singing.

ZEPHANIAH 3:1-5, 14-17

*Related texts:* PSALM 25; 34:1-5; ISAIAH 40; ROMANS 10:9-11

## *The Call of Jeremiah: Part 1*

The words of Jeremiah the son of Hilkiah, of the priests that *were* in Anathoth in the land of Benjamin: to whom the word of the LORD came in the days of Josiah the son of Amon king of Judah, in the thirteenth year of his reign. It came also in the days of Jehoiakim the son of Josiah king of Judah, unto the end of the eleventh year of Zedekiah the son of Josiah king of Judah, unto the carrying away of Jerusalem captive in the fifth month.

**THE ONE
MINUTE
BIBLE**

Then the word of the LORD came unto me, saying,

Before I formed thee in the belly I knew thee;
   and before thou camest forth out of the womb
      I sanctified thee,
   *and* I ordained thee a prophet unto the nations.

Then said I, Ah, Lord GOD! Behold, I cannot speak: for I *am* a child.

But the LORD said unto me, Say not, I *am* a child: for thou shalt go to all that I shall send thee, and whatsoever I command thee thou shalt speak. Be not afraid of their faces: for I *am* with thee to deliver thee, saith the LORD.

Then the LORD put forth his hand, and touched my mouth. And the LORD said unto me, Behold, I have put my words in thy mouth. See, I have this day set thee over the nations and over the kingdoms, to root out, and to pull down, and to destroy, and to throw down, to build, and to plant.

JEREMIAH 1:1-10

*Related texts:* EXODUS 4:10-12; PSALM 136; ISAIAH 6; LUKE 1:13-16; 1 TIMOTHY 4:12

283

## *The Call of Jeremiah: Part 2*

**THE ONE
MINUTE
BIBLE**

And the word of the LORD came unto me the second time, saying, What seest thou?

And I said, I see a seething pot; and the face thereof *is* toward the north.

Then the LORD said unto me, Out of the north an evil shall break forth upon all the inhabitants of the land. For, lo, I will call all the families of the kingdoms of the north, saith the LORD;

> And they shall come, and they shall set every one his
> throne
> at the entering of the gates of Jerusalem,
> and against all the walls thereof round about,
> and against all the cities of Judah.
> And I will utter my judgments against them
> touching all their wickedness, who have
> forsaken me,
> and have burned incense unto other gods,
> and worshipped the works of their own hands.

Thou therefore gird up thy loins, and arise, and speak unto them all that I command thee: be not dismayed at their faces, lest I confound thee before them. For, behold, I have made thee this day a defenced city, and an iron pillar, and brazen walls against the whole land, against the kings of Judah, against the princes thereof, against the priests thereof, and against the people of the land. And they shall fight against thee; but they shall not prevail against thee; for I *am* with thee, saith the LORD, to deliver thee.

JEREMIAH 1:13-19

***Related texts:*** DEUTERONOMY 28; JOSHUA 1; EZEKIEL 11; 24; 33:1-20; 1 JOHN 5:3-4

# *Jeremiah Is Saved by Micah's Prophecy*

THE ONE
MINUTE
BIBLE

In the beginning of the reign of Jehoiakim the son of Josiah king of Judah came this word from the LORD, saying, And thou shalt say unto them, Thus saith the LORD; If ye will not hearken to me, to walk in my law, which I have set before you, to hearken to the words of my servants the prophets, whom I sent unto you, both rising up early, and sending *them*, but ye have not hearkened; then will I make this house like Shiloh, and will make this city a curse to all the nations of the earth.

Now it came to pass, when Jeremiah had made an end of speaking all that the LORD had commanded *him* to speak unto all the people, that the priests and the prophets and all the people took him, saying, Thou shalt surely die. Why hast thou prophesied in the name of the LORD, saying, This house shall be like Shiloh, and this city shall be desolate without an inhabitant? And all the people were gathered against Jeremiah in the house of the LORD.

Then rose up certain of the elders of the land, and spake to all the assembly of the people, saying, Micah the Morasthite prophesied in the days of Hezekiah king of Judah, and spake to all the people of Judah, saying, Thus saith the LORD of hosts;

Zion shall be plowed *like* a field,
  and Jerusalem shall become heaps,
  and the mountain of the house as the high places
    of a forest.

Did Hezekiah king of Judah and all Judah put him at all to death? Did he not fear the LORD, and besought the LORD, and the LORD repented him of the evil which he had pronounced against them? Thus might we procure great evil against our souls.

JEREMIAH 26:1, 4-6, 8-9, 17-19

*Related texts:* JEREMIAH 18:1-11; 19:1–20:2; 38:1-13;
LAMENTATIONS 3:52-57; MICAH 3:9-12; MATTHEW 16:13-14

## Judah Goes into Exile

**THE ONE
MINUTE
BIBLE**

Zedekiah *was* one and twenty years old when he began to reign, and reigned eleven years in Jerusalem. And he did *that which was* evil in the sight of the Lord his God, *and* humbled not himself before Jeremiah the prophet *speaking* from the mouth of the Lord.

And the Lord God of their fathers sent to them by his messengers, rising up betimes, and sending; because he had compassion on his people, and on his dwelling place: but they mocked the messengers of God, and despised his words, and misused his prophets, until the wrath of the Lord arose against his people, till *there was* no remedy. Therefore he brought upon them the king of the Chaldees, who slew their young men with the sword in the house of their sanctuary, and had no compassion upon young man or maiden, old man, or him that stooped for age: he gave *them* all into his hand.

And all the vessels of the house of God, great and small, and the treasures of the house of the Lord, and the treasures of the king, and of his princes; all *these* he brought to Babylon. And they burnt the house of God, and brake down the wall of Jerusalem, and burnt all the palaces thereof with fire, and destroyed all the goodly vessels thereof.

And them that had escaped from the sword carried he away to Babylon; where they were servants to him and his sons until the reign of the kingdom of Persia: to fulfil the word of the Lord by the mouth of Jeremiah, until the land had enjoyed her sabbaths: *for* as long as she lay desolate she kept sabbath, to fulfil threescore and ten years.

2 Chronicles 36:11-12, 15-21

---

***Related texts:*** Leviticus 26:1-43; 2 Kings 20:12-18; 25; Isaiah 39; Jeremiah 25; 38; 52; Matthew 1:1-17

## *Lament over Fallen Jerusalem*

**THE ONE
MINUTE
BIBLE**

How doth the city sit solitary,
   *that was* full of people!
*How* is she become as a widow!
   She *that was* great among the nations,
*and* princess among the provinces,
   *how* is she become tributary!
She weepeth sore in the night,
   and her tears *are* on her cheeks:
among all her lovers
   she hath none to comfort *her*:
all her friends have dealt treacherously with her,
   they are become her enemies.


And I said, My strength and my hope
   is perished from the LORD:
remembering mine affliction and my misery,
   the wormwood and the gall.
My soul hath *them* still in remembrance,
   and is humbled in me.
This I recall to my mind,
   therefore have I hope.
*It is of* the LORD's mercies that we are not consumed,
   because his compassions fail not.
*They are* new every morning:
   great *is* thy faithfulness.
The LORD *is* my portion, saith my soul;
   therefore will I hope in him.
The LORD *is* good unto them that wait for him,
   to the soul *that* seeketh him.
*It is* good that *a man* should both hope and quietly wait
   for the salvation of the LORD.

LAMENTATIONS 1:1-2; 3:18-26

*Related texts:* PSALM 137; EZEKIEL 19; 24; MATTHEW 23:33-39

## The LORD Promises Vengeance on Babylon

**THE ONE
MINUTE
BIBLE**

Behold, his soul *which* is lifted up
  is not upright in him:
    but the just shall live by his faith.
Yea also, because he transgresseth by wine,
  *he is* a proud man, neither keepeth at home,
who enlargeth his desire as hell,
  and *is* as death, and cannot be satisfied,
but gathereth unto him all nations,
  and heapeth unto him all people.

Shall not all these take up a parable against him, and a
taunting proverb against him, and say,
Woe to him that increaseth *that which is* not his!
  How long?
  And to him that ladeth himself with thick clay!

When I heard, my belly trembled;
  my lips quivered at the voice:
rottenness entered into my bones,
  and I trembled in myself,
that I might rest in the day of trouble:
  when he cometh up unto the people,
  he will invade them with his troops.
Although the fig tree shall not blossom,
  neither *shall* fruit *be* in the vines;
the labour of the olive shall fail,
  and the fields shall yield no meat;
the flock shall be cut off from the fold,
  and *there shall be* no herd in the stalls:
yet I will rejoice in the LORD,
  I will joy in the God of my salvation.
The LORD God *is* my strength,
  and he will make my feet like hinds' *feet*,
  and he will make me to walk upon mine high places.

HABAKKUK 2:4-6; 3:16-19a

*Related texts:* GENESIS 9:5-6; 12:1-3; ROMANS 1:16-17;
GALATIANS 3:8-14; HEBREWS 10:32-39

## *Obadiah: The Day of the LORD*

Shall I not in that day, saith the LORD,
  even destroy the wise *men* out of Edom,
  and understanding out of the mount of Esau?
For *thy* violence against thy brother Jacob
  shame shall cover thee,
  and thou shalt be cut off for ever.
In the day that thou stoodest on the other side,
  in the day that the strangers carried away captive his
    forces,
and foreigners entered into his gates,
  and cast lots upon Jerusalem,
  even thou *wast* as one of them.
But thou shouldest not have looked on the day of thy
    brother
  in the day that he became a stranger;
neither shouldest thou have rejoiced over the children
    of Judah
  in the day of their destruction;
neither shouldest thou have spoken proudly
  in the day of distress.

For the day of the LORD *is* near
  upon all the heathen:
as thou hast done, it shall be done unto thee:
  thy reward shall return upon thine own head.
For as ye have drunk upon my holy mountain,
  *so* shall all the heathen drink continually,
yea, they shall drink, and they shall swallow down,
  and they shall be as though they had not been.
But upon mount Zion shall be deliverance,
  and there shall be holiness;
and the house of Jacob
  shall possess their possessions.

OBADIAH 1:8, 10-12, 15-17

*Related texts:* ISAIAH 13; JOEL 3; 2 PETER 3

## Ezekiel Sees the Restoration of Israel

**THE ONE MINUTE BIBLE**

The hand of the LORD was upon me, and carried me out in the spirit of the LORD, and set me down in the midst of the valley which *was* full of bones.

Again he said unto me, Prophesy upon these bones, and say unto them, O ye dry bones, hear the word of the LORD. Thus saith the Lord GOD unto these bones; Behold, I will cause breath to enter into you, and ye shall live: and I will lay sinews upon you, and will bring up flesh upon you, and cover you with skin, and put breath in you, and ye shall live; and ye shall know that I *am* the LORD.

So I prophesied as I was commanded: and as I prophesied, there was a noise, and behold a shaking, and the bones came together, bone to his bone.

Then said he unto me, Prophesy unto the wind, prophesy, son of man, and say to the wind, Thus saith the Lord GOD; Come from the four winds, O breath, and breathe upon these slain, that they may live. So I prophesied as he commanded me, and the breath came into them, and they lived, and stood up upon their feet, an exceeding great army.

Then he said unto me, Son of man, these bones are the whole house of Israel: behold, they say, Our bones are dried, and our hope is lost: we are cut off for our parts. Therefore prophesy and say unto them, Thus saith the Lord GOD; Behold, O my people, I will open your graves, and cause you to come up out of your graves, and bring you into the land of Israel. And shall put my spirit in you, and ye shall live, and I shall place you in your own land: then shall ye know that I the LORD have spoken *it*, and performed *it*, saith the LORD.

EZEKIEL 37:1, 4-7, 9-12, 14

*Related texts:* DEUTERONOMY 30:1-10; PSALM 80; ISAIAH 40; EZEKIEL 36; ACTS 17:24-25; 2 THESSALONIANS 2:7-8

## The Writing on the Wall

Belshazzar the king made a great feast to a thousand of his lords, and drank wine before the thousand. Belshazzar, whiles he tasted the wine, commanded to bring the golden and silver vessels which his father Nebuchadnezzar had taken out of the temple which *was* in Jerusalem; that the king, and his princes, his wives, and his concubines, might drink therein. They drank wine, and praised the gods of gold, and of silver, of brass, of iron, of wood, and of stone.

In the same hour came forth fingers of a man's hand, and wrote over against the candlestick upon the plaster of the wall of the king's palace: and the king saw the part of the hand that wrote. Then the king's countenance was changed, and his thoughts troubled him, so that the joints of his loins were loosed, and his knees smote one against another.

*Now* the queen, by reason of the words of the king and his lords, came into the banquet house: *and* the queen spake and said, O king, live for ever: let not thy thoughts trouble thee, nor let thy countenance be changed: there is a man in thy kingdom, in whom *is* the spirit of the holy gods; and in the days of thy father light and understanding and wisdom, like the wisdom of the gods, was found in him; whom the king Nebuchadnezzar thy father, the king, *I say,* thy father, made master of the magicians, astrologers, Chaldeans, *and* soothsayers; forasmuch as an excellent spirit, and knowledge, and understanding, interpreting of dreams, and showing of hard sentences, and dissolving of doubts, were found in the same Daniel, whom the king named Belteshazzar: now let Daniel be called, and he will show the interpretation.

DANIEL 5:1-2, 4-6, 10-12

*Related texts:* GENESIS 41; DANIEL 1–4; JOEL 2:28-32; ACTS 2:1-21

## Daniel Interprets the Writing

**THE ONE
MINUTE
BIBLE**

Then was Daniel brought in before the king. *And* the king spake and said unto Daniel, *Art* thou that Daniel, which *art* of the children of the captivity of Judah, whom the king my father brought out of Jewry? And I have heard of thee, that thou canst make interpretations, and dissolve doubts: now if thou canst read the writing, and make known to me the interpretation thereof, thou shalt be clothed with scarlet, and *have* a chain of gold about thy neck, and shalt be the third ruler in the kingdom.

Then Daniel answered and said before the king, Let thy gifts be to thyself, and give thy rewards to another; yet I will read the writing unto the king, and make known to him the interpretation.

Thou hast praised the gods of silver, and gold, of brass, iron, wood, and stone, which see not, nor hear, nor know: and the God in whose hand thy breath *is*, and whose *are* all thy ways, hast thou not glorified: then was the part of the hand sent from him; and this writing was written.

And this *is* the writing that was written,
  MENE, MENE, TEKEL, UPHARSIN.
This *is* the interpretation of the thing:
  MENE; God hath numbered thy kingdom,
    and finished it.
  TEKEL; Thou art weighed in the balances,
    and art found wanting.
  PERES; Thy kingdom is divided,
    and given to the Medes and Persians.
In that night was Belshazzar the king of the Chaldeans slain. And Darius the Median took the kingdom, *being* about threescore and two years old.

DANIEL 5:13, 16-17, 23b-28, 30-31

*Related texts:* ISAIAH 47; DANIEL 4; MATTHEW 24:14-22;
1 CORINTHIANS 12

## Cyrus Sends Israel Home

Now in the first year of Cyrus king of Persia, that the word of the LORD by the mouth of Jeremiah might be fulfilled, the LORD stirred up the spirit of Cyrus king of Persia, that he made a proclamation throughout all his kingdom, and *put it* also in writing, saying,
Thus saith Cyrus king of Persia,

**THE ONE MINUTE BIBLE**

The LORD God of heaven hath given me all the kingdoms of the earth; and he hath charged me to build him an house at Jerusalem, which *is* in Judah. Who *is there* among you of all his people? His God be with him, and let him go up to Jerusalem, which *is* in Judah, and build the house of the LORD God of Israel, (he *is* the God,) which *is* in Jerusalem. And whosoever remaineth in any place where he sojourneth, let the men of his place help him with silver, and with gold, and with goods, and with beasts, beside the freewill offering for the house of God that *is* in Jerusalem.

Then rose up the chief of the fathers of Judah and Benjamin, and the priests, and the Levites, with all *them* whose spirit God had raised, to go up to build the house of the LORD which *is* in Jerusalem. And all they that *were* about them strengthened their hands with vessels of silver, with gold, with goods, and with beasts, and with precious things, beside all *that* was willingly offered. Also Cyrus the king brought forth the vessels of the house of the LORD, which Nebuchadnezzar had brought forth out of Jerusalem, and had put them in the house of his gods.

EZRA 1:1-7

*Related texts:* 2 CHRONICLES 36:22-23; JEREMIAH 25:11-12; 29:10-14

293

# Haggai: Rebuild the Temple!

**THE ONE
MINUTE
BIBLE**

Thus speaketh the LORD of hosts, saying, This people say, The time is not come, the time that the LORD's house should be built.

Then came the word of the LORD by Haggai the prophet, saying, *Is it* time for you, O ye, to dwell in your ceiled houses, and this house *lie* waste?

Now therefore thus saith the LORD of hosts; Consider your ways. Ye have sown much, and bring in little; ye eat, but ye have not enough; ye drink, but ye are not filled with drink; ye clothe you, but there is none warm; and he that earneth wages earneth wages *to put it* into a bag with holes.

Thus saith the LORD of hosts; Consider your ways. Go up to the mountain, and bring wood, and build the house; and I will take pleasure in it, and I will be glorified, saith the LORD. Ye looked for much, and, lo, *it came* to little; and when ye brought *it* home, I did blow upon it. Why? saith the LORD of hosts. Because of mine house that *is* waste, and ye run every man unto his own house. Therefore the heaven over you is stayed from dew, and the earth is stayed *from* her fruit. And I called for a drought upon the land, and upon the mountains, and upon the corn, and upon the new wine, and upon the oil, and upon *that* which the ground bringeth forth, and upon men, and upon cattle, and upon all the labour of the hands.

Then Zerubbabel the son of Shealtiel, and Joshua the son of Josedech, the high priest, with all the remnant of the people, obeyed the voice of the LORD their God, and the words of Haggai the prophet, as the LORD their God had sent him, and the people did fear before the LORD.

HAGGAI 1:2-12

---

*Related texts:* HAGGAI 2; ZECHARIAH 1–6; 1 CORINTHIANS 3:9-17; 2 CORINTHIANS 6:14-16; EPHESIANS 2:11-22

## *Zechariah Encourages the Exiles*

Upon the four and twentieth day of the eleventh month, which *is* the month Sebat, in the second year of Darius, came the word of the LORD unto Zechariah, the son of Berechiah, the son of Iddo the prophet, saying, I saw by night, and behold a man riding upon a red horse, and he stood among the myrtle trees that *were* in the bottom; and behind him *were there* red horses, speckled, and white.

And they answered the angel of the LORD that stood among the myrtle trees, and said, We have walked to and fro through the earth, and, behold, all the earth sitteth still, and is at rest.

Then the angel of the LORD answered and said, O LORD of hosts, how long wilt thou not have mercy on Jerusalem and on the cities of Judah, against which thou hast had indignation these threescore and ten years? And the LORD answered the angel that talked with me *with* good words *and* comfortable words.

So the angel that communed with me said unto me, Cry thou, saying, Thus saith the LORD of hosts; I am jealous for Jerusalem and for Zion with a great jealousy. And I am very sore displeased with the heathen *that are* at ease: for I was but a little displeased, and they helped forward the affliction.

Therefore thus saith the LORD; I am returned to Jerusalem with mercies: my house shall be built in it, saith the LORD of hosts, and a line shall be stretched forth upon Jerusalem.

Cry yet, saying, Thus saith the LORD of hosts; My cities through prosperity shall yet be spread abroad; and the LORD shall yet comfort Zion, and shall yet choose Jerusalem.

**THE ONE MINUTE BIBLE**

ZECHARIAH 1:7-8, 11-17

*Related texts:* ISAIAH 40:1-2; ZECHARIAH 1–6; 1 CORINTHIANS 14:3; 2 CORINTHIANS 1:3-7

## The Exiles Rebuild the Temple

**THE ONE
MINUTE
BIBLE**

Now when the adversaries of Judah and Benjamin heard that the children of the captivity builded the temple unto the LORD God of Israel; then they came to Zerubbabel, and to the chief of the fathers, and said unto them, Let us build with you: for we seek your God, as ye *do*; and we do sacrifice unto him since the days of Esarhaddon king of Assur, which brought us up hither.

But Zerubbabel, and Jeshua, and the rest of the chief of the fathers of Israel, said unto them, Ye have nothing to do with us to build an house unto our God; but we ourselves together will build unto the LORD God of Israel, as king Cyrus the king of Persia hath commanded us.

Then the people of the land weakened the hands of the people of Judah, and troubled them in building, and hired counsellors against them, to frustrate their purpose, all the days of Cyrus king of Persia, even until the reign of Darius king of Persia.

Then Tatnai, governor on this side the river, Shethar-boznai, and their companions, according to that which Darius the king had sent, so they did speedily. And the elders of the Jews builded, and they prospered through the prophesying of Haggai the prophet and Zechariah the son of Iddo. And they builded, and finished *it*, according to the commandment of the God of Israel, and according to the commandment of Cyrus, and Darius, and Artaxerxes king of Persia. And this house was finished on the third day of the month Adar, which was in the sixth year of the reign of Darius the king.

EZRA 4:1-5; 6:13-15

*Related texts:* EZRA 3–6; EZEKIEL 40–48; HAGGAI 1–2; JOHN 2:13-21

*The Bible is always...with me. Indeed,
I am not apt to dip pen in ink without
first looking into the Book of Books.*
**Hayyim Nahman Bialik (1873-1934)**
HEBREW POET

*This book...is the best gift God has
given to man.... But for it we could
not know right from wrong.*
**Abraham Lincoln (1809-1865)**
UNITED STATES PRESIDENT

*The Bible, that great medicine chest
of humanity.This is called with cause
the Holy Scripture. He who lost his God
may find Him again in this book, and
he who has never known Him will
inhale here the breath of God's word.*
**Heinrich Heine (1797-1856)**
GERMAN POET

## Nehemiah Prays for the Exiles

THE ONE
MINUTE
BIBLE

The words of Nehemiah the son of Hachaliah.

And it came to pass in the month Chisleu, in the twentieth year, as I was in Shushan the palace, that Hanani, one of my brethren, came, he and *certain* men of Judah; and I asked them concerning the Jews that had escaped, which were left of the captivity, and concerning Jerusalem.

And they said unto me, The remnant that are left of the captivity there in the province *are* in great affliction and reproach: the wall of Jerusalem also *is* broken down, and the gates thereof are burned with fire.

And it came to pass, when I heard these words, that I sat down and wept, and mourned *certain* days, and fasted, and prayed before the God of heaven, and said,

I beseech thee, O LORD God of heaven, the great and terrible God, that keepeth covenant and mercy for them that love him and observe his commandments: let thine ear now be attentive, and thine eyes open, that thou mayest hear the prayer of thy servant, which I pray before thee now, day and night, for the children of Israel thy servants, and confess the sins of the children of Israel, which we have sinned against thee: both I and my father's house have sinned. We have dealt very corruptly against thee, and have not kept the commandments, nor the statutes, nor the judgments, which thou commandedst thy servant Moses.

Remember, I beseech thee, the word that thou commandedst thy servant Moses, saying, *If* ye transgress, I will scatter you abroad among the nations: but *if* ye turn unto me, and keep my commandments, and do them; though there were of you cast out unto the uttermost part of the heaven, *yet* will I gather them from thence, and will bring them unto the place that I have chosen to set my name there.

NEHEMIAH 1:1-9

---

*Related texts:* LEVITICUS 26:14-46; DEUTERONOMY 7:6-15; 28:15-68; DANIEL 9:1-19; JAMES 5:13-16

## The Exiles Rebuild Jerusalem's Wall

**THE ONE
MINUTE
BIBLE**

So built we the wall; and all the wall was joined together unto the half thereof: for the people had a mind to work.

But it came to pass, *that* when Sanballat, and Tobiah, and the Arabians, and the Ammonites, and the Ashdodites, heard that the walls of Jerusalem were made up, *and* that the breaches began to be stopped, then they were very wroth, and conspired all of them together to come *and* to fight against Jerusalem, and to hinder it. Nevertheless we made our prayer unto our God, and set a watch against them day and night, because of them.

And it came to pass from that time forth, *that* the half of my servants wrought in the work, and the other half of them held both the spears, the shields, and the bows, and the habergeons; and the rulers *were* behind all the house of Judah. They which builded on the wall, and they that bare burdens, with those that laded, *every one* with one of his hands wrought in the work, and with the other *hand* held a weapon. For the builders, every one had his sword girded by his side, and *so* builded.

So the wall was finished in the twenty and fifth *day* of *the* month Elul, in fifty and two days. And it came to pass, that when all our enemies heard *thereof*, and all the heathen that *were* about us saw *these things*, they were much cast down in their own eyes: for they perceived that this work was wrought of our God.

NEHEMIAH 4:6-9, 16-18a; 6:15-16

---

***Related texts:*** NEHEMIAH 2–6; PSALMS 27; 51:18-19; 127:1; JOHN 16:33; 1 JOHN 4:4

## *Pray for the Peace of Jerusalem*

A Song of degrees of David.

I was glad when they said unto me,
Let us go into the house of the LORD.
Our feet shall stand
within thy gates, O Jerusalem.

Jerusalem is builded as a city
that is compact together:
whither the tribes go up,
the tribes of the LORD,
unto the testimony of Israel,
to give thanks unto the name of the LORD.
For there are set thrones of judgment,
the thrones of the house of David.

Pray for the peace of Jerusalem:
they shall prosper that love thee.
Peace be within thy walls,
*and* prosperity within thy palaces.
For my brethren and companions' sakes,
I will now say, Peace *be* within thee.
Because of the house of the LORD our God
I will seek thy good.

PSALM 122

---

*Related texts:* PSALM 85; ZECHARIAH 9:9-17; LUKE 13:34-35;
EPHESIANS 2:11-22

**THE ONE
MINUTE
BIBLE**

## Ezra Reads the Law to the Exiles

And Ezra the priest brought the law before the congregation both of men and women, and all that could hear with understanding, upon the first day of the seventh month. And he read therein before the street that *was* before the water gate from the morning until midday, before the men and the women, and those that could understand; and the ears of all the people *were* attentive unto the book of the law.

And Ezra opened the book in the sight of all the people; (for he was above all the people;) and when he opened it, all the people stood up: and Ezra blessed the Lord, the great God. And all the people answered, Amen, Amen, with lifting up their hands: and they bowed their heads, and worshipped the Lord with *their* faces to the ground.

Also ... the Levites caused the people to understand the law: and the people *stood* in their place. So they read in the book in the law of God distinctly, and gave the sense, and caused *them* to understand the reading.

And Nehemiah, which *is* the Tirshatha, and Ezra the priest the scribe, and the Levites that taught the people, said unto all the people, This day *is* holy unto the Lord your God; mourn not, nor weep. For all the people wept, when they heard the words of the law.

Then he said unto them, Go your way, eat the fat, and drink the sweet, and send portions unto them for whom nothing is prepared: for *this* day *is* holy unto our Lord: neither be ye sorry; for the joy of the Lord is your strength.

Nehemiah 8:2-3, 5-10

---

***Related texts:*** Deuteronomy 16:13-15; Ezra 6:19-22; Isaiah 58; Matthew 13:18-23; Acts 17:10-11

## Persia Needs a New Queen

THE ONE
MINUTE
BIBLE

Now it came to pass in the days of Ahasuerus, (this *is* Ahasuerus which reigned, from India even unto Ethiopia, *over* an hundred and seven and twenty provinces:) that in those days, when the king Ahasuerus sat on the throne of his kingdom, which *was* in Shushan the palace, in the third year of his reign, he made a feast unto all his princes and his servants.

On the seventh day, when the heart of the king was merry with wine, he commanded ... the seven chamberlains that served in the presence of Ahasuerus the king, to bring Vashti the queen before the king with the crown royal, to show the people and the princes her beauty: for she *was* fair to look on. But the queen Vashti refused to come at the king's commandment by *his* chamberlains: therefore was the king very wroth, and his anger burned in him.

And Memucan answered before the king and the princes, Vashti the queen hath not done wrong to the king only, but also to all the princes, and to all the people that *are* in all the provinces of the king Ahasuerus.

If it please the king, let there go a royal commandment from him, and let it be written among the laws of the Persians and the Medes, that it be not altered, That Vashti come no more before king Ahasuerus; and let the king give her royal estate unto another that is better than she. And when the king's decree which he shall make shall be published throughout all his empire, (for it is great,) all the wives shall give to their husbands honour, both to great and small.

ESTHER 1:1-3a, 10-12, 16, 19-20

*Related texts:* EZRA 4:1-6; PROVERBS 31:1-9; DANIEL 9:1-2; 1 CORINTHIANS 6:9-10

# Esther Becomes Queen of Persia

**THE ONE
MINUTE
BIBLE**

*Now* in Shushan the palace there was a certain Jew, whose name *was* Mordecai, the son of Jair, the son of Shimei, the son of Kish, a Benjamite; who had been carried away from Jerusalem with the captivity which had been carried away with Jeconiah king of Judah, whom Nebuchadnezzar the king of Babylon had carried away. And he brought up Hadassah, that *is*, Esther, his uncle's daughter: for she had neither father nor mother, and the maid *was* fair and beautiful; whom Mordecai, when her father and mother were dead, took for his own daughter.

So it came to pass, when the king's commandment and his decree was heard, and when many maidens were gathered together unto Shushan the palace, to the custody of Hegai, that Esther was brought also unto the king's house, to the custody of Hegai, keeper of the women. And the maiden pleased him, and she obtained kindness of him; and he speedily gave her her things for purification, with such things as belonged to her, and seven maidens, *which were* meet to be given her, out of the king's house: and he preferred her and her maids unto the best *place* of the house of the women.

Esther had not showed her people nor her kindred: for Mordecai had charged her that she should not show *it*.

And the king loved Esther above all the women, and she obtained grace and favour in his sight more than all the virgins; so that he set the royal crown upon her head, and made her queen instead of Vashti.

ESTHER 2:5-10, 17

---

*Related texts:* GENESIS 39; 41; NEHEMIAH 1:1-11; 1 PETER 3:1-6

# Haman Plots to Kill the Jews

THE ONE
MINUTE
BIBLE

After these things did king Ahasuerus promote Haman the son of Hammedatha the Agagite, and advanced him, and set his seat above all the princes that *were* with him. And all the king's servants, that *were* in the king's gate, bowed, and reverenced Haman: for the king had so commanded concerning him. But Mordecai bowed not, nor did *him* reverence.

And when Haman saw that Mordecai bowed not, nor did him reverence, then was Haman full of wrath. And he thought scorn to lay hands on Mordecai alone; for they had showed him the people of Mordecai: wherefore Haman sought to destroy all the Jews that *were* throughout the whole kingdom of Ahasuerus, *even* the people of Mordecai.

And Haman said unto king Ahasuerus, There is a certain people scattered abroad and dispersed among the people in all the provinces of thy kingdom; and their laws *are* diverse from all people; neither keep they the king's laws: therefore it *is* not for the king's profit to suffer them. If it please the king, let it be written that they may be destroyed: and I will pay ten thousand talents of silver to the hands of those that have the charge of the business, to bring *it* into the king's treasuries.

And the king took his ring from his hand, and gave it unto Haman the son of Hammedatha the Agagite, the Jews' enemy. And the king said unto Haman, The silver *is* given to thee, the people also, to do with them as it seemeth good to thee.

ESTHER 3:1-2, 5-6, 8-11

---

***Related texts:*** GENESIS 12:1-3; DEUTERONOMY 30:1-7; ESTHER 4–6; PSALM 44:1-8; DANIEL 3; 6; ROMANS 9–11

# *Haman's Downfall*

**THE ONE
MINUTE
BIBLE**

So the king and Haman came to banquet with Esther the queen. And the king said again unto Esther on the second day at the banquet of wine, What *is* thy petition, queen Esther? And it shall be granted thee: and what *is* thy request? And it shall be performed, *even* to the half of the kingdom.

Then Esther the queen answered and said, If I have found favour in thy sight, O king, and if it please the king, let my life be given me at my petition, and my people at my request: for we are sold, I and my people, to be destroyed, to be slain, and to perish. But if we had been sold for bondmen and bondwomen, I had held my tongue, although the enemy could not countervail the king's damage.

Then the king Ahasuerus answered and said unto Esther the queen, Who is he, and where is he, that durst presume in his heart to do so?

And Esther said, The adversary and enemy *is* this wicked Haman. Then Haman was afraid before the king and the queen.

And Harbonah, one of the chamberlains, said before the king, Behold also, the gallows fifty cubits high, which Haman had made for Mordecai, who had spoken good for the king, standeth in the house of Haman.

Then the king said, Hang him thereon. So they hanged Haman on the gallows that he had prepared for Mordecai. Then was the king's wrath pacified.

ESTHER 7:1-6, 9-10

---

***Related texts:*** DEUTERONOMY 23:3-5; ESTHER 8–10; JOEL 3:1-8; OBADIAH 15; REVELATION 19:11–20:10

## *Malachi: Messenger of the Covenant*

Behold, I will send my messenger, and he shall prepare the way before me: and the Lord, whom ye seek, shall suddenly come to his temple, even the messenger of the covenant, whom ye delight in: behold, he shall come, saith the LORD of hosts.

But who may abide the day of his coming? And who shall stand when he appeareth? For he *is* like a refiner's fire, and like fullers' soap: and he shall sit *as* a refiner and purifier of silver: and he shall purify the sons of Levi, and purge them as gold and silver, that they may offer unto the LORD an offering in righteousness. Then shall the offering of Judah and Jerusalem be pleasant unto the LORD, as in the days of old, and as in former years.

For, behold, the day cometh, that shall burn as an oven; and all the proud, yea, and all that do wickedly, shall be stubble: and the day that cometh shall burn them up, saith the LORD of hosts, that it shall leave them neither root nor branch. But unto you that fear my name shall the Sun of righteousness arise with healing in his wings; and ye shall go forth, and grow up as calves of the stall. And ye shall tread down the wicked; for they shall be ashes under the soles of your feet in the day that I shall do *this*, saith the LORD of hosts.

Behold, I will send you Elijah the prophet before the coming of the great and dreadful day of the LORD: and he shall turn the heart of the fathers to the children, and the heart of the children to their fathers, lest I come and smite the earth with a curse.

MALACHI 3:1-4; 4:1-3, 5-6

THE ONE
MINUTE
BIBLE

*Related texts:* ISAIAH 60; LUKE 1:1-17; MATTHEW 3:1-12; 17:10-13

**THE ONE
MINUTE
BIBLE**

## *The Promise of Jesus' Coming*

And now, saith the LORD
    that formed me from the womb *to be* his servant,
to bring Jacob again to him,
    Though Israel be not gathered,
yet shall I be glorious in the eyes of the LORD,
    and my God shall be my strength.
And he said,
It is a light thing that thou shouldest be my servant
    to raise up the tribes of Jacob,
    and to restore the preserved of Israel:
I will also give thee for a light to the Gentiles,
    that thou mayest be my salvation unto the end
        of the earth.

But thou, Bethlehem Ephratah,
    *though* thou be little among the thousands of Judah,
*yet* out of thee shall he come forth unto me
    *that is* to be ruler in Israel;
whose goings forth *have been* from of old,
    from everlasting.

Therefore will he give them up,
    until the time *that* she which travaileth hath brought
        forth:
then the remnant of his brethren shall return
    unto the children of Israel.
And he shall stand and feed
    in the strength of the LORD,
    in the majesty of the name of the LORD his God;
and they shall abide: for now shall he be great
    unto the ends of the earth.
    And this *man* shall be the peace.

ISAIAH 49:5-6; MICAH 5:2-5a

*Related texts:* GENESIS 35:14-19; RUTH 4:10-17; 1 SAMUEL 17:12;
MATTHEW 2:1-6

## *Jesus: Son of God, Son of Man*

I saw in the night visions, and, behold, *one* like the Son of man came with the clouds of heaven, and came to the Ancient of days, and they brought him near before him. And there was given him dominion, and glory, and a kingdom, that all people, nations, and languages, should serve him: his dominion *is* an everlasting dominion, which shall not pass away, and his kingdom *that* which shall not be destroyed.

**THE ONE MINUTE BIBLE**

God, who at sundry times and in divers manners spake in time past unto the fathers by the prophets, hath in these last days spoken unto us by *his* Son, whom he hath appointed heir of all things, by whom also he made the worlds; who being the brightness of *his* glory, and the express image of his person, and upholding all things by the word of his power, when he had by himself purged our sins, sat down on the right hand of the Majesty on high; being made so much better than the angels, as he hath by inheritance obtained a more excellent name than they.

For unto which of the angels said he at any time,

Thou art my Son,
    this day have I begotten thee?

And again,

I will be to him a Father,
    and he shall be to me a Son?

DANIEL 7:13-14; HEBREWS 1:1-5

***Related texts:*** 2 SAMUEL 7:14; 1 CHRONICLES 17:13; PSALM 2:7; MATTHEW 23:63-64; MARK 14:61-62; LUKE 22:67-70; JOHN 1:32-34

## Jesus Christ Is Born

**THE ONE
MINUTE
BIBLE**

Now the birth of Jesus Christ was on this wise: when as his mother Mary was espoused to Joseph, before they came together, she was found with child of the Holy Ghost. Then Joseph her husband, being a just *man*, and not willing to make her a public example, was minded to put her away privily.

But while he thought on these things, behold, the angel of the Lord appeared unto him in a dream, saying, Joseph, thou son of David, fear not to take unto thee Mary thy wife: for that which is conceived in her is of the Holy Ghost. And she shall bring forth a son, and thou shalt call his name JESUS: for he shall save his people from their sins.

Now all this was done, that it might be fulfilled which was spoken of the Lord by the prophet, saying, Behold, a virgin shall be with child, and shall bring forth a son, and they shall call his name Emmanuel, which being interpreted is, God with us.

Then Joseph being raised from sleep did as the angel of the Lord had bidden him, and took unto him his wife: and knew her not till she had brought forth her firstborn son: and he called his name JESUS.

MATTHEW 1:18-25

*Related texts:* ISAIAH 7:14; MATTHEW 2; LUKE 1–2; JOHN 4:1-42

## The Boy Jesus in the Temple

Now Jesus' parents went to Jerusalem every year at the feast of the passover. And when he was twelve years old, they went up to Jerusalem after the custom of the feast. And when they had fulfilled the days, as they returned, the child Jesus tarried behind in Jerusalem; and Joseph and his mother knew not *of it*. But they, supposing him to have been in the company, went a day's journey; and they sought him among *their* kinsfolk and acquaintance. And when they found him not, they turned back again to Jerusalem, seeking him.

And it came to pass, that after three days they found him in the temple, sitting in the midst of the doctors, both hearing them, and asking them questions. And all that heard him were astonished at his understanding and answers. And when they saw him, they were amazed: and his mother said unto him, Son, why hast thou thus dealt with us? Behold, thy father and I have sought thee sorrowing.

And he said unto them, How is it that ye sought me? Wist ye not that I must be about my Father's business? And they understood not the saying which he spake unto them.

And he went down with them, and came to Nazareth, and was subject unto them: but his mother kept all these sayings in her heart. And Jesus increased in wisdom and stature, and in favour with God and man.

LUKE 2:41-52

---

*Related texts:* 1 SAMUEL 2:21, 26; PSALMS 26:8; 27:4; 65;
MATTHEW 2:13-23; JOHN 2:13-17; 2 CORINTHIANS 4:18–5:4

## *Jesus Is Baptized*

**THE ONE
MINUTE
BIBLE**

The beginning of the gospel of Jesus Christ, the Son of God; as it is written in the prophets,

Behold, I send my messenger before thy face,
    which shall prepare thy way before thee.
The voice of one crying in the wilderness,
Prepare ye the way of the Lord,
    make his paths straight.

John did baptize in the wilderness, and preach the baptism of repentance for the remission of sins. And there went out unto him all the land of Judaea, and they of Jerusalem, and were all baptized of him in the river of Jordan, confessing their sins. And John was clothed with camel's hair, and with a girdle of a skin about his loins; and he did eat locusts and wild honey; and preached, saying, There cometh one mightier than I after me, the latchet of whose shoes I am not worthy to stoop down and unloose. I indeed have baptized you with water: but he shall baptize you with the Holy Ghost.

And it came to pass in those days, that Jesus came from Nazareth of Galilee, and was baptized of John in Jordan. And straightway coming up out of the water, he saw the heavens opened, and the Spirit like a dove descending upon him: and there came a voice from heaven, *saying*, Thou art my beloved Son, in whom I am well pleased.

MARK 1:1-11

*Related texts:* ISAIAH 40:3; MALACHI 3:1; MATTHEW 3; LUKE 3;
JOHN 1:19-34

# Jesus Is Tempted by the Devil

Then was Jesus led up of the Spirit into the wilderness to be tempted of the devil. And when he had fasted forty days and forty nights, he was afterward an hungered. And when the tempter came to him, he said, If thou be the Son of God, command that these stones be made bread.

But he answered and said, It is written, Man shall not live by bread alone, but by every word that proceedeth out of the mouth of God.

Then the devil taketh him up into the holy city, and setteth him on a pinnacle of the temple, and saith unto him, If thou be the Son of God, cast thyself down: for it is written,

He shall give his angels charge concerning thee:
　　and in *their* hands they shall bear thee up,
　lest at any time thou dash thy foot against a stone.

Jesus said unto him, It is written again, Thou shalt not tempt the Lord thy God.

Again, the devil taketh him up into an exceeding high mountain, and showeth him all the kingdoms of the world, and the glory of them; and saith unto him, All these things will I give thee, if thou wilt fall down and worship me.

Then saith Jesus unto him, Get thee hence, Satan: for it is written, Thou shalt worship the Lord thy God, and him only shalt thou serve.

Then the devil leaveth him, and, behold, angels came and ministered unto him.

MATTHEW 4:1-11

---

*Related texts:* DEUTERONOMY 6:13, 16; 8:3; PSALM 91:11-12;
MARK 1:12-13; LUKE 4:1-13

## Jesus' First Miracle

**THE ONE
MINUTE
BIBLE**

And the third day there was a marriage in Cana of Galilee; and the mother of Jesus was there: and both Jesus was called, and his disciples, to the marriage. And when they wanted wine, the mother of Jesus saith unto him, They have no wine.

Jesus saith unto her, Woman, what have I to do with thee? Mine hour is not yet come.

His mother saith unto the servants, Whatsoever he saith unto you, do *it.*

Jesus saith unto them, Fill the waterpots with water. And they filled them up to the brim.

And he saith unto them, Draw out now, and bear unto the governor of the feast. And they bare *it.*

When the ruler of the feast had tasted the water that was made wine, and knew not whence it was: (but the servants which drew the water knew;) the governor of the feast called the bridegroom, and saith unto him, Every man at the beginning doth set forth good wine; and when men have well drunk, then that which is worse: *but* thou hast kept the good wine until now.

This beginning of miracles did Jesus in Cana of Galilee, and manifested forth his glory; and his disciples believed on him.

And there are also many other things which Jesus did, the which, if they should be written every one, I suppose that even the world itself could not contain the books that should be written. Amen.

JOHN 2:1-5, 7-11; 21:25

*Related texts:* ISAIAH 55; JOEL 3:16-18; AMOS 9:11-15; JOHN 20:30-31

314

## *You Must Be Born Again*

THE ONE
MINUTE
BIBLE

There was a man of the Pharisees, named Nicodemus, a ruler of the Jews: the same came to Jesus by night, and said unto him, Rabbi, we know that thou art a teacher come from God: for no man can do these miracles that thou doest, except God be with him.

Jesus answered and said unto him, Verily, verily, I say unto thee, Except a man be born again, he cannot see the kingdom of God.

Nicodemus saith unto him, How can a man be born when he is old? Can he enter the second time into his mother's womb, and be born?

Jesus answered, Verily, verily, I say unto thee, Except a man be born of water and *of* the Spirit, he cannot enter into the kingdom of God.

Nicodemus answered and said unto him, How can these things be?

Jesus answered and said unto him, Art thou a master of Israel, and knowest not these things? If I have told you earthly things, and ye believe not, how shall ye believe, if I tell you *of* heavenly things? And no man hath ascended up to heaven, but he that came down from heaven, *even* the Son of man which is in heaven. And as Moses lifted up the serpent in the wilderness, even so must the Son of man be lifted up: that whosoever believeth in him should not perish, but have eternal life.

For God so loved the world, that he gave his only begotten Son, that whosoever believeth in him should not perish, but have everlasting life.

JOHN 3:1-5, 9-10, 12-16

*Related texts:* NUMBERS 21:1-9; JOHN 1:1-13; 1 PETER 1;
1 JOHN 2:28-29; 3:1-10; 4:7-8; 5

## *Jesus Calls His First Disciples*

**THE ONE
MINUTE
BIBLE**

   And it came to pass, that, as the people pressed upon Jesus to hear the word of God, he stood by the lake of Gennesaret, and saw two ships standing by the lake: but the fishermen were gone out of them, and were washing *their* nets. And he entered into one of the ships, which was Simon's, and prayed him that he would thrust out a little from the land. And he sat down, and taught the people out of the ship.

   Now when he had left speaking, he said unto Simon, Launch out into the deep, and let down your nets for a draught.

   And Simon answering said unto him, Master, we have toiled all the night, and have taken nothing: nevertheless at thy word I will let down the net.

   And when they had this done, they enclosed a great multitude of fishes: and their net brake. And they beckoned unto *their* partners, which were in the other ship, that they should come and help them. And they came, and filled both the ships, so that they began to sink.

   When Simon Peter saw *it*, he fell down at Jesus' knees, saying, Depart from me; for I am a sinful man, O Lord. For he was astonished, and all that were with him, at the draught of the fishes which they had taken: and so *was* also James, and John, the sons of Zebedee, which were partners with Simon.

   And Jesus said unto Simon, Fear not; from henceforth thou shalt catch men. And when they had brought their ships to land, they forsook all, and followed him.

Luke 5:1-11

***Related texts:*** Psalm 51:1-13; Matthew 4:18-22; Mark 1:16-20; John 1:35-51

316

## *Healing Illness; Forgiving Sin*

**THE ONE MINUTE BIBLE**

And it came to pass on a certain day, as Jesus was teaching, that there were Pharisees and doctors of the law sitting by, which were come out of every town of Galilee, and Judaea, and Jerusalem: and the power of the Lord was *present* to heal them. And, behold, men brought in a bed a man which was taken with a palsy: and they sought *means* to bring him in, and to lay *him* before him. And when they could not find by what *way* they might bring him in because of the multitude, they went upon the housetop, and let him down through the tiling with *his* couch into the midst before Jesus.

And when he saw their faith, he said unto him, Man, thy sins are forgiven thee.

And the scribes and the Pharisees began to reason, saying, Who is this which speaketh blasphemies? Who can forgive sins, but God alone?

But when Jesus perceived their thoughts, he answering said unto them, What reason ye in your hearts? Whether is easier, to say, Thy sins be forgiven thee; or to say, Rise up and walk? But that ye may know that the Son of man hath power upon earth to forgive sins, (he said unto the sick of the palsy,) I say unto thee, Arise, and take up thy couch, and go into thine house. And immediately he rose up before them, and took up that whereon he lay, and departed to his own house, glorifying God. And they were all amazed, and they glorified God, and were filled with fear, saying, We have seen strange things to day.

LUKE 5:17-26

*Related texts:* PSALM 25:1-11; MICAH 7:18; MATTHEW 9:1-8; MARK 2:1-12

**THE ONE**
**M I N U T E**
**B I B L E**

# Jesus Controls Storms and Spirits

And when Jesus was entered into a ship, his disciples followed him. And, behold, there arose a great tempest in the sea, insomuch that the ship was covered with the waves: but he was asleep. And his disciples came to *him*, and awoke him, saying, Lord, save us: we perish.

And he saith unto them, Why are ye fearful, O ye of little faith? Then he arose, and rebuked the winds and the sea; and there was a great calm.

But the men marvelled, saying, What manner of man is this, that even the winds and the sea obey him!

And when he was come to the other side into the country of the Gergesenes, there met him two possessed with devils, coming out of the tombs, exceeding fierce, so that no man might pass by that way. And, behold, they cried out, saying, What have we to do with thee, Jesus, thou Son of God? Art thou come hither to torment us before the time?

And there was a good way off from them an herd of many swine feeding. So the devils besought him, saying, If thou cast us out, suffer us to go away into the herd of swine.

And he said unto them, Go. And when they were come out, they went into the herd of swine: and, behold, the whole herd of swine ran violently down a steep place into the sea, and perished in the waters.

MATTHEW 8:23-32

*Related texts:* DEUTERONOMY 14:8; ISAIAH 65:1-4; JONAH 1; MARK 4:35-5:20; LUKE 8:22-39

## *Faith and Healing*

While Jesus spake these things unto them, behold, there came a certain ruler, and worshipped him, saying, My daughter is even now dead: but come and lay thy hand upon her, and she shall live. And Jesus arose, and followed him, and *so did* his disciples.

And, behold, a woman, which was diseased with an issue of blood twelve years, came behind *him*, and touched the hem of his garment: for she said within herself, If I may but touch his garment, I shall be whole.

But Jesus turned him about, and when he saw her, he said, Daughter, be of good comfort; thy faith hath made thee whole. And the woman was made whole from that hour.

And when Jesus came into the ruler's house, and saw the minstrels and the people making a noise, he said unto them, Give place: for the maid is not dead, but sleepeth. And they laughed him to scorn. But when the people were put forth, he went in, and took her by the hand, and the maid arose. And the fame hereof went abroad into all that land.

Is any among you afflicted? Let him pray. Is any merry? Let him sing psalms. Is any sick among you? Let him call for the elders of the church; and let them pray over him, anointing him with oil in the name of the Lord: and the prayer of faith shall save the sick, and the Lord shall raise him up; and if he have committed sins, they shall be forgiven him. Confess *your* faults one to another, and pray one for another, that ye may be healed. The effectual fervent prayer of a righteous man availeth much.

MATTHEW 9:18-26; JAMES 5:13-16

**THE ONE MINUTE BIBLE**

*Related texts:* HABAKKUK 2:4; MATTHEW 9:27-30; MARK 5:21-43; LUKE 7:1-10, 36-50; 8:22-25, 40-56; 17:11-19; 18:35-43

## *Jesus Responds to Lack of Faith*

**THE ONE
MINUTE
BIBLE**

Jesus and his disciples went into a house. And the multitude cometh together again, so that they could not so much as eat bread. And when his friends heard *of it*, they went out to lay hold on him: for they said, He is beside himself.

And the scribes which came down from Jerusalem said, He hath Beelzebub, and by the prince of the devils casteth he out devils.

And he called them *unto him*, and said unto them in parables, How can Satan cast out Satan? And if a kingdom be divided against itself, that kingdom cannot stand. And if a house be divided against itself, that house cannot stand. And if Satan rise up against himself, and be divided, he cannot stand, but hath an end. No man can enter into a strong man's house, and spoil his goods, except he will first bind the strong man; and then he will spoil his house.

Verily I say unto you, All sins shall be forgiven unto the sons of men, and blasphemies wherewith soever they shall blaspheme: but he that shall blaspheme against the Holy Ghost hath never forgiveness, but is in danger of eternal damnation.

Because they said, He hath an unclean spirit.

MARK 3:19b-30

---

*Related texts:* EXODUS 22:28; PSALM 106:1-37; MATTHEW 12:22-37;
13:53-58; MARK 6:1-6; LUKE 11:14-23; 12:10

## *Jesus Feeds Five Thousand*

When Jesus then lifted up *his* eyes, and saw a great company come unto him, he saith unto Philip, Whence shall we buy bread, that these may eat? And this he said to prove him: for he himself knew what he would do.

Philip answered him, Two hundred pennyworth of bread is not sufficient for them, that every one of them may take a little.

One of his disciples, Andrew, Simon Peter's brother, saith unto him, There is a lad here, which hath five barley loaves, and two small fishes: but what are they among so many?

And Jesus said, Make the men sit down. Now there was much grass in the place. So the men sat down, in number about five thousand. And Jesus took the loaves; and when he had given thanks, he distributed to the disciples, and the disciples to them that were set down; and likewise of the fishes as much as they would.

When they were filled, he said unto his disciples, Gather up the fragments that remain, that nothing be lost. Therefore they gathered *them* together, and filled twelve baskets with the fragments of the five barley loaves, which remained over and above unto them that had eaten.

Then those men, when they had seen the miracle that Jesus did, said, This is of a truth that prophet that should come into the world.

JOHN 6:5-14

*Related texts:* DEUTERONOMY 8:2-3; MATTHEW 14:13-21; MARK 6:32-44; LUKE 9:10-17

## *Who Is Jesus?*

**THE ONE
MINUTE
BIBLE**

When Jesus came into the coasts of Caesarea Philippi, he asked his disciples, saying, Whom do men say that I the Son of man am?

And they said, Some *say that thou art* John the Baptist: some, Elias; and others, Jeremias, or one of the prophets.

He saith unto them, But whom say ye that I am?

And Simon Peter answered and said, Thou art the Christ, the Son of the living God.

And Jesus answered and said unto him, Blessed art thou, Simon Bar-jona: for flesh and blood hath not revealed *it* unto thee, but my Father which is in heaven. And I say also unto thee, That thou art Peter, and upon this rock I will build my church; and the gates of hell shall not prevail against it. And I will give unto thee the keys of the kingdom of heaven: and whatsoever thou shalt bind on earth shall be bound in heaven: and whatsoever thou shalt loose on earth shall be loosed in heaven. Then charged he his disciples that they should tell no man that he was Jesus the Christ.

From that time forth began Jesus to show unto his disciples, how that he must go unto Jerusalem, and suffer many things of the elders and chief priests and scribes, and be killed, and be raised again the third day.

MATTHEW 16:13-21

*Related texts:* ISAIAH 52:14-15; MARK 8:27-33; LUKE 9:18-22; JOHN 6:67-71

## *The Transfiguration*

**THE ONE
MINUTE
BIBLE**

And after six days Jesus taketh *with him* Peter, and James, and John, and leadeth them up into an high mountain apart by themselves: and he was transfigured before them. And his raiment became shining, exceeding white as snow; so as no fuller on earth can white them. And there appeared unto them Elias with Moses: and they were talking with Jesus.

And Peter answered and said to Jesus, Master, it is good for us to be here: and let us make three tabernacles; one for thee, and one for Moses, and one for Elias. For he wist not what to say; for they were sore afraid.

And there was a cloud that overshadowed them: and a voice came out of the cloud, saying, This is my beloved Son: hear him.

And suddenly, when they had looked round about, they saw no man any more, save Jesus only with themselves.

And as they came down from the mountain, he charged them that they should tell no man what things they had seen, till the Son of man were risen from the dead. And they kept that saying with themselves, questioning one with another what the rising from the dead should mean.

And the Word was made flesh, and dwelt among us, (and we beheld his glory, the glory as of the only begotten of the Father,) full of grace and truth.

MARK 9:2-10; JOHN 1:14

---

***Related texts:*** EXODUS 40:33-35; MATTHEW 17:1-9; LUKE 9:28-36;
ROMANS 16:25-27; 1 TIMOTHY 1:17; JUDE 24-25

## Small Faith–Large Results

**THE ONE
MINUTE
BIBLE**

And when they were come to the multitude, there came to Jesus a *certain* man, kneeling down to him, and saying, Lord, have mercy on my son: for he is lunatick, and sore vexed: for ofttimes he falleth into the fire, and oft into the water. And I brought him to thy disciples, and they could not cure him.

Then Jesus answered and said, O faithless and perverse generation, how long shall I be with you? How long shall I suffer you? Bring him hither to me. And Jesus rebuked the devil; and he departed out of him: and the child was cured from that very hour.

Then came the disciples to Jesus apart, and said, Why could not we cast him out?

And Jesus said unto them, Because of your unbelief: for verily I say unto you, If ye have faith as a grain of mustard seed, ye shall say unto this mountain, Remove hence to yonder place; and it shall remove; and nothing shall be impossible unto you. Howbeit this kind goeth not out but by prayer and fasting.

And while they abode in Galilee, Jesus said unto them, The Son of man shall be betrayed into the hands of men: and they shall kill him, and the third day he shall be raised again. And they were exceeding sorry.

[Jesus said,] Verily, verily, I say unto you, He that believeth on me, the works that I do shall he do also; and greater *works* than these shall he do; because I go unto my Father. And whatsoever ye shall ask in my name, that will I do, that the Father may be glorified in the Son.

MATTHEW 17:14-23; JOHN 14:12-13

*Related texts:* 1 SAMUEL 16:14-23; MARK 9:14-32; LUKE 9:37-45; ROMANS 4:18-21; 11:1-23; HEBREWS 3:16-19

## *Jesus Teaches His Disciples to Pray*

And it came to pass, that, as he was praying in a certain place, when he ceased, one of his disciples said unto him, Lord, teach us to pray, as John also taught his disciples.

And he said unto them, When ye pray, say,

Our Father which art in heaven,
Hallowed be thy name.
Thy kingdom come.
Thy will be done, as in heaven, so in earth.
Give us day by day our daily bread.
And forgive us our sins;
 for we also forgive every one that is indebted to us.
And lead us not into temptation;
but deliver us from evil.

And he said unto them, Which of you shall have a friend, and shall go unto him at midnight, and say unto him, Friend, lend me three loaves; for a friend of mine in his journey is come to me, and I have nothing to set before him?

And he from within shall answer and say, Trouble me not: the door is now shut, and my children are with me in bed; I cannot rise and give thee. I say unto you, Though he will not rise and give him, because he is his friend, yet because of his importunity he will rise and give him as many as he needeth.

And I say unto you, Ask, and it shall be given you; seek, and ye shall find; knock, and it shall be opened unto you. For every one that asketh receiveth; and he that seeketh findeth; and to him that knocketh it shall be opened.

LUKE 11:1-10

**THE ONE MINUTE BIBLE**

*Related texts:* PSALM 89:19-29; ISAIAH 9:6-7; MATTHEW 6:6-13; 7:7-11; REVELATION 3:14-22

**THE ONE
MINUTE
BIBLE**

*October 28*

## Jesus Welcomes Little Children

Then there arose a reasoning among the disciples, which of them should be greatest. And Jesus, perceiving the thought of their heart, took a child, and set him by him, and said unto them, Whosoever shall receive this child in my name receiveth me: and whosoever shall receive me receiveth him that sent me: for he that is least among you all, the same shall be great.

And they brought young children to him, that he should touch them: and *his* disciples rebuked those that brought *them*. But when Jesus saw *it*, he was much displeased, and said unto them, Suffer the little children to come unto me, and forbid them not: for of such is the kingdom of God. Verily I say unto you, Whosoever shall not receive the kingdom of God as a little child, he shall not enter therein. And he took them up in his arms, put *his* hands upon them, and blessed them.

In that hour Jesus rejoiced in spirit, and said, I thank thee, O Father, Lord of heaven and earth, that thou hast hid these things from the wise and prudent, and hast revealed them unto babes: even so, Father; for so it seemed good in thy sight.
All things are delivered to me of my Father: and no man knoweth who the Son is, but the Father; and who the Father is, but the Son, and *he* to whom the Son will reveal *him*.

LUKE 9:46-48; MARK 10:13-16; LUKE 10:21-22

*Related texts:* PSALM 127:3-5; MATTHEW 18:1-14; 19:13-15;
MARK 9:33-37; LUKE 18:15-17

326

# Jesus Heals on the Sabbath

And he was teaching in one of the synagogues on the sabbath. And, behold, there was a woman which had a spirit of infirmity eighteen years, and was bowed together, and could in no wise lift up *herself*. And when Jesus saw her, he called *her to him*, and said unto her, Woman, thou art loosed from thine infirmity. And he laid *his* hands on her: and immediately she was made straight, and glorified God.

And the ruler of the synagogue answered with indignation, because that Jesus had healed on the sabbath day, and said unto the people, There are six days in which men ought to work: in them therefore come and be healed, and not on the sabbath day.

The Lord then answered him, and said, *Thou* hypocrite, doth not each one of you on the sabbath loose his ox or *his* ass from the stall, and lead *him* away to watering? And ought not this woman, being a daughter of Abraham, whom Satan hath bound, lo, these eighteen years, be loosed from this bond on the sabbath day?

And when he had said these things, all his adversaries were ashamed: and all the people rejoiced for all the glorious things that were done by him.

LUKE 13:10-17

*Related texts:* EXODUS 20:8-11; MATTHEW 12:1-14; MARK 2:23–3:6; LUKE 6:1-11; 14:1-6; JOHN 5:1-18

# Jesus Teaches on Divorce and Celibacy

**THE ONE
MINUTE
BIBLE**

The Pharisees also came unto Jesus, tempting him, and saying unto him, Is it lawful for a man to put away his wife for every cause?

And he answered and said unto them, Have ye not read, that he which made *them* at the beginning made them male and female, and said, For this cause shall a man leave father and mother, and shall cleave to his wife: and they twain shall be one flesh? Wherefore they are no more twain, but one flesh. What therefore God hath joined together, let not man put asunder.

They say unto him, Why did Moses then command to give a writing of divorcement, and to put her away?

He saith unto them, Moses because of the hardness of your hearts suffered you to put away your wives: but from the beginning it was not so. And I say unto you, Whosoever shall put away his wife, except *it be* for fornication, and shall marry another, committeth adultery: and whoso marrieth her which is put away doth commit adultery.

His disciples say unto him, If the case of the man be so with *his* wife, it is not good to marry.

But he said unto them, All *men* cannot receive this saying, save *they* to whom it is given. For there are some eunuchs, which were so born from *their* mother's womb: and there are some eunuchs, which were made eunuchs of men: and there be eunuchs, which have made themselves eunuchs for the kingdom of heaven's sake. He that is able to receive *it*, let him receive *it*.

MATTHEW 19:3-12

***Related texts:*** GENESIS 1:27; 2:24; DEUTERONOMY 24:1-4; MALACHI 2:13-16; MARK 10:2-12; LUKE 16:18

## *Treasure in Heaven*

**THE ONE MINUTE BIBLE**

And a certain ruler asked him, saying, Good Master, what shall I do to inherit eternal life?

And Jesus said unto him, Why callest thou me good? None *is* good, save one, *that is*, God. Thou knowest the commandments, Do not commit adultery, Do not kill, Do not steal, Do not bear false witness, Honour thy father and thy mother.

And he said, All these have I kept from my youth up.

Now when Jesus heard these things, he said unto him, Yet lackest thou one thing: sell all that thou hast, and distribute unto the poor, and thou shalt have treasure in heaven: and come, follow me.

And when he heard this, he was very sorrowful: for he was very rich. And when Jesus saw that he was very sorrowful, he said, How hardly shall they that have riches enter into the kingdom of God! For it is easier for a camel to go through a needle's eye, than for a rich man to enter into the kingdom of God.

And they that heard *it* said, Who then can be saved?

And he said, The things which are impossible with men are possible with God.

Then Peter said, Lo, we have left all, and followed thee.

And he said unto them, Verily I say unto you, There is no man that hath left house, or parents, or brethren, or wife, or children, for the kingdom of God's sake, who shall not receive manifold more in this present time, and in the world to come life everlasting.

LUKE 18:18-30

*Related texts:* EXODUS 20:12-16; DEUTERONOMY 5:16-20; MATTHEW 19:16-30; MARK 10:17-31; 1 CORINTHIANS 13:3

*The Bible is alive, it speaks to me.*
**Martin Luther (1483-1546)**
GERMAN THEOLOGIAN AND REFORMER

*He rightly reads Scripture who turns words into deeds.*
**St. Bernard of Clairvaux (1090-1153)**
FRENCH MONK

*The Bible holds up before us ideals that are within sight of the weakest and the lowliest, and yet so high that the best and noblest are kept with their faces turned ever upward.*
**William Jennings Bryan (1860-1925)**
AMERICAN ORATOR AND POLITICIAN

## *Jesus Visits a Sinner*

And *Jesus* entered and passed through Jericho. And, behold, *there was* a man named Zacchaeus, which was the chief among the publicans, and he was rich. And he sought to see Jesus who he was; and could not for the press, because he was little of stature. And he ran before, and climbed up into a sycamore tree to see him: for he was to pass that *way*.

And when Jesus came to the place, he looked up, and saw him, and said unto him, Zacchaeus, make haste, and come down; for to day I must abide at thy house. And he made haste, and came down, and received him joyfully.

And when they saw *it*, they all murmured, saying, That he was gone to be guest with a man that is a sinner.

And Zacchaeus stood, and said unto the Lord; Behold, Lord, the half of my goods I give to the poor; and if I have taken any thing from any man by false accusation, I restore *him* fourfold.

And Jesus said unto him, This day is salvation come to this house, forsomuch as he also is a son of Abraham. For the Son of man is come to seek and to save that which was lost.

And as it is appointed unto men once to die, but after this the judgment: so Christ was once offered to bear the sins of many; and unto them that look for him shall he appear the second time without sin unto salvation.

LUKE 19:1-10; HEBREWS 9:27-28

*Related texts:* EZEKIEL 34:7-16; MARK 2:14-17; LUKE 7:36-47

## *Jesus Anointed for Burial*

**THE ONE
MINUTE
BIBLE**

Then Jesus six days before the passover came to Bethany, where Lazarus was which had been dead, whom he raised from the dead. There they made him a supper; and Martha served: but Lazarus was one of them that sat at the table with him. Then took Mary a pound of ointment of spikenard, very costly, and anointed the feet of Jesus, and wiped his feet with her hair: and the house was filled with the odour of the ointment.

Then saith one of his disciples, Judas Iscariot, Simon's *son*, which should betray him, Why was not this ointment sold for three hundred pence, and given to the poor? This he said, not that he cared for the poor; but because he was a thief, and had the bag, and bare what was put therein.

Then said Jesus, Let her alone: against the day of my burying hath she kept this. For the poor always ye have with you; but me ye have not always.

Much people of the Jews therefore knew that he was there: and they came not for Jesus' sake only, but that they might see Lazarus also, whom he had raised from the dead. But the chief priests consulted that they might put Lazarus also to death; because that by reason of him many of the Jews went away, and believed on Jesus.

JOHN 12:1-11

*Related texts:* PSALM 16:9-11; MATTHEW 26:6-13; MARK 14:3-9; LUKE 7:36-50; JOHN 11

## The Triumphal Entry

THE ONE
MINUTE
BIBLE

And it came to pass, when he was come nigh to Bethphage and Bethany, at the mount called *the mount* of Olives, he sent two of his disciples, saying, Go ye into the village over against *you*; in the which at your entering ye shall find a colt tied, whereon yet never man sat: loose him, and bring *him hither*. And if any man ask you, Why do ye loose *him*? thus shall ye say unto him, Because the Lord hath need of him.

And they that were sent went their way, and found even as he had said unto them. And as they were loosing the colt, the owners thereof said unto them, Why loose ye the colt?

And they said, The Lord hath need of him.

And they brought him to Jesus: and they cast their garments upon the colt, and they set Jesus thereon. And as he went, they spread their clothes in the way.

And when he was come nigh, even now at the descent of the mount of Olives, the whole multitude of the disciples began to rejoice and praise God with a loud voice for all the mighty works that they had seen; saying,

Blessed *be* the King that cometh in the name of the Lord:
peace in heaven, and glory in the highest.

And some of the Pharisees from among the multitude said unto him, Master, rebuke thy disciples.

And he answered and said unto them, I tell you that, if these should hold their peace, the stones would immediately cry out.

LUKE 19:29-40

*Related texts:* PSALM 118; MATTHEW 21:1-9; MARK 11:1-10; JOHN 12:12-19

## The Parable of the Vineyard

**THE ONE
MINUTE
BIBLE**

Then began Jesus to speak to the people this parable; A certain man planted a vineyard, and let it forth to husbandmen, and went into a far country for a long time. And at the season he sent a servant to the husbandmen, that they should give him of the fruit of the vineyard: but the husbandmen beat him, and sent *him* away empty. And again he sent another servant: and they beat him also, and entreated *him* shamefully, and sent *him* away empty. And again he sent a third: and they wounded him also, and cast *him* out.

Then said the lord of the vineyard, What shall I do? I will send my beloved son: it may be they will reverence *him* when they see him.

But when the husbandmen saw him, they reasoned among themselves, saying, This is the heir: come, let us kill him, that the inheritance may be ours. So they cast him out of the vineyard, and killed *him*.

What therefore shall the lord of the vineyard do unto them? He shall come and destroy these husbandmen, and shall give the vineyard to others.

And when they heard *it*, they said, God forbid.

And he beheld them, and said, What is this then that is written,

The stone which the builders rejected,
　the same is become the head of the corner?

Whosoever shall fall upon that stone shall be broken; but on whomsoever it shall fall, it will grind him to powder.

And the chief priests and the scribes the same hour sought to lay hands on him; and they feared the people: for they perceived that he had spoken this parable against them.

LUKE 20:9-19

***Related texts:*** PSALM 118; MATTHEW 21:33-46; MARK 12:1-12

## *The Last Supper*

Then one of the twelve, called Judas Iscariot, went unto the chief priests, and said *unto them*, What will ye give me, and I will deliver him unto you? And they covenanted with him for thirty pieces of silver. And from that time he sought opportunity to betray him.

Now the first *day* of the *feast of* unleavened bread the disciples came to Jesus, saying unto him, Where wilt thou that we prepare for thee to eat the passover?

And he said, Go into the city to such a man, and say unto him, The Master saith, My time is at hand; I will keep the passover at thy house with my disciples. And the disciples did as Jesus had appointed them; and they made ready the passover.

Now when the even was come, he sat down with the twelve. And as they did eat, he said, Verily I say unto you, that one of you shall betray me.

And they were exceeding sorrowful, and began every one of them to say unto him, Lord, is it I?

And he answered and said, He that dippeth *his* hand with me in the dish, the same shall betray me. The Son of man goeth as it is written of him: but woe unto that man by whom the Son of man is betrayed! It had been good for that man if he had not been born.

Then Judas, which betrayed him, answered and said, Master, is it I?

He said unto him, Thou hast said.

MATTHEW 26:14-25

*Related texts:* PSALM 41:9; PROVERBS 11:13; MARK 14:10-25; LUKE 22:3-23; JOHN 13–17

## Faithless Friends

**THE ONE
MINUTE
BIBLE**

And Jesus saith unto them, All ye shall be offended because of me this night: for it is written,

> I will smite the shepherd,
>     and the sheep shall be scattered.

But after that I am risen, I will go before you into Galilee.

But Peter said unto him, Although all shall be offended, yet *will* not I.

And Jesus saith unto him, Verily I say unto thee, That this day, *even* in this night, before the cock crow twice, thou shalt deny me thrice.

But he spake the more vehemently, If I should die with thee, I will not deny thee in any wise. Likewise also said they all.

And they came to a place which was named Gethsemane: and he saith to his disciples, Sit ye here, while I shall pray. And he taketh with him Peter and James and John, and began to be sore amazed, and to be very heavy; and saith unto them, My soul is exceeding sorrowful unto death: tarry ye here, and watch.

And he went forward a little, and fell on the ground, and prayed that, if it were possible, the hour might pass from him. And he said, Abba, Father, all things *are* possible unto thee; take away this cup from me: nevertheless not what I will, but what thou wilt.

And he cometh, and findeth them sleeping, and saith unto Peter, Simon, sleepest thou? Couldest not thou watch one hour? Watch ye and pray, lest ye enter into temptation. The spirit truly *is* ready, but the flesh *is* weak.

Mark 14:27-38

---

***Related texts:*** Zechariah 13:7; Mark 14:26-42; Luke 22:31-46; John 13:36-38

## Betrayal and Denial

And while he yet spake, behold a multitude, and he that was called Judas, one of the twelve, went before them, and drew near unto Jesus to kiss him. But Jesus said unto him, Judas, betrayest thou the Son of man with a kiss?

Then took they him, and led *him*, and brought him into the high priest's house. And Peter followed afar off. And when they had kindled a fire in the midst of the hall, and were set down together, Peter sat down among them. But a certain maid beheld him as he sat by the fire, and earnestly looked upon him, and said, This man was also with him.

And he denied him, saying, Woman, I know him not.

And after a little while another saw him, and said, Thou art also of them.

And Peter said, Man, I am not.

And about the space of one hour after another confidently affirmed, saying, Of a truth this *fellow* also was with him: for he is a Galilaean.

And Peter said, Man, I know not what thou sayest. And immediately, while he yet spake, the cock crew. And the Lord turned, and looked upon Peter. And Peter remembered the word of the Lord, how he had said unto him, Before the cock crow, thou shalt deny me thrice. And Peter went out, and wept bitterly.

LUKE 22:47-48, 54-62

*Related texts:* PSALM 42; MATTHEW 26:47-56, 69-75; MARK 14:43-53, 66-72; JOHN 18:2-12, 25-27

## Jesus Is Sentenced to Death

**THE ONE
MINUTE
BIBLE**

And the chief priests and all the council sought for witness against Jesus to put him to death; and found none. For many bare false witness against him, but their witness agreed not together.

And there arose certain, and bare false witness against him, saying, We heard him say, I will destroy this temple that is made with hands, and within three days I will build another made without hands. But neither so did their witness agree together.

And the high priest stood up in the midst, and asked Jesus, saying, Answerest thou nothing? What *is it which* these witness against thee? But he held his peace, and answered nothing.

Again the high priest asked him, and said unto him, Art thou the Christ, the Son of the Blessed?

And Jesus said, I am: and ye shall see the Son of man sitting on the right hand of power, and coming in the clouds of heaven.

Then the high priest rent his clothes, and saith, What need we any further witnesses? Ye have heard the blasphemy: what think ye?

And they all condemned him to be guilty of death. And some began to spit on him, and to cover his face, and to buffet him, and to say unto him, Prophesy: and the servants did strike him with the palms of their hands.

Mark 14:55-65

***Related texts:*** Exodus 20:16; Daniel 7:13-14; Matthew 26:59-67; Mark 14:55-65; Luke 23:63-71; John 18:19-24

## *Jesus Is Crucified*

**THE ONE
MINUTE
BIBLE**

And when they were come to the place, which is called Calvary, there they crucified him, and the malefactors, one on the right hand, and the other on the left. Then said Jesus, Father, forgive them; for they know not what they do. And they parted his raiment, and cast lots.

And the people stood beholding. And the rulers also with them derided *him*, saying, He saved others; let him save himself, if he be Christ, the chosen of God.

And one of the malefactors which were hanged railed on him, saying, If thou be Christ, save thyself and us.

But the other answering rebuked him, saying, Dost not thou fear God, seeing thou art in the same condemnation? And we indeed justly; for we receive the due reward of our deeds: but this man hath done nothing amiss.

And he said unto Jesus, Lord, remember me when thou comest into thy kingdom.

And Jesus said unto him, Verily I say unto thee, To day shalt thou be with me in paradise.

And it was about the sixth hour, and there was a darkness over all the earth until the ninth hour. And the sun was darkened, and the veil of the temple was rent in the midst. And when Jesus had cried with a loud voice, he said, Father, into thy hands I commend my spirit: and having said thus, he gave up the ghost.

Now when the centurion saw what was done, he glorified God, saying, Certainly this was a righteous man.

LUKE 23:33-35, 39-47

*Related texts:* PSALM 22; MATTHEW 27; MARK 15; LUKE 23; JOHN 18:28-19:42

## *The Resurrection*

**THE ONE
MINUTE
BIBLE**

The first *day* of the week cometh Mary Magdalene early, when it was yet dark, unto the sepulchre, and seeth the stone taken away from the sepulchre. Then she runneth, and cometh to Simon Peter, and to the other disciple, whom Jesus loved, and saith unto them, They have taken away the Lord out of the sepulchre, and we know not where they have laid him.

Peter therefore went forth, and that other disciple, and came to the sepulchre. So they ran both together: and the other disciple did outrun Peter, and came first to the sepulchre. And he stooping down, *and* looking in, saw the linen clothes lying; yet went he not in. Then cometh Simon Peter following him, and went into the sepulchre, and seeth the linen clothes lie, and the napkin, that was about his head, not lying with the linen clothes, but wrapped together in a place by itself. Then went in also that other disciple, which came first to the sepulchre, and he saw, and believed. For as yet they knew not the scripture, that he must rise again from the dead.

Then the same day at evening, being the first *day* of the week, when the doors were shut where the disciples were assembled for fear of the Jews, came Jesus and stood in the midst, and saith unto them, Peace *be* unto you. And when he had so said, he showed unto them *his* hands and his side. Then were the disciples glad, when they saw the Lord.

JOHN 20:1-9, 19-20

***Related texts:*** PSALM 16:9-11; ISAIAH 53:9-12; MATTHEW 28; MARK 16; LUKE 24; JOHN 20–21

## *Alive in Christ*

Beware lest any man spoil you through philosophy and vain deceit, after the tradition of men, after the rudiments of the world, and not after Christ.

For in him dwelleth all the fulness of the Godhead bodily. And ye are complete in him, which is the head of all principality and power: in whom also ye are circumcised with the circumcision made without hands, in putting off the body of the sins of the flesh by the circumcision of Christ: buried with him in baptism, wherein also ye are risen with *him* through the faith of the operation of God, who hath raised him from the dead.

And you, being dead in your sins and the uncircumcision of your flesh, hath he quickened together with him, having forgiven you all trespasses; blotting out the handwriting of ordinances that was against us, which was contrary to us, and took it out of the way, nailing it to his cross; *and* having spoiled principalities and powers, he made a show of them openly, triumphing over them in it.

Let no man therefore judge you in meat, or in drink, or in respect of an holyday, or of the new moon, or of the sabbath *days*: which are a shadow of things to come; but the body *is* of Christ.

COLOSSIANS 2:8-17

**THE ONE MINUTE BIBLE**

*Related texts:* ISAIAH 1:11-14; ACTS 2:22-36; ROMANS 6:1-11; 1 CORINTHIANS 15:12-58

# Jesus Returns to the Father

**THE ONE
MINUTE
BIBLE**

The former treatise have I made, O Theophilus, of all that Jesus began both to do and teach, until the day in which he was taken up, after that he through the Holy Ghost had given commandments unto the apostles whom he had chosen: to whom also he showed himself alive after his passion by many infallible proofs, being seen of them forty days, and speaking of the things pertaining to the kingdom of God: and, being assembled together with *them*, commanded them that they should not depart from Jerusalem, but wait for the promise of the Father, which, *saith he*, ye have heard of me. For John truly baptized with water; but ye shall be baptized with the Holy Ghost not many days hence.

When they therefore were come together, they asked of him, saying, Lord, wilt thou at this time restore again the kingdom to Israel?

And he said unto them, It is not for you to know the times or the seasons, which the Father hath put in his own power. But ye shall receive power, after that the Holy Ghost is come upon you: and ye shall be witnesses unto me both in Jerusalem, and in all Judaea, and in Samaria, and unto the uttermost part of the earth.

And when he had spoken these things, while they beheld, he was taken up; and a cloud received him out of their sight.

And while they looked stedfastly toward heaven as he went up, behold, two men stood by them in white apparel; which also said, Ye men of Galilee, why stand ye gazing up into heaven? This same Jesus, which is taken up from you into heaven, shall so come in like manner as ye have seen him go into heaven.

ACTS 1:1-11

*Related texts:* 1 CHRONICLES 16:8, 23-31; PSALMS 67; 72; ISAIAH 45:22-23; 49:6; LUKE 24:50-53

## The Gift of the Holy Spirit

And when the day of Pentecost was fully come, they were all with one accord in one place. And suddenly there came a sound from heaven as of a rushing mighty wind, and it filled all the house where they were sitting. And there appeared unto them cloven tongues like as of fire, and it sat upon each of them. And they were all filled with the Holy Ghost, and began to speak with other tongues, as the Spirit gave them utterance.

And there were dwelling at Jerusalem Jews, devout men, out of every nation under heaven. Now when this was noised abroad, the multitude came together, and were confounded, because that every man heard them speak in his own language. And they were all amazed and marvelled, saying one to another, Behold, are not all these which speak Galilaeans? And how hear we every man in our own tongue, wherein we were born? Parthians, and Medes, and Elamites, and the dwellers in Mesopotamia, and in Judaea, and Cappadocia, in Pontus, and Asia, Phrygia, and Pamphylia, in Egypt, and in the parts of Libya about Cyrene, and strangers of Rome, Jews and proselytes, Cretes and Arabians, we do hear them speak in our tongues the wonderful works of God.

And they were all amazed, and were in doubt, saying one to another, What meaneth this?

Others mocking said, These men are full of new wine.

ACTS 2:1-13

**THE ONE MINUTE BIBLE**

***Related texts:*** LEVITICUS 23:4-16; MATTHEW 3:1-12; JOHN 14:15-26; 15:26-27; 16:12-15

## Peter's First Sermon

**THE ONE
MINUTE
BIBLE**

But Peter, standing up with the eleven, lifted up his voice, and said unto them, Ye men of Judaea, and all *ye* that dwell at Jerusalem, be this known unto you, and hearken to my words: for these are not drunken, as ye suppose, seeing it is *but* the third hour of the day. But this is that which was spoken by the prophet Joel;

And it shall come to pass in the last days, saith God,
I will pour out of my Spirit upon all flesh:
and your sons and your daughters shall prophesy,
and your young men shall see visions,
and your old men shall dream dreams:
and on my servants and on my handmaidens
I will pour out in those days of my Spirit;
and they shall prophesy.
And it shall come to pass, *that* whosoever shall call
on the name of the Lord shall be saved.

Ye men of Israel, hear these words; Jesus of Nazareth, a man approved of God among you by miracles and wonders and signs, which God did by him in the midst of you, as ye yourselves also know: him, being delivered by the determinate counsel and foreknowledge of God, ye have taken, and by wicked hands have crucified and slain: whom God hath raised up, having loosed the pains of death: because it was not possible that he should be holden of it.

Then Peter said unto them, Repent, and be baptized every one of you in the name of Jesus Christ for the remission of sins, and ye shall receive the gift of the Holy Ghost.

ACTS 2:14-18, 21-24, 38

---

*Related texts:* EZEKIEL 36:16-28; 39:21-29; JOEL 2:28-32;
ROMANS 10:1-13

## *Peter Heals a Crippled Beggar*

Now Peter and John went up together into the temple at the hour of prayer, *being* the ninth *hour*. And a certain man lame from his mother's womb was carried, whom they laid daily at the gate of the temple which is called Beautiful, to ask alms of them that entered into the temple; who seeing Peter and John about to go into the temple asked an alms. And Peter, fastening his eyes upon him with John, said, Look on us. And he gave heed unto them, expecting to receive something of them.

Then Peter said, Silver and gold have I none; but such as I have give I thee: in the name of Jesus Christ of Nazareth rise up and walk. And he took him by the right hand, and lifted *him* up: and immediately his feet and ankle bones received strength. And he leaping up stood, and walked, and entered with them into the temple, walking, and leaping, and praising God. And all the people saw him walking and praising God: and they knew that it was he which sat for alms at the Beautiful gate of the temple: and they were filled with wonder and amazement at that which had happened unto him.

And as they spake unto the people, the priests, and the captain of the temple, and the Sadducees, came upon them, being grieved that they taught the people, and preached through Jesus the resurrection from the dead. And they laid hands on them, and put *them* in hold unto the next day: for it was now eventide. Howbeit many of them which heard the word believed; and the number of the men was about five thousand.

ACTS 3:1-10; 4:1-4

*Related texts:* JEREMIAH 37:15; 38:6; MATTHEW 15:29-31; 21:1-16; JOHN 5; 14:12-14

## *Obey God Before People*

**THE ONE
MINUTE
BIBLE**

Now when the rulers, and elders, and scribes saw the boldness of Peter and John, and perceived that they were unlearned and ignorant men, they marvelled; and they took knowledge of them, that they had been with Jesus. And beholding the man which was healed standing with them, they could say nothing against it. But when they had commanded them to go aside out of the council, they conferred among themselves, saying, What shall we do to these men? For that indeed a notable miracle hath been done by them *is* manifest to all them that dwell in Jerusalem; and we cannot deny *it*. But that it spread no further among the people, let us straitly threaten them, that they speak henceforth to no man in this name.

And they called them, and commanded them not to speak at all nor teach in the name of Jesus. But Peter and John answered and said unto them, Whether it be right in the sight of God to hearken unto you more than unto God, judge ye. For we cannot but speak the things which we have seen and heard.

So when they had further threatened them, they let them go, finding nothing how they might punish them, because of the people: for all *men* glorified God for that which was done. For the man was above forty years old, on whom this miracle of healing was showed.

And being let go, they went to their own company, and reported all that the chief priests and elders had said unto them.

Acts 4:13-23

*Related texts:* Jeremiah 20:9; Matthew 5:10-12; Acts 5:17-42

## *Stephen Is Martyred for His Testimony*

And the word of God increased; and the number of the disciples multiplied in Jerusalem greatly; and a great company of the priests were obedient to the faith.

And Stephen, full of faith and power, did great wonders and miracles among the people. Then there arose certain of the synagogue, which is called *the* synagogue of the Libertines, and Cyrenians, and Alexandrians, and of them of Cilicia and of Asia, disputing with Stephen. And they were not able to resist the wisdom and the spirit by which he spake.

Then they suborned men, which said, We have heard him speak blasphemous words against Moses, and *against* God.

And they stirred up the people, and the elders, and the scribes, and came upon *him*, and caught him, and brought *him* to the council.

But Stephen, being full of the Holy Ghost, looked up stedfastly into heaven, and saw the glory of God, and Jesus standing on the right hand of God, and said, Behold, I see the heavens opened, and the Son of man standing on the right hand of God.

Then they cried out with a loud voice, and stopped their ears, and ran upon him with one accord, and cast *him* out of the city, and stoned *him*: and the witnesses laid down their clothes at a young man's feet, whose name was Saul.

And they stoned Stephen, calling upon *God*, and saying, Lord Jesus, receive my spirit. And he kneeled down, and cried with a loud voice, Lord, lay not this sin to their charge. And when he had said this, he fell asleep.

And Saul was consenting unto his death.

ACTS 6:7-12; 7:55-8:1a

**THE ONE MINUTE BIBLE**

*Related texts:* LEVITICUS 24:10-16; MARK 13:9-13; JOHN 16:1-4; ACTS 7:1-54; 8:1-4

## Saul Meets Jesus

**THE ONE
MINUTE
BIBLE**

And at that time there was a great persecution against the church which was at Jerusalem; and they were all scattered abroad throughout the regions of Judaea and Samaria, except the apostles. And devout men carried Stephen *to his burial*, and made great lamentation over him. As for Saul, he made havock of the church, entering into every house, and haling men and women committed *them* to prison. Therefore they that were scattered abroad went every where preaching the word.

And Saul, yet breathing out threatenings and slaughter against the disciples of the Lord, went unto the high priest, and desired of him letters to Damascus to the synagogues, that if he found any of this way, whether they were men or women, he might bring them bound unto Jerusalem. And as he journeyed, he came near Damascus: and suddenly there shined round about him a light from heaven: and he fell to the earth, and heard a voice saying unto him, Saul, Saul, why persecutest thou me?

And he said, Who art thou, Lord?

And the Lord said, I am Jesus whom thou persecutest: *it is* hard for thee to kick against the pricks.

And he trembling and astonished said, Lord, what wilt thou have me to do?

And the Lord *said* unto him, Arise, and go into the city, and it shall be told thee what thou must do.

And the men which journeyed with him stood speechless, hearing a voice, but seeing no man. And Saul arose from the earth; and when his eyes were opened, he saw no man: but they led him by the hand, and brought *him* into Damascus. And he was three days without sight, and neither did eat nor drink.

ACTS 8:1b-4; 9:1-9

*Related texts:* DANIEL 8:26-27; LUKE 1:18-20; ACTS 22:1-21; 26:1-29

350

## Saul Begins to Preach About Jesus

And there was a certain disciple at Damascus, named Ananias; and to him said the Lord in a vision, Ananias.

And he said, Behold, I *am here*, Lord.

And the Lord *said* unto him, Arise, and go into the street which is called Straight, and inquire in the house of Judas for *one* called Saul, of Tarsus: for, behold, he prayeth, and hath seen in a vision a man named Ananias coming in, and putting *his* hand on him, that he might receive his sight.

**THE ONE MINUTE BIBLE**

Then Ananias answered, Lord, I have heard by many of this man, how much evil he hath done to thy saints at Jerusalem: and here he hath authority from the chief priests to bind all that call on thy name.

But the Lord said unto him, Go thy way: for he is a chosen vessel unto me, to bear my name before the Gentiles, and kings, and the children of Israel.

And Ananias went his way, and entered into the house; and putting his hands on him said, Brother Saul, the Lord, *even* Jesus, that appeared unto thee in the way as thou camest, hath sent me, that thou mightest receive thy sight, and be filled with the Holy Ghost. And immediately there fell from his eyes as it had been scales: and he received sight forthwith, and arose, and was baptized. And when he had received meat, he was strengthened.

Then was Saul certain days with the disciples which were at Damascus. And straightway he preached Christ in the synagogues, that he is the Son of God.

ACTS 9:10-15, 17-20

---

*Related texts:* GENESIS 20; NUMBERS 12; 1 CORINTHIANS 15:1-11; GALATIANS 1:11-24

## The First Missionary Journey

**THE ONE MINUTE BIBLE**

Now there were in the church that was at Antioch certain prophets and teachers; as Barnabas, and Simeon that was called Niger, and Lucius of Cyrene, and Manaen, which had been brought up with Herod the tetrarch, and Saul. As they ministered to the Lord, and fasted, the Holy Ghost said, Separate me Barnabas and Saul for the work whereunto I have called them. And when they had fasted and prayed, and laid *their* hands on them, they sent *them* away.

So they, being sent forth by the Holy Ghost, departed unto Seleucia; and from thence they sailed to Cyprus. And when they were at Salamis, they preached the word of God in the synagogues of the Jews: and they had also John to *their* minister.

And when they had gone through the isle unto Paphos, they found a certain sorcerer, a false prophet, a Jew, whose name *was* Bar-jesus: which was with the deputy of the country, Sergius Paulus, a prudent man; who called for Barnabas and Saul, and desired to hear the word of God. But Elymas the sorcerer (for so is his name by interpretation) withstood them, seeking to turn away the deputy from the faith. Then Saul, (who also *is called* Paul,) filled with the Holy Ghost, set his eyes on him, and said, O full of all subtlety and all mischief, *thou* child of the devil, *thou* enemy of all righteousness, wilt thou not cease to pervert the right ways of the Lord? And now, behold, the hand of the Lord *is* upon thee, and thou shalt be blind, not seeing the sun for a season.

And immediately there fell on him a mist and a darkness; and he went about seeking some to lead him by the hand. Then the deputy, when he saw what was done, believed, being astonished at the doctrine of the Lord.

ACTS 13:1-12

*Related texts:* NUMBERS 27:22-23; DEUTERONOMY 34:9; MATTHEW 19:13-15; LUKE 4:40; ACTS 6:1-6; 8:5-25; 1 TIMOTHY 4:11-14

# Paul and Barnabas Among the Gentiles

And there sat a certain man at Lystra, impotent in his feet, being a cripple from his mother's womb, who never had walked: the same heard Paul speak: who stedfastly beholding him, and perceiving that he had faith to be healed, said with a loud voice, Stand upright on thy feet. And he leaped and walked.

And there came thither *certain* Jews from Antioch and Iconium, who persuaded the people, and, having stoned Paul, drew *him* out of the city, supposing he had been dead. Howbeit, as the disciples stood round about him, he rose up, and came into the city: and the next day he departed with Barnabas to Derbe.

And when they had preached the gospel to that city, and had taught many, they returned again to Lystra, and *to* Iconium, and Antioch, confirming the souls of the disciples, *and* exhorting them to continue in the faith, and that we must through much tribulation enter into the kingdom of God. And when they had ordained them elders in every church, and had prayed with fasting, they commended them to the Lord, on whom they believed.

And thence they sailed to Antioch, from whence they had been recommended to the grace of God for the work which they fulfilled. And when they were come, and had gathered the church together, they rehearsed all that God had done with them, and how he had opened the door of faith unto the Gentiles. And there they abode long time with the disciples.

ACTS 14:8-10, 19-23, 26-28

**THE ONE MINUTE BIBLE**

---

*Related texts:* EXODUS 17:1-4; NUMBERS 14:1-10; 1 SAMUEL 30:6; JOHN 8:31-59; ACTS 7:52-60; 14:1-7; ROMANS 1:1-17; EPHESIANS 2:11-22

## *In Everything Give Thanks*

Give thanks unto the LORD, call upon his name,
    make known his deeds among the people.
Sing unto him, sing psalms unto him,
    talk ye of all his wondrous works.

**THE ONE
MINUTE
BIBLE**

O come, let us sing unto the LORD:
    let us make a joyful noise to the rock of our salvation.
Let us come before his presence with thanksgiving,
    and make a joyful noise unto him with psalms.

For the LORD *is* a great God,
    and a great King above all gods.
In his hand *are* the deep places of the earth:
    the strength of the hills *is* his also.
The sea *is* his, and he made it:
    and his hands formed the dry *land*.

O come, let us worship and bow down:
    let us kneel before the LORD our maker.
For he *is* our God;
    and we *are* the people of his pasture,
    and the sheep of his hand.

Rejoice evermore. Pray without ceasing. In every thing give thanks: for this is the will of God in Christ Jesus concerning you.

1 CHRONICLES 16:8-9; PSALM 95:1-7a; 1 THESSALONIANS 5:16-18

*Related texts:* NEHEMIAH 12:27-43; PSALMS 77; 135:1-7; 148; LUKE 22:14-19

## *Give Thanks for God's Provision*

O give thanks unto the LORD, for *he is* good:
　for his mercy *endureth* for ever.
Let the redeemed of the LORD say *so*,
　whom he hath redeemed from the hand of the enemy;
and gathered them out of the lands,
　from the east, and from the west, from the north, and
　　from the south.

They wandered in the wilderness in a solitary way;
　they found no city to dwell in.
Hungry and thirsty,
　their soul fainted in them.
Then they cried unto the LORD in their trouble,
　*and he* delivered them out of their distresses.
And he led them forth by the right way,
　that they might go to a city of habitation.
Oh that *men* would praise the LORD *for* his goodness,
　and *for* his wonderful works to the children of men!
For he satisfieth the longing soul,
　and filleth the hungry soul with goodness.

Oh that *men* would praise the LORD *for* his goodness,
　and *for* his wonderful works to the children of men!
And let them sacrifice the sacrifices of thanksgiving,
　and declare his works with rejoicing.

PSALM 107:1-9, 21-22

*Related texts:* 2 CHRONICLES 20:14-26; PSALMS 104; 118; 145;
MATTHEW 6:25-34

## Give Thanks to God Among His People

**THE ONE MINUTE BIBLE**

A Psalm of praise.

Make a joyful noise unto the LORD, all ye lands.
　　Serve the LORD with gladness:
　　come before his presence with singing.
Know ye that the LORD he *is* God:
　　*it is* he *that* hath made us, and not we ourselves;
　　*we* are his people, and the sheep of his pasture.

Enter into his gates with thanksgiving,
　　*and* into his courts with praise:
　　be thankful unto him, *and* bless his name.
For the LORD *is* good; his mercy *is* everlasting;
　　and his truth *endureth* to all generations.

And let the peace of God rule in your hearts, to the which also ye are called in one body; and be ye thankful. Let the word of Christ dwell in you richly in all wisdom; teaching and admonishing one another in psalms and hymns and spiritual songs, singing with grace in your hearts to the Lord. And whatsoever ye do in word or deed, *do* all in the name of the Lord Jesus, giving thanks to God and the Father by him.

PSALM 100; COLOSSIANS 3:15-17

*Related texts:* 2 CHRONICLES 6:41; PSALMS 65; 84; 96; EPHESIANS 5:18-20; 3 JOHN 11

# *Give Thanks to God for His Enduring Love*

O give thanks unto the LORD; for *he is* good:
    for his mercy *endureth* for ever.
O give thanks unto the God of gods:
    for his mercy *endureth* for ever.
O give thanks to the Lord of lords:
    for his mercy *endureth* for ever.

**THE ONE
MINUTE
BIBLE**

We give thanks to God and the Father of our Lord
Jesus Christ, praying always for you, since we heard of
your faith in Christ Jesus, and of the love *which ye have*
to all the saints, for the hope which is laid up for you in
heaven, whereof ye heard before in the word of the
truth of the gospel; which is come unto you, as *it is* in
all the world; and bringeth forth fruit, as *it doth* also in
you, since the day ye heard *of* it, and knew the grace of
God in truth.

I thank my God, making mention of thee always in
my prayers, hearing of thy love and faith, which thou
hast toward the Lord Jesus, and toward all saints; that
the communication of thy faith may become effectual by
the acknowledging of every good thing which is in you
in Christ Jesus. For we have great joy and consolation
in thy love, because the bowels of the saints are
refreshed by thee, brother.

PSALM 136:1-3; COLOSSIANS 1:3-6; PHILEMON 1:4-7

***Related texts:*** 1 CHRONICLES 16:34-36; 2 CHRONICLES 5–7;
PSALMS 118:1-4; 136:4-26; 2 CORINTHIANS 9:10-15

**THE ONE**
**MINUTE**
**BIBLE**

# Receive God's Good Gifts with Thanksgiving

Now the Spirit speaketh expressly, that in the latter times some shall depart from the faith, giving heed to seducing spirits, and doctrines of devils; speaking lies in hypocrisy; having their conscience seared with a hot iron; forbidding to marry, *and commanding to* abstain from meats, which God hath created to be received with thanksgiving of them which believe and know the truth. For every creature of God *is* good, and nothing to be refused, if it be received with thanksgiving: for it is sanctified by the word of God and prayer.

If thou put the brethren in remembrance of these things, thou shalt be a good minister of Jesus Christ, nourished up in the words of faith and of good doctrine, whereunto thou hast attained. But refuse profane and old wives' fables, and exercise thyself *rather* unto godliness. For bodily exercise profiteth little: but godliness is profitable unto all things, having promise of the life that now is, and of that which is to come.

This *is* a faithful saying and worthy of all acceptation. For therefore we both labour and suffer reproach, because we trust in the living God, who is the Saviour of all men, specially of those that believe.

These things command and teach.

1 TIMOTHY 4:1-11

*Related texts:* 1 CHRONICLES 16:4-14; ROMANS 8:18-28; 14; 1 CORINTHIANS 10

## Give Thanks to God in Heaven

And immediately I was in the spirit; and, behold, a throne was set in heaven, and *one* sat on the throne. And he that sat was to look upon like a jasper and a sardine stone: and *there was* a rainbow round about the throne, in sight like unto an emerald. And round about the throne *were* four and twenty seats: and upon the seats I saw four and twenty elders sitting, clothed in white raiment; and they had on their heads crowns of gold. And out of the throne proceeded lightnings and thunderings and voices: and *there were* seven lamps of fire burning before the throne, which are the seven Spirits of God. And before the throne *there was* a sea of glass like unto crystal.

And in the midst of the throne, and round about the throne, *were* four beasts full of eyes before and behind. And they rest not day and night, saying,

> Holy, holy, holy,
> Lord God Almighty,
> which was, and is, and is to come.

And when those beasts give glory and honour and thanks to him that sat on the throne, who liveth for ever and ever, the four and twenty elders fall down before him that sat on the throne, and worship him that liveth for ever and ever, and cast their crowns before the throne, saying,

> Thou art worthy, O Lord,
>     to receive glory and honour and power:
> for thou hast created all things,
>     and for thy pleasure they are
>     and were created.

REVELATION 4:2-6, 8b-11

*Related texts:* EXODUS 24:1-11; ISAIAH 6; PSALMS 103:20-22; 148; MARK 10:17-18

## THE ONE MINUTE BIBLE

# *Let Everything Praise the Lord!*

Praise ye the LORD.

Praise God in his sanctuary:
    praise him in the firmament of his power.
Praise him for his mighty acts:
    praise him according to his excellent greatness.
Praise him with the sound of the trumpet:
    praise him with the psaltery and harp.
Praise him with the timbrel and dance:
    praise him with stringed instruments and organs.
Praise him upon the loud cymbals:
    praise him upon the high sounding cymbals.

Let every thing that hath breath praise the LORD.

Praise ye the LORD.

And be not drunk with wine, wherein is excess; but be filled with the Spirit; speaking to yourselves in psalms and hymns and spiritual songs, singing and making melody in your heart to the Lord; giving thanks always for all things unto God and the Father in the name of our Lord Jesus Christ.

PSALM 150; EPHESIANS 5:18-20

***Related texts:*** EXODUS 15:1-21; 1 CHRONICLES 15–16; COLOSSIANS 3:16-17

## *Jews and Gentiles Are One in Christ*

If ye have heard of the dispensation of the grace of
God which is given me to you-ward: how that by
revelation he made known unto me the mystery; (as I
wrote afore in few words, whereby, when ye read, ye
may understand my knowledge in the mystery of Christ)
which in other ages was not made known unto the sons
of men, as it is now revealed unto his holy apostles and
prophets by the Spirit; that the Gentiles should be
fellowheirs, and of the same body, and partakers of his
promise in Christ by the gospel:

Whereof I was made a minister, according to the gift
of the grace of God given unto me by the effectual
working of his power. Unto me, who am less than the
least of all saints, is this grace given, that I should
preach among the Gentiles the unsearchable riches of
Christ; and to make all *men* see what *is* the fellowship of
the mystery, which from the beginning of the world hath
been hid in God, who created all things by Jesus Christ:
to the intent that now unto the principalities and
powers in heavenly *places* might be known by the
church the manifold wisdom of God, according to the
eternal purpose which he purposed in Christ Jesus our
Lord: in whom we have boldness and access with
confidence by the faith of him.

EPHESIANS 3:2-12

**THE ONE
MINUTE
BIBLE**

***Related texts:*** ISAIAH 49:1-6; ACTS 15; GALATIANS 3:25-29;
EPHESIANS 2:11-22

## *Spiritual Gifts*

**THE ONE
MINUTE
BIBLE**

Now concerning spiritual *gifts*, brethren, I would not have you ignorant. Ye know that ye were Gentiles, carried away unto these dumb idols, even as ye were led. Wherefore I give you to understand, that no man speaking by the Spirit of God calleth Jesus accursed: and *that* no man can say that Jesus is the Lord, but by the Holy Ghost.

Now there are diversities of gifts, but the same Spirit. And there are differences of administrations, but the same Lord. And there are diversities of operations, but it is the same God which worketh all in all.

But the manifestation of the Spirit is given to every man to profit withal. For to one is given by the Spirit the word of wisdom; to another the word of knowledge by the same Spirit; to another faith by the same Spirit; to another the gifts of healing by the same Spirit; to another the working of miracles; to another prophecy; to another discerning of spirits; to another *divers* kinds of tongues; to another the interpretation of tongues: but all these worketh that one and the selfsame Spirit, dividing to every man severally as he will.

For as the body is one, and hath many members, and all the members of that one body, being many, are one body: so also *is* Christ. For by one Spirit are we all baptized into one body, whether *we be* Jews or Gentiles, whether *we be* bond or free; and have been all made to drink into one Spirit.

1 Corinthians 12:1-13

***Related texts:*** Exodus 31:1-6; 35:30–36:2; Romans 12:1-8; 1 Corinthians 13–14; Ephesians 4:1-16; Hebrews 2:1-4; 1 Peter 4:7-11

*I believe that the intention of Holy Writ
was to persuade men of the truths necessary
to salvation; such as neither science nor
other means could render credible, but
only the voice of the Holy Spirit.*
**Galileo (1564-1642)**
ITALIAN ASTRONOMER

*I feel that a comprehensive study of the Bible
is a liberal education for anyone. Nearly all
of the great men of our country have been
well versed in the teachings of the Bible.*
**Franklin D. Roosevelt (1882-1945)**
UNITED STATES PRESIDENT

*I have found in the Bible words for my
inmost thoughts, songs for my joy, utterance
for my hidden griefs and pleading for
my shame and feebleness.*
**Samuel Taylor Coleridge (1772-1834)**
ENGLISH POET

## Future Hope, Future Reward

For we know that if our earthly house of *this* tabernacle were dissolved, we have a building of God, an house not made with hands, eternal in the heavens. For in this we groan, earnestly desiring to be clothed upon with our house which is from heaven: if so be that being clothed we shall not be found naked. For we that are in *this* tabernacle do groan, being burdened: not for that we would be unclothed, but clothed upon, that mortality might be swallowed up of life. Now he that hath wrought us for the selfsame thing *is* God, who also hath given unto us the earnest of the Spirit.

Therefore *we are* always confident, knowing that, whilst we are at home in the body, we are absent from the Lord: (for we walk by faith, not by sight:) we are confident, *I say*, and willing rather to be absent from the body, and to be present with the Lord. Wherefore we labour, that, whether present or absent, we may be accepted of him. For we must all appear before the judgment seat of Christ; that every one may receive the things *done* in *his* body, according to that he hath done, whether *it be* good or bad.

2 Corinthians 5:1-10

*Related texts:* Ecclesiastes 12; John 11:20-27; Romans 14:1-13; Philippians 1:20-26; 1 Corinthians 15:35-54

# Sealed for Salvation

**THE ONE
MINUTE
BIBLE**

Blessed *be* the God and Father of our Lord Jesus Christ, who hath blessed us with all spiritual blessings in heavenly *places* in Christ: according as he hath chosen us in him before the foundation of the world, that we should be holy and without blame before him in love: having predestinated us unto the adoption of children by Jesus Christ to himself, according to the good pleasure of his will, to the praise of the glory of his grace, wherein he hath made us accepted in the beloved.

In whom we have redemption through his blood, the forgiveness of sins, according to the riches of his grace; wherein he hath abounded toward us in all wisdom and prudence; having made known unto us the mystery of his will, according to his good pleasure which he hath purposed in himself: that in the dispensation of the fulness of times he might gather together in one all things in Christ, both which are in heaven, and which are on earth; *even* in him.

In whom also we have obtained an inheritance, being predestinated according to the purpose of him who worketh all things after the counsel of his own will: that we should be to the praise of his glory, who first trusted in Christ. In whom ye also *trusted*, after that ye heard the word of truth, the gospel of your salvation: in whom also after that ye believed, ye were sealed with that holy Spirit of promise, which is the earnest of our inheritance until the redemption of the purchased possession, unto the praise of his glory.

EPHESIANS 1:3-14

---

*Related texts:* PSALM 113; ROMANS 8:29-39; EPHESIANS 2:4-10; REVELATION 3:5; 13:8; 17:8; 20:15

## *Humility and Glory*

If *there be* therefore any consolation in Christ, if any comfort of love, if any fellowship of the Spirit, if any bowels and mercies, fulfil ye my joy, that ye be likeminded, having the same love, *being* of one accord, of one mind. *Let* nothing *be done* through strife or vainglory; but in lowliness of mind let each esteem other better than themselves. Look not every man on his own things, but every man also on the things of others.

Let this mind be in you, which was also in Christ Jesus:

Who, being in the form of God,
thought it not robbery to be equal with God:
but made himself of no reputation,
and took upon him the form of a servant,
and was made in the likeness of men:
and being found in fashion as a man,
he humbled himself,
and became obedient unto death,
even the death of the cross.
Wherefore God also hath highly exalted him,
and given him a name which is above every name:
that at the name of Jesus every knee should bow,
of *things* in heaven, and *things* in earth, and *things*
under the earth;
and *that* every tongue should confess that Jesus
Christ *is* Lord,
to the glory of God the Father.

PHILIPPIANS 2:1-11

**THE ONE MINUTE BIBLE**

---

*Related texts:* ISAIAH 45:22-25; JOHN 13:1-15; ROMANS 14:11-12; 1 CORINTHIANS 15:20-28; PHILIPPIANS 2:19-21; 1 PETER 5:5-6

**THE ONE
MINUTE
BIBLE**

## To Know Christ

If any other man thinketh that he hath whereof he might trust in the flesh, I more: circumcised the eighth day, of the stock of Israel, *of* the tribe of Benjamin, an Hebrew of the Hebrews; as touching the law, a Pharisee; concerning zeal, persecuting the church; touching the righteousness which is in the law, blameless.

But what things were gain to me, those I counted loss for Christ. Yea doubtless, and I count all things *but* loss for the excellency of the knowledge of Christ Jesus my Lord: for whom I have suffered the loss of all things, and do count them *but* dung, that I may win Christ, and be found in him, not having mine own righteousness, which is of the law, but that which is through the faith of Christ, the righteousness which is of God by faith: that I may know him, and the power of his resurrection, and the fellowship of his sufferings, being made conformable unto his death; if by any means I might attain unto the resurrection of the dead.

Not as though I had already attained, either were already perfect: but I follow after, if that I may apprehend that for which also I am apprehended of Christ Jesus. Brethren, I count not myself to have apprehended: but *this* one thing *I do*, forgetting those things which are behind, and reaching forth unto those things which are before, I press toward the mark for the prize of the high calling of God in Christ Jesus.

PHILIPPIANS 3:4b-14

*Related texts:* PSALM 18:30-33; MATTHEW 5:43-48; MARK 8:34-37; ACTS 22:1-21; COLOSSIANS 1:24; HEBREWS 12:1-3

## *The Supremacy of Christ*

Christ is the image of the invisible God, the firstborn of every creature: for by him were all things created, that are in heaven, and that are in earth, visible and invisible, whether *they be* thrones, or dominions, or principalities, or powers: all things were created by him, and for him: and he is before all things, and by him all things consist. And he is the head of the body, the church: who is the beginning, the firstborn from the dead; that in all *things* he might have the preeminence. For it pleased *the Father* that in him should all fulness dwell; and, having made peace through the blood of his cross, by him to reconcile all things unto himself; by him, *I say*, whether *they be* things in earth, or things in heaven.

And you, that were sometime alienated and enemies in *your* mind by wicked works, yet now hath he reconciled in the body of his flesh through death, to present you holy and unblameable and unreproveable in his sight: if ye continue in the faith grounded and settled, and *be* not moved away from the hope of the gospel, which ye have heard, *and* which was preached to every creature which is under heaven; whereof I Paul am made a minister.

THE ONE
MINUTE
BIBLE

COLOSSIANS 1:15-23

*Related texts:* GENESIS 1:26; JOHN 1:1-18; ROMANS 5:9-11; 2 CORINTHIANS 5:17-21; COLOSSIANS 2:9-10; HEBREWS 1:1-3

## Meeting the Lord in the Air

**THE ONE
MINUTE
BIBLE**

But I would not have you to be ignorant, brethren, concerning them which are asleep, that ye sorrow not, even as others which have no hope. For if we believe that Jesus died and rose again, even so them also which sleep in Jesus will God bring with him. For this we say unto you by the word of the Lord, that we which are alive *and* remain unto the coming of the Lord shall not prevent them which are asleep. For the Lord himself shall descend from heaven with a shout, with the voice of the archangel, and with the trump of God: and the dead in Christ shall rise first: then we which are alive *and* remain shall be caught up together with them in the clouds, to meet the Lord in the air: and so shall we ever be with the Lord. Wherefore comfort one another with these words.

But of the times and the seasons, brethren, ye have no need that I write unto you. For yourselves know perfectly that the day of the Lord so cometh as a thief in the night. For when they shall say, Peace and safety; then sudden destruction cometh upon them, as travail upon a woman with child; and they shall not escape.

But ye, brethren, are not in darkness, that that day should overtake you as a thief.

1 THESSALONIANS 4:13-5:4

*Related texts:* DANIEL 12:1-3; MATTHEW 24; 2 PETER 3; REVELATION 3:1-6

## *Work Is Good*

Now we command you, brethren, in the name of our Lord Jesus Christ, that ye withdraw yourselves from every brother that walketh disorderly, and not after the tradition which he received of us. For yourselves know how ye ought to follow us: for we behaved not ourselves disorderly among you; neither did we eat any man's bread for nought; but wrought with labour and travail night and day, that we might not be chargeable to any of you: not because we have not power, but to make ourselves an ensample unto you to follow us. For even when we were with you, this we commanded you, that if any would not work, neither should he eat.

For we hear that there are some which walk among you disorderly, working not at all, but are busybodies. Now them that are such we command and exhort by our Lord Jesus Christ, that with quietness they work, and eat their own bread. But ye, brethren, be not weary in well doing.

And if any man obey not our word by this epistle, note that man, and have no company with him, that he may be ashamed. Yet count *him* not as an enemy, but admonish *him* as a brother.

2 THESSALONIANS 3:6-15

*Related texts:* GENESIS 1:26-30; 2:15; 1 CORINTHIANS 9; 2 CORINTHIANS 12:12-18; 1 THESSALONIANS 2:1-12

**THE ONE
MINUTE
BIBLE**

## Godliness and Contentment

If any man teach otherwise, and consent not to wholesome words, *even* the words of our Lord Jesus Christ, and to the doctrine which is according to godliness; he is proud, knowing nothing, but doting about questions and strifes of words, whereof cometh envy, strife, railings, evil surmisings, perverse disputings of men of corrupt minds, and destitute of the truth, supposing that gain is godliness: from such withdraw thyself.

But godliness with contentment is great gain. For we brought nothing into *this* world, *and it is* certain we can carry nothing out. And having food and raiment let us be therewith content. But they that will be rich fall into temptation and a snare, and *into* many foolish and hurtful lusts, which drown men in destruction and perdition. For the love of money is the root of all evil: which while some coveted after, they have erred from the faith, and pierced themselves through with many sorrows.

Charge them that are rich in this world, that they be not highminded, nor trust in uncertain riches, but in the living God, who giveth us richly all things to enjoy; that they do good, that they be rich in good works, ready to distribute, willing to communicate; laying up in store for themselves a good foundation against the time to come, that they may lay hold on eternal life.

1 TIMOTHY 6:3-10, 17-19

---

*Related texts:* PSALM 112:4; PROVERBS 11:24-26; 14:31; 19:17; 22:9; 28:8; LUKE 12:13-34; 16:1-15; PHILIPPIANS 4:10-14

## *The Profit of the Scriptures*

**THE ONE
MINUTE
BIBLE**

This know also, that in the last days perilous times shall come. For men shall be lovers of their own selves, covetous, boasters, proud, blasphemers, disobedient to parents, unthankful, unholy, without natural affection, trucebreakers, false accusers, incontinent, fierce, despisers of those that are good, traitors, heady, highminded, lovers of pleasures more than lovers of God; having a form of godliness, but denying the power thereof: from such turn away.

But thou hast fully known my doctrine, manner of life, purpose, faith, longsuffering, charity, patience, persecutions, afflictions, which came unto me at Antioch, at Iconium, at Lystra; what persecutions I endured: but out of *them* all the Lord delivered me. Yea, and all that will live godly in Christ Jesus shall suffer persecution. But evil men and seducers shall wax worse and worse, deceiving, and being deceived.

But continue thou in the things which thou hast learned and hast been assured of, knowing of whom thou hast learned *them*; and that from a child thou hast known the holy scriptures, which are able to make thee wise unto salvation through faith which is in Christ Jesus. All scripture *is* given by inspiration of God, and *is* profitable for doctrine, for reproof, for correction, for instruction in righteousness: that the man of God may be perfect, thoroughly furnished unto all good works.

2 Timothy 3:1-5, 10-17

*Related texts:* Isaiah 40:6-8; Matthew 5:10-12; Acts 14;
2 Corinthians 4; 12:1-10; 1 Peter 1:23–2:3

## *Jesus: Our High Priest*

**THE ONE MINUTE BIBLE**

Seeing then that we have a great high priest, that is passed into the heavens, Jesus the Son of God, let us hold fast *our* profession. For we have not an high priest which cannot be touched with the feeling of our infirmities; but was in all points tempted like as *we are*, *yet* without sin. Let us therefore come boldly unto the throne of grace, that we may obtain mercy, and find grace to help in time of need.

Who in the days of his flesh, when he had offered up prayers and supplications with strong crying and tears unto him that was able to save him from death, and was heard in that he feared; though he were a Son, yet learned he obedience by the things which he suffered; and being made perfect, he became the author of eternal salvation unto all them that obey him; called of God an high priest after the order of Melchisedec.

Wherefore in all things it behoved him to be made like unto *his* brethren, that he might be a merciful and faithful high priest in things *pertaining* to God, to make reconciliation for the sins of the people. For in that he himself hath suffered being tempted, he is able to succour them that are tempted.

HEBREWS 4:14-16; 5:7-10; 2:17-18

*Related texts:* GENESIS 14:18-20; PSALM 110; MATTHEW 4:1-11

## *Heroes of Faith: Part 1*

Now faith is the substance of things hoped for, the evidence of things not seen. For by it the elders obtained a good report.

Through faith we understand that the worlds were framed by the word of God, so that things which are seen were not made of things which do appear.

By faith Abel offered unto God a more excellent sacrifice than Cain, by which he obtained witness that he was righteous, God testifying of his gifts: and by it he being dead yet speaketh.

By faith Enoch was translated that he should not see death; and was not found, because God had translated him: for before his translation he had this testimony, that he pleased God. But without faith *it is* impossible to please *him*: for he that cometh to God must believe that he is, and *that* he is a rewarder of them that diligently seek him.

By faith Noah, being warned of God of things not seen as yet, moved with fear, prepared an ark to the saving of his house; by the which he condemned the world, and became heir of the righteousness which is by faith.

By faith Abraham, when he was called to go out into a place which he should after receive for an inheritance, obeyed; and he went out, not knowing whither he went.

HEBREWS 11:1-8

**THE ONE MINUTE BIBLE**

*Related texts:* GENESIS 1; 4:1-16; 5:23-24; 6–8; 12; JUDE 14-15

*December 12*

## Heroes of Faith: Part 2

**THE ONE
MINUTE
BIBLE**

Through faith also Sara herself received strength to conceive seed, and was delivered of a child when she was past age, because she judged him faithful who had promised. Therefore sprang there even of one, and him as good as dead, *so many* as the stars of the sky in multitude, and as the sand which is by the sea shore innumerable.

By faith Abraham, when he was tried, offered up Isaac: and he that had received the promises offered up his only begotten *son*, of whom it was said, That in Isaac shall thy seed be called: accounting that God *was* able to raise *him* up, even from the dead; from whence also he received him in a figure.

By faith Moses, when he was come to years, refused to be called the son of Pharaoh's daughter; choosing rather to suffer affliction with the people of God, than to enjoy the pleasures of sin for a season; esteeming the reproach of Christ greater riches than the treasures in Egypt: for he had respect unto the recompense of the reward. By faith he forsook Egypt, not fearing the wrath of the king: for he endured, as seeing him who is invisible.

And these all, having obtained a good report through faith, received not the promise: God having provided some better thing for us, that they without us should not be made perfect.

HEBREWS 11:11-12, 17-19, 24-27, 39-40

*Related texts:* GENESIS 21–22; EXODUS 2–3; HEBREWS 10:36-39

## *Wisdom in Trials*

My brethren, count it all joy when ye fall into divers temptations; knowing *this*, that the trying of your faith worketh patience. But let patience have *her* perfect work, that ye may be perfect and entire, wanting nothing. If any of you lack wisdom, let him ask of God, that giveth to all *men* liberally, and upbraideth not; and it shall be given him. But let him ask in faith, nothing wavering. For he that wavereth is like a wave of the sea driven with the wind and tossed. For let not that man think that he shall receive any thing of the Lord. A double minded man *is* unstable in all his ways.

Blessed *is* the man that endureth temptation: for when he is tried, he shall receive the crown of life, which the Lord hath promised to them that love him.

Let no man say when he is tempted, I am tempted of God: for God cannot be tempted with evil, neither tempteth he any man: but every man is tempted, when he is drawn away of his own lust, and enticed. Then when lust hath conceived, it bringeth forth sin: and sin, when it is finished, bringeth forth death.

JAMES 1:2-8, 12-15

**THE ONE**
**MINUTE**
**BIBLE**

---

*Related texts:* JOB 1–42; MATTHEW 6:9-13; 21:18-22;
1 CORINTHIANS 10:12-13

## Controlling the Tongue

**THE ONE
MINUTE
BIBLE**

My brethren, be not many masters, knowing that we shall receive the greater condemnation. For in many things we offend all. If any man offend not in word, the same *is* a perfect man, *and* able also to bridle the whole body.

Behold, we put bits in the horses' mouths, that they may obey us; and we turn about their whole body. Behold also the ships, which though *they be* so great, and *are* driven of fierce winds, yet are they turned about with a very small helm, whithersoever the governor listeth. Even so the tongue is a little member, and boasteth great things. Behold, how great a matter a little fire kindleth! And the tongue *is* a fire, a world of iniquity: so is the tongue among our members, that it defileth the whole body, and setteth on fire the course of nature; and it is set on fire of hell.

For every kind of beasts, and of birds, and of serpents, and of things in the sea, is tamed, and hath been tamed of mankind: but the tongue can no man tame; *it is* an unruly evil, full of deadly poison.

Therewith bless we God, even the Father; and therewith curse we men, which are made after the similitude of God. Out of the same mouth proceedeth blessing and cursing. My brethren, these things ought not so to be. Doth a fountain send forth at the same place sweet *water* and bitter? Can the fig tree, my brethren, bear olive berries? Either a vine, figs? So *can* no fountain both yield salt water and fresh.

JAMES 3:1-12

*Related texts:* PSALM 12; PROVERBS 6:16-19; 10:18-21, 31-32; 12:17-19, 22

## The Promise of Salvation

Blessed *be* the God and Father of our Lord Jesus Christ, which according to his abundant mercy hath begotten us again unto a lively hope by the resurrection of Jesus Christ from the dead, to an inheritance incorruptible, and undefiled, and that fadeth not away, reserved in heaven for you, who are kept by the power of God through faith unto salvation ready to be revealed in the last time.

Wherein ye greatly rejoice, though now for a season, if need be, ye are in heaviness through manifold temptations: that the trial of your faith, being much more precious than of gold that perisheth, though it be tried with fire, might be found unto praise and honour and glory at the appearing of Jesus Christ: whom having not seen, ye love; in whom, though now ye see *him* not, yet believing, ye rejoice with joy unspeakable and full of glory: receiving the end of your faith, *even* the salvation of *your* souls.

Of which salvation the prophets have inquired and searched diligently, who prophesied of the grace *that should come* unto you: searching what, or what manner of time the Spirit of Christ which was in them did signify, when it testified beforehand the sufferings of Christ, and the glory that should follow. Unto whom it was revealed, that not unto themselves, but unto us they did minister the things, which are now reported unto you by them that have preached the gospel unto you with the Holy Ghost sent down from heaven; which things the angels desire to look into.

1 PETER 1:3-12

*Related texts:* ISAIAH 52:13-53:12; ZECHARIAH 13:7-9; HEBREWS 1–2; JAMES 1

## Living Stones and the Cornerstone

**THE ONE
MINUTE
BIBLE**

Wherefore laying aside all malice, and all guile, and hypocrisies, and envies, and all evil speakings, as newborn babes, desire the sincere milk of the word, that ye may grow thereby: if so be ye have tasted that the Lord *is* gracious.

To whom coming, *as unto* a living stone, disallowed indeed of men, but chosen of God, *and* precious, ye also, as lively stones, are built up a spiritual house, an holy priesthood, to offer up spiritual sacrifices, acceptable to God by Jesus Christ. Wherefore also it is contained in the scripture,

> Behold, I lay in Sion
>     a chief corner stone, elect, precious:
> and he that believeth on him
>     shall not be confounded.

Unto you therefore which believe *he is* precious: but unto them which be disobedient,

> the stone which the builders disallowed,
>     the same is made the head of the corner,

> and a stone of stumbling,
>     and a rock of offence,

*even to them* which stumble at the word, being disobedient: whereunto also they were appointed.

But ye *are* a chosen generation, a royal priesthood, an holy nation, a peculiar people; that ye should show forth the praises of him who hath called you out of darkness into his marvellous light: which in time past *were* not a people, but *are* now the people of God: which had not obtained mercy, but now have obtained mercy.

1 Peter 2:1-10

***Related texts:*** Psalms 34; 118:22-29; Isaiah 28:16-17;
Matthew 16:13-19; Luke 20:9-19; Hebrews 5:11-14

## *The Morning Star*

**THE ONE
MINUTE
BIBLE**

For we have not followed cunningly devised fables, when we made known unto you the power and coming of our Lord Jesus Christ, but were eyewitnesses of his majesty. For he received from God the Father honour and glory, when there came such a voice to him from the excellent glory, This is my beloved Son, in whom I am well pleased. And this voice which came from heaven we heard, when we were with him in the holy mount.

We have also a more sure word of prophecy; whereunto ye do well that ye take heed, as unto a light that shineth in a dark place, until the day dawn, and the day star arise in your hearts: knowing this first, that no prophecy of the scripture is of any private interpretation. For the prophecy came not in old time by the will of man: but holy men of God spake *as they were* moved by the Holy Ghost.

Thy word *is* a lamp unto my feet,
    and a light unto my path.

I Jesus have sent mine angel to testify unto you these things in the churches. I am the root and the offspring of David, *and* the bright and morning star.

2 PETER 1:16-21; PSALM 119:105; REVELATION 22:16

---

*Related texts:* JEREMIAH 26; AMOS 3:1-8; ISAIAH 61; MARK 9:2-9; LUKE 1:1-4

## *Love One Another*

**THE ONE
MINUTE
BIBLE**

My little children, these things write I unto you, that ye sin not. And if any man sin, we have an advocate with the Father, Jesus Christ the righteous: and he is the propitiation for our sins: and not for ours only, but also for *the sins of* the whole world.

And hereby we do know that we know him, if we keep his commandments. He that saith, I know him, and keepeth not his commandments, is a liar, and the truth is not in him. But whoso keepeth his word, in him verily is the love of God perfected: hereby know we that we are in him. He that saith he abideth in him ought himself also so to walk, even as he walked.

Brethren, I write no new commandment unto you, but an old commandment which ye had from the beginning. The old commandment is the word which ye have heard from the beginning. Again, a new commandment I write unto you, which thing is true in him and in you: because the darkness is past, and the true light now shineth.

[Jesus said,] A new commandment I give unto you, That ye love one another; as I have loved you, that ye also love one another. By this shall all *men* know that ye are my disciples, if ye have love one to another.

1 John 2:1-8; John 13:34-35

---

***Related texts:*** 1 Kings 8:46-51; Psalm 119:9-11; John 14:15; Hebrews 2:17-18; 4:14-16; 7-9; 1 John 3:11-24

## *The Love of the Father*

Love not the world, neither the things *that are* in the world. If any man love the world, the love of the Father is not in him. For all that *is* in the world, the lust of the flesh, and the lust of the eyes, and the pride of life, is not of the Father, but is of the world. And the world passeth away, and the lust thereof: but he that doeth the will of God abideth for ever.

Behold, what manner of love the Father hath bestowed upon us, that we should be called the sons of God: therefore the world knoweth us not, because it knew him not.

Whosoever believeth that Jesus is the Christ is born of God: and every one that loveth him that begat loveth him also that is begotten of him. By this we know that we love the children of God, when we love God, and keep his commandments. For this is the love of God, that we keep his commandments: and his commandments are not grievous. For whatsoever is born of God overcometh the world: and this is the victory that overcometh the world, *even* our faith. Who is he that overcometh the world, but he that believeth that Jesus is the Son of God?

1 John 2:15-17; 3:1; 5:1-5

***Related texts:*** Deuteronomy 30:11-16; John 15:17-25; 1 John 4:7-21

## *Antichrists*

**THE ONE
MINUTE
BIBLE**

Little children, it is the last time: and as ye have heard that antichrist shall come, even now are there many antichrists; whereby we know that it is the last time. They went out from us, but they were not of us; for if they had been of us, they would *no doubt* have continued with us: but *they went out*, that they might be made manifest that they were not all of us.

But ye have an unction from the Holy One, and ye know all things. I have not written unto you because ye know not the truth, but because ye know it, and that no lie is of the truth. Who is a liar but he that denieth that Jesus is the Christ? He is antichrist, that denieth the Father and the Son. Whosoever denieth the Son, the same hath not the Father: *[but] he that acknowledgeth the Son hath the Father also.*

For many deceivers are entered into the world, who confess not that Jesus Christ is come in the flesh. This is a deceiver and an antichrist. Look to yourselves, that we lose not those things which we have wrought, but that we receive a full reward. Whosoever transgresseth, and abideth not in the doctrine of Christ, hath not God. He that abideth in the doctrine of Christ, he hath both the Father and the Son. If there come any unto you, and bring not this doctrine, receive him not into *your* house, neither bid him God speed: for he that biddeth him God speed is partaker of his evil deeds.

1 JOHN 2:18-23; 2 JOHN 7-11

*Related texts:* PROVERBS 13:5; ISAIAH 44:24-25; JEREMIAH 14:14-15; 2 TIMOTHY 3; 2 PETER 2-3

## *The Salvation We Share*

Beloved, when I gave all diligence to write unto you of the common salvation, it was needful for me to write unto you, and exhort *you* that ye should earnestly contend for the faith which was once delivered unto the saints. For there are certain men crept in unawares, who were before of old ordained to this condemnation, ungodly men, turning the grace of our God into lasciviousness, and denying the only Lord God, and our Lord Jesus Christ.

But, beloved, remember ye the words which were spoken before of the apostles of our Lord Jesus Christ; how that they told you there should be mockers in the last time, who should walk after their own ungodly lusts. These be they who separate themselves, sensual, having not the Spirit.

But ye, beloved, building up yourselves on your most holy faith, praying in the Holy Ghost, keep yourselves in the love of God, looking for the mercy of our Lord Jesus Christ unto eternal life.

And of some have compassion, making a difference: and others save with fear, pulling *them* out of the fire; hating even the garment spotted by the flesh.

Now unto him that is able to keep you from falling, and to present *you* faultless before the presence of his glory with exceeding joy, to the only wise God our Saviour, *be* glory and majesty, dominion and power, both now and ever. Amen.

JUDE 3-4, 17-25

*Related texts:* AMOS 4:11; ZECHARIAH 3; ACTS 20:28-31; 2 PETER 3; 1 TIMOTHY 4:1-6

## The Lord's Anointed King

**THE ONE
MINUTE
BIBLE**

Why do the heathen rage,
  and the people imagine a vain thing?
The kings of the earth set themselves,
  and the rulers take counsel together,
against the Lord,
  and against his anointed, *saying*,
Let us break their bands asunder,
  and cast away their cords from us.

He that sitteth in the heavens shall laugh:
  the Lord shall have them in derision.
Then shall he speak unto them in his wrath,
  and vex them in his sore displeasure.
Yet have I set my king
  upon my holy hill of Zion.

I will declare the decree: the Lord hath said unto me,

Thou *art* my Son;
  this day have I begotten thee.
Ask of me,
  and I shall give *thee* the heathen *for* thine inheritance,
  and the uttermost parts of the earth *for* thy possession.
Thou shalt break them with a rod of iron;
  thou shalt dash them in pieces like a potter's vessel.

Be wise now therefore, O ye kings:
  be instructed, ye judges of the earth.
Serve the Lord with fear,
  and rejoice with trembling.
Kiss the Son, lest he be angry,
  and ye perish *from* the way,
when his wrath is kindled but a little.
  Blessed *are* all they that put their trust in him.

Psalm 2

---

***Related texts:*** 2 Samuel 7; 1 Chronicles 17; Mark 1:1-11;
Revelation 2:18-29

## David's Son and Lord

A Psalm of David.

The L<small>ORD</small> said unto my Lord,
 Sit thou at my right hand,
until I make thine enemies
 thy footstool.
The L<small>ORD</small> shall send the rod of thy strength out of Zion:
 rule thou in the midst of thine enemies.
Thy people *shall be* willing
 in the day of thy power,
in the beauties of holiness
 from the womb of the morning:
 thou hast the dew of thy youth.
The L<small>ORD</small> hath sworn,
 and will not repent,
Thou *art* a priest for ever
 after the order of Melchizedek.
The Lord at thy right hand
 shall strike through kings in the day of his wrath.
He shall judge among the heathen,
 he shall fill *the places* with the dead bodies;
 he shall wound the heads over many countries.
He shall drink of the brook in the way:
 therefore shall he lift up the head.

And they truly were many priests, because they were
not suffered to continue by reason of death: but this
*man*, because he continueth ever, hath an
unchangeable priesthood. Wherefore he is able also to
save them to the uttermost that come unto God by him,
seeing he ever liveth to make intercession for them.

For such an high priest became us, *who is* holy,
harmless, undefiled, separate from sinners, and made
higher than the heavens.

P<small>SALM</small> 110; H<small>EBREWS</small> 7:23-26

---

***Related texts:*** G<small>ENESIS</small> 14:18-20; M<small>ATTHEW</small> 22:41-46;
H<small>EBREWS</small> 5:1-10; 7

# Christ Is Born

**THE ONE MINUTE BIBLE**

And Joseph also went up from Galilee, out of the city of Nazareth, into Judaea, unto the city of David, which is called Bethlehem; (because he was of the house and lineage of David:) to be taxed with Mary his espoused wife, being great with child. And so it was, that, while they were there, the days were accomplished that she should be delivered. And she brought forth her firstborn son, and wrapped him in swaddling clothes, and laid him in a manger; because there was no room for them in the inn.

And there were in the same country shepherds abiding in the field, keeping watch over their flock by night. And, lo, the angel of the Lord came upon them, and the glory of the Lord shone round about them: and they were sore afraid. And the angel said unto them, Fear not: for, behold, I bring you good tidings of great joy, which shall be to all people. For unto you is born this day in the city of David a Saviour, which is Christ the Lord. And this *shall be* a sign unto you; ye shall find the babe wrapped in swaddling clothes, lying in a manger.

And suddenly there was with the angel a multitude of the heavenly host praising God, and saying,

Glory to God in the highest,
   and on earth peace, good will toward men.

LUKE 2:4-14

---

*Related texts:* 2 SAMUEL 7:8-17; PSALM 89:20-37; ISAIAH 9:6-7; MATTHEW 1:18-25; LUKE 1-2

## *The Gifts of the Magi*

Now when Jesus was born in Bethlehem of Judaea in the days of Herod the king, behold, there came wise men from the east to Jerusalem, saying, Where is he that is born King of the Jews? For we have seen his star in the east, and are come to worship him.

When Herod the king had heard *these things*, he was troubled, and all Jerusalem with him. And when he had gathered all the chief priests and scribes of the people together, he demanded of them where Christ should be born. And they said unto him, In Bethlehem of Judaea: for thus it is written by the prophet,

And thou Bethlehem, *in* the land of Juda,
     art not the least among the princes of Juda:
for out of thee shall come a Governor,
     that shall rule my people Israel.

Then Herod, when he had privily called the wise men, inquired of them diligently what time the star appeared. And he sent them to Bethlehem, and said, Go and search diligently for the young child; and when ye have found *him*, bring me word again, that I may come and worship him also.

When they had heard the king, they departed; and, lo, the star, which they saw in the east, went before them, till it came and stood over where the young child was. When they saw the star, they rejoiced with exceeding great joy. And when they were come into the house, they saw the young child with Mary his mother, and fell down, and worshipped him: and when they had opened their treasures, they presented unto him gifts; gold, and frankincense, and myrrh. And being warned of God in a dream that they should not return to Herod, they departed into their own country another way.

MATTHEW 2:1-12

***Related texts:*** EXODUS 30:22-33; MICAH 5:2-5; MARK 15:16-24;
LUKE 1–2; JOHN 12:1-7; HEBREWS 13:15-21

# New Heavens and a New Earth

**THE ONE
MINUTE
BIBLE**

For, behold, I create
    new heavens and a new earth:
and the former shall not be remembered,
    nor come into mind.
But be ye glad and rejoice for ever
    *in that* which I create:
for, behold, I create Jerusalem a rejoicing,
    and her people a joy.
And I will rejoice in Jerusalem,
    and joy in my people:
and the voice of weeping shall be no more heard in her,
    nor the voice of crying.

There shall be no more thence
    an infant of days,
    nor an old man that hath not filled his days:
for the child shall die
    an hundred years old;
but the sinner *being* an hundred years old
    shall be accursed.
They shall not labour in vain,
    nor bring forth for trouble;
for they *are* the seed of the blessed of the LORD,
    and their offspring with them.
And it shall come to pass, that before they call,
    I will answer;
    and while they are yet speaking, I will hear.
The wolf and the lamb shall feed together,
    and the lion shall eat straw like the bullock:
    and dust *shall be* the serpent's meat.
They shall not hurt nor destroy
    in all my holy mountain,
                saith the LORD.

ISAIAH 65:17-20, 23-25

***Related texts:*** GENESIS 3:1-14; ISAIAH 66:22-24; 2 PETER 3:1-14; REVELATION 21:1-5

# Ezekiel Sees the Glory Return to Jerusalem

Afterward he brought me to the gate, *even* the gate that looketh toward the east: and, behold, the glory of the God of Israel came from the way of the east: and his voice *was* like a noise of many waters: and the earth shined with his glory. And *it was* according to the appearance of the vision which I saw, *even* according to the vision that I saw when I came to destroy the city: and the visions *were* like the vision that I saw by the river Chebar; and I fell upon my face. And the glory of the LORD came into the house by the way of the gate whose prospect *is* toward the east. So the spirit took me up, and brought me into the inner court; and, behold, the glory of the LORD filled the house.

And I heard *him* speaking unto me out of the house; and the man stood by me. And he said unto me, Son of man, the place of my throne, and the place of the soles of my feet, where I will dwell in the midst of the children of Israel for ever, and my holy name, shall the house of Israel no more defile, *neither* they, nor their kings, by their whoredom, nor by the carcases of their kings in their high places. In their setting of their threshold by my thresholds, and their post by my posts, and the wall between me and them, they have even defiled my holy name by their abominations that they have committed: wherefore I have consumed them in mine anger. Now let them put away their whoredom, and the carcases of their kings, far from me, and I will dwell in the midst of them for ever.

EZEKIEL 43:1-9

*Related texts:* EZEKIEL 1; 3; 8–11; ZECHARIAH 14; REVELATION 21:1-4

## His Face Was Like the Sun

**THE ONE
MINUTE
BIBLE**

I John, who also am your brother, and companion in tribulation, and in the kingdom and patience of Jesus Christ, was in the isle that is called Patmos, for the word of God, and for the testimony of Jesus Christ. I was in the Spirit on the Lord's day, and heard behind me a great voice, as of a trumpet, saying, I am Alpha and Omega, the first and the last: and, What thou seest, write in a book, and send *it* unto the seven churches which are in Asia; unto Ephesus, and unto Smyrna, and unto Pergamos, and unto Thyatira, and unto Sardis, and unto Philadelphia, and unto Laodicea.

And I turned to see the voice that spake with me. And being turned, I saw seven golden candlesticks; and in the midst of the seven candlesticks *one* like unto the Son of man, clothed with a garment down to the foot, and girt about the paps with a golden girdle. His head and *his* hairs *were* white like wool, as white as snow; and his eyes *were* as a flame of fire; and his feet like unto fine brass, as if they burned in a furnace; and his voice as the sound of many waters. And he had in his right hand seven stars: and out of his mouth went a sharp twoedged sword: and his countenance *was* as the sun shineth in his strength.

And when I saw him, I fell at his feet as dead. And he laid his right hand upon me, saying unto me, Fear not; I am the first and the last: *I am* he that liveth, and was dead; and, behold, I am alive for evermore, Amen; and have the keys of hell and of death.

Write the things which thou hast seen, and the things which are, and the things which shall be hereafter.

REVELATION 1:9-19

*Related texts:* PSALM 149; DANIEL 7; 2 TIMOTHY 3; HEBREWS 4:12-13; REVELATION 2–11; 19:11-21

## The Saints and the Serpent

And I saw an angel come down from heaven, having the key of the bottomless pit and a great chain in his hand. And he laid hold on the dragon, that old serpent, which is the Devil, and Satan, and bound him a thousand years, and cast him into the bottomless pit, and shut him up, and set a seal upon him, that he should deceive the nations no more, till the thousand years should be fulfilled: and after that he must be loosed a little season.

And I saw thrones, and they sat upon them, and judgment was given unto them: and *I saw* the souls of them that were beheaded for the witness of Jesus, and for the word of God, and which had not worshipped the beast, neither his image, neither had received *his* mark upon their foreheads, or in their hands; and they lived and reigned with Christ a thousand years. But the rest of the dead lived not again until the thousand years were finished. This *is* the first resurrection. Blessed and holy *is* he that hath part in the first resurrection: on such the second death hath no power, but they shall be priests of God and of Christ, and shall reign with him a thousand years.

And when the thousand years are expired, Satan shall be loosed out of his prison, and shall go out to deceive the nations which are in the four quarters of the earth, Gog and Magog, to gather them together to battle: the number of whom *is* as the sand of the sea. And they went up on the breadth of the earth, and compassed the camp of the saints about, and the beloved city: and fire came down from God out of heaven, and devoured them. And the devil that deceived them was cast into the lake of fire and brimstone, where the beast and the false prophet *are*, and shall be tormented day and night for ever and ever.

REVELATION 20:1-10

*Related texts:* GENESIS 3:1-15; EZEKIEL 38–39; 1 CORINTHIANS 6:1-3; REVELATION 12-13; 17-19

*December 30*

## Judgment Day

**THE ONE
MINUTE
BIBLE**

And I saw a great white throne, and him that sat on it, from whose face the earth and the heaven fled away; and there was found no place for them. And I saw the dead, small and great, stand before God; and the books were opened: and another book was opened, which is *the book* of life: and the dead were judged out of those things which were written in the books, according to their works. And the sea gave up the dead which were in it; and death and hell delivered up the dead which were in them: and they were judged every man according to their works. And death and hell were cast into the lake of fire. This is the second death. And whosoever was not found written in the book of life was cast into the lake of fire.

And I saw a new heaven and a new earth: for the first heaven and the first earth were passed away; and there was no more sea. And I John saw the holy city, new Jerusalem, coming down from God out of heaven, prepared as a bride adorned for her husband. And I heard a great voice out of heaven saying, Behold, the tabernacle of God *is* with men, and he will dwell with them, and they shall be his people, and God himself shall be with them, *and be* their God. And God shall wipe away all tears from their eyes; and there shall be no more death, neither sorrow, nor crying, neither shall there be any more pain: for the former things are passed away.

Revelation 20:11-21:4

---

*Related texts:* Isaiah 65:17-25; 66:22-24; Daniel 12:1-3; John 1:14-18; 2 Peter 3:1-14

394

## *Jesus Is Coming Soon!*

Behold, I come quickly: blessed *is* he that keepeth the sayings of the prophecy of this book.

And, behold, I come quickly; and my reward *is* with me, to give every man according as his work shall be. I am Alpha and Omega, the beginning and the end, the first and the last.

Blessed *are* they that do his commandments, that they may have right to the tree of life, and may enter in through the gates into the city. For without *are* dogs, and sorcerers, and whoremongers, and murderers, and idolaters, and whosoever loveth and maketh a lie.

I Jesus have sent mine angel to testify unto you these things in the churches. I am the root and the offspring of David, *and* the bright and morning star.

And the Spirit and the bride say, Come. And let him that heareth say, Come. And let him that is athirst come. And whosoever will, let him take the water of life freely.

He which testifieth these things saith, Surely I come quickly.

Amen. Even so, come, Lord Jesus.

The grace of our Lord Jesus Christ *be* with you all. Amen.

REVELATION 22:7, 12-17, 20-21

**THE ONE
MINUTE
BIBLE**

---

*Related texts:* PSALMS 1; 37; MATTHEW 16:24-27; LUKE 12:35-40;
1 THESSALONIANS 4:13-5:11; REVELATION 1:1-3

# Daily Bible Reading Plan - I

| Day | Date | AM | PM | Day | Date | AM | PM |
|-----|------|------|------|-----|------|------|------|
| 1 | Jan 1 | Ge 1-2 | Mt 1 | 61 | Mar 1 | Nu 26-27 | Mk 8:22-38 |
| 2 | Jan 2 | Ge 3-5 | Mt 2 | 62 | Mar 2 | Nu 28-29 | Mk 9:1-29 |
| 3 | Jan 3 | Ge 6-8 | Mt 3 | 63 | Mar 3 | Nu 30-31 | Mk 9:30-50 |
| 4 | Jan 4 | Ge 9-11 | Mt 4 | 64 | Mar 4 | Nu 32-33 | Mk 10:1-31 |
| 5 | Jan 5 | Ge 12-14 | Mt 5:1-26 | 65 | Mar 5 | Nu 34-36 | Mk 10:32-52 |
| 6 | Jan 6 | Ge 15-17 | Mt 5:27-48 | 66 | Mar 6 | Dt 1-2 | Mk 11:1-19 |
| 7 | Jan 7 | Ge 18-19 | Mt 6 | 67 | Mar 7 | Dt 3-4 | Mk 11:20-33 |
| 8 | Jan 8 | Ge 20-22 | Mt 7 | 68 | Mar 8 | Dt 5-7 | Mk 12:1-27 |
| 9 | Jan 9 | Ge 23-24 | Mt 8 | 69 | Mar 9 | Dt 8-10 | Mk 12:28-44 |
| 10 | Jan 10 | Ge 25-26 | Mt 9:1-17 | 70 | Mar 10 | Dt 11-13 | Mk 13:1-13 |
| 11 | Jan 11 | Ge 27-28 | Mt 9:18-38 | 71 | Mar 11 | Dt 14-16 | Mk 13:14-37 |
| 12 | Jan 12 | Ge 29-30 | Mt 10:1-23 | 72 | Mar 12 | Dt 17-19 | Mk 14:1-25 |
| 13 | Jan 13 | Ge 31-32 | Mt 10:24-42 | 73 | Mar 13 | Dt 20-22 | Mk 14:26-50 |
| 14 | Jan 14 | Ge 33-35 | Mt 11 | 74 | Mar 14 | Dt 23-25 | Mk 14:51-72 |
| 15 | Jan 15 | Ge 36-37 | Mt 12:1-21 | 75 | Mar 15 | Dt 26-27 | Mk 15:1-26 |
| 16 | Jan 16 | Ge 38-40 | Mt 12:22-50 | 76 | Mar 16 | Dt 28 | Mk 15:27-47 |
| 17 | Jan 17 | Ge 41 | Mt 13:1-32 | 77 | Mar 17 | Dt 29-30 | Mk 16 |
| 18 | Jan 18 | Ge 42-43 | Mt 13:33-58 | 78 | Mar 18 | Dt 31-32 | Lk 1:1-23 |
| 19 | Jan 19 | Ge 44-45 | Mt 14:1-21 | 79 | Mar 19 | Dt 33-34 | Lk 1:24-56 |
| 20 | Jan 20 | Ge 46-48 | Mt 14:22-36 | 80 | Mar 20 | Jos 1-3 | Lk 1:57-80 |
| 21 | Jan 21 | Ge 49-50 | Mt 15:1-20 | 81 | Mar 21 | Jos 4-6 | Lk 2:1-24 |
| 22 | Jan 22 | Ex 1-3 | Mt 15:21-39 | 82 | Mar 22 | Jos 7-8 | Lk 2:25-52 |
| 23 | Jan 23 | Ex 4-6 | Mt 16 | 83 | Mar 23 | Jos 9-10 | Lk 3 |
| 24 | Jan 24 | Ex 7-8 | Mt 17 | 84 | Mar 24 | Jos 11-13 | Lk 4:1-32 |
| 25 | Jan 25 | Ex 9-10 | Mt 18:1-20 | 85 | Mar 25 | Jos 14-15 | Lk 4:33-44 |
| 26 | Jan 26 | Ex 11-12 | Mt 18:21-35 | 86 | Mar 26 | Jos 16-18 | Lk 5:1-16 |
| 27 | Jan 27 | Ex 13-15 | Mt 19:1-15 | 87 | Mar 27 | Jos 19-20 | Lk 5:17-39 |
| 28 | Jan 28 | Ex 16-18 | Mt 19:16-30 | 88 | Mar 28 | Jos 21-22 | Lk 6:1-26 |
| 29 | Jan 29 | Ex 19-21 | Mt 20:1-16 | 89 | Mar 29 | Jos 23-24 | Lk 6:27-49 |
| 30 | Jan 30 | Ex 22-24 | Mt 20:17-34 | 90 | Mar 30 | Jdg 1-2 | Lk 7:1-30 |
| 31 | Jan 31 | Ex 25-26 | Mt 21:1-22 | 91 | Mar 31 | Jdg 3-5 | Lk 7:31-50 |
| 32 | Feb 1 | Ex 27-28 | Mt 21:23-46 | 92 | Apr 1 | Jdg 6-7 | Lk 8:1-21 |
| 33 | Feb 2 | Ex 29-30 | Mt 22:1-22 | 93 | Apr 2 | Jdg 8-9 | Lk 8:22-56 |
| 34 | Feb 3 | Ex 31-33 | Mt 22:23-46 | 94 | Apr 3 | Jdg 10-11 | Lk 9:1-36 |
| 35 | Feb 4 | Ex 34-36 | Mt 23:1-22 | 95 | Apr 4 | Jdg 12-14 | Lk 9:37-62 |
| 36 | Feb 5 | Ex 37-38 | Mt 23:23-39 | 96 | Apr 5 | Jdg 15-17 | Lk 10:1-24 |
| 37 | Feb 6 | Ex 39-40 | Mt 24:1-22 | 97 | Apr 6 | Jdg 18-19 | Lk 10:25-42 |
| 38 | Feb 7 | Lev 1-3 | Mt 24:23-51 | 98 | Apr 7 | Jdg 20-21 | Lk 11:1-28 |
| 39 | Feb 8 | Lev 4-6 | Mt 25:1-30 | 99 | Apr 8 | Ruth | Lk 11:29-54 |
| 40 | Feb 9 | Lev 7-9 | Mt 25:31-46 | 100 | Apr 9 | 1Sa 1-3 | Lk 12:1-34 |
| 41 | Feb 10 | Lev 10-12 | Mt 26:1-19 | 101 | Apr 10 | 1Sa 4-6 | Lk 12:35-59 |
| 42 | Feb 11 | Lev 13 | Mt 26:20-54 | 102 | Apr 11 | 1Sa 7-9 | Lk 13:1-21 |
| 43 | Feb 12 | Lev 14 | Mt 26:55-75 | 103 | Apr 12 | 1Sa 10-12 | Lk 13:22-35 |
| 44 | Feb 13 | Lev 15-17 | Mt 27:1-31 | 104 | Apr 13 | 1Sa 13-14 | Lk 14:1-24 |
| 45 | Feb 14 | Lev 18-19 | Mt 27:32-66 | 105 | Apr 14 | 1Sa 15-16 | Lk 14:25-35 |
| 46 | Feb 15 | Lev 20-21 | Mt 28 | 106 | Apr 15 | 1Sa 17-18 | Lk 15:1-10 |
| 47 | Feb 16 | Lev 22-23 | Mk 1:1-22 | 107 | Apr 16 | 1Sa 19-21 | Lk 15:11-32 |
| 48 | Feb 17 | Lev 24-25 | Mk 1:23-45 | 108 | Apr 17 | 1Sa 22-24 | Lk 16:1-18 |
| 49 | Feb 18 | Lev 26-27 | Mk 2 | 109 | Apr 18 | 1Sa 25-26 | Lk 16:19-31 |
| 50 | Feb 19 | Nu 1-2 | Mk 3:1-21 | 110 | Apr 19 | 1Sa 27-29 | Lk 17:1-19 |
| 51 | Feb 20 | Nu 3-4 | Mk 3:22-35 | 111 | Apr 20 | 1Sa 30-31 | Lk 17:20-37 |
| 52 | Feb 21 | Nu 5-6 | Mk 4:1-20 | 112 | Apr 21 | 2Sa 1-3 | Lk 18:1-17 |
| 53 | Feb 22 | Nu 7 | Mk 4:21-41 | 113 | Apr 22 | 2Sa 4-6 | Lk 18:18-43 |
| 54 | Feb 23 | Nu 8-10 | Mk 5:1-20 | 114 | Apr 23 | 2Sa 7-9 | Lk 19:1-28 |
| 55 | Feb 24 | Nu 11-13 | Mk 5:21-43 | 115 | Apr 24 | 2Sa 10-12 | Lk 19:29-48 |
| 56 | Feb 25 | Nu 14-15 | Mk 6:1-32 | 116 | Apr 25 | 2Sa 13-14 | Lk 20:1-26 |
| 57 | Feb 26 | Nu 16-17 | Mk 6:33-56 | 117 | Apr 26 | 2Sa 15-16 | Lk 20:27-47 |
| 58 | Feb 27 | Nu 18-20 | Mk 7:1-13 | 118 | Apr 27 | 2Sa 17-18 | Lk 21:1-19 |
| 59 | Feb 28 | Nu 21-22 | Mk 7:14-37 | 119 | Apr 28 | 2Sa 19-20 | Lk 21:20-38 |
| 60 | Feb 29 | Nu 23-25 | Mk 8:1-21 | 120 | Apr 29 | 2Sa 21-22 | Lk 22:1-30 |
| | | | | 121 | Apr 30 | 2Sa 23-24 | Lk 22:31-53 |

# DAILY BIBLE READING PLAN - I

| Day | Date | AM | PM | Day | Date | AM | PM |
|-----|------|-----|-----|-----|------|-----|-----|
| 122 | May 1 | 1Ki 1-2 | Lk 22:54-71 | 183 | Jul 1 | Job 21-22 | Acts 10:1-23 |
| 123 | May 2 | 1Ki 3-5 | Lk 23:1-26 | 184 | Jul 2 | Job 23-25 | Acts 10:24-48 |
| 124 | May 3 | 1Ki 6-7 | Lk 23:27-38 | 185 | Jul 3 | Job 26-28 | Acts 11 |
| 125 | May 4 | 1Ki 8-9 | Lk 23:39-56 | 186 | Jul 4 | Job 29-30 | Acts 12 |
| 126 | May 5 | 1Ki 10-11 | Lk 24:1-35 | 187 | Jul 5 | Job 31-32 | Acts 13:1-23 |
| 127 | May 6 | 1Ki 12-13 | Lk 24:36-53 | 188 | Jul 6 | Job 33-34 | Acts 13:24-52 |
| 128 | May 7 | 1Ki 14-15 | Jn 1:1-28 | 189 | Jul 7 | Job 35-37 | Acts 14 |
| 129 | May 8 | 1Ki 16-18 | Jn 1:29-51 | 190 | Jul 8 | Job 38-39 | Acts 15:1-21 |
| 130 | May 9 | 1Ki 19-20 | Jn 2 | 191 | Jul 9 | Job 40-42 | Acts 15:22-41 |
| 131 | May 10 | 1Ki 21-22 | Jn 3:1-21 | 192 | Jul 10 | Ps 1-3 | Acts 16:1-15 |
| 132 | May 11 | 2Ki 1-3 | Jn 3:22-36 | 193 | Jul 11 | Ps 4-6 | Acts 16:16-40 |
| 133 | May 12 | 2Ki 4-5 | Jn 4:1-30 | 194 | Jul 12 | Ps 7-9 | Acts 17:1-15 |
| 134 | May 13 | 2Ki 6-8 | Jn 4:31-54 | 195 | Jul 13 | Ps 10-12 | Acts 17:16-34 |
| 135 | May 14 | 2Ki 9-11 | Jn 5:1-24 | 196 | Jul 14 | Ps 13-16 | Acts 18 |
| 136 | May 15 | 2Ki 12-14 | Jn 5:25-47 | 197 | Jul 15 | Ps 17-18 | Acts 19:1-20 |
| 137 | May 16 | 2Ki 15-17 | Jn 6:1-21 | 198 | Jul 16 | Ps 19-21 | Acts 19:21-41 |
| 138 | May 17 | 2Ki 18-19 | Jn 6:22-44 | 199 | Jul 17 | Ps 22-24 | Acts 20:1-16 |
| 139 | May 18 | 2Ki 20-22 | Jn 6:45-71 | 200 | Jul 18 | Ps 25-27 | Acts 20:17-38 |
| 140 | May 19 | 2Ki 23-25 | Jn 7:1-31 | 201 | Jul 19 | Ps 28-30 | Acts 21:1-14 |
| 141 | May 20 | 1Ch 1-2 | Jn 7:32-53 | 202 | Jul 20 | Ps 31-33 | Acts 21:15-40 |
| 142 | May 21 | 1Ch 3-5 | Jn 8:1-20 | 203 | Jul 21 | Ps 34-35 | Acts 22 |
| 143 | May 22 | 1Ch 6-7 | Jn 8:21-36 | 204 | Jul 22 | Ps 36-37 | Acts 23:1-11 |
| 144 | May 23 | 1Ch 8-10 | Jn 8:37-59 | 205 | Jul 23 | Ps 38-40 | Acts 23:12-35 |
| 145 | May 24 | 1Ch 11-13 | Jn 9:1-23 | 206 | Jul 24 | Ps 41-43 | Acts 24 |
| 146 | May 25 | 1Ch 14-16 | Jn 9:24-41 | 207 | Jul 25 | Ps 44-46 | Acts 25 |
| 147 | May 26 | 1Ch 17-19 | Jn 10:1-21 | 208 | Jul 26 | Ps 47-49 | Acts 26 |
| 148 | May 27 | 1Ch 20-22 | Jn 10:22-42 | 209 | Jul 27 | Ps 50-52 | Acts 27:1-25 |
| 149 | May 28 | 1Ch 23-25 | Jn 11:1-17 | 210 | Jul 28 | Ps 53-55 | Acts 27:26-44 |
| 150 | May 29 | 1Ch 26-27 | Jn 11:18-46 | 211 | Jul 29 | Ps 56-58 | Acts 28:1-15 |
| 151 | May 30 | 1Ch 28-29 | Jn 11:47-57 | 212 | Jul 30 | Ps 59-61 | Acts 28:16-31 |
| 152 | May 31 | 2Ch 1-3 | Jn 12:1-19 | 213 | Jul 31 | Ps62-64 | Rom 1 |
| | | | | | | | |
| 153 | Jun 1 | 2Ch 4-6 | Jn 12:20-50 | 214 | Aug 1 | Ps65-67 | Rom 2 |
| 154 | Jun 2 | 2Ch 7-9 | Jn 13:1-17 | 215 | Aug 2 | Ps 68-69 | Rom 3 |
| 155 | Jun 3 | 2Ch 10-12 | Jn 13:18-38 | 216 | Aug 3 | Ps70-72 | Rom 4 |
| 156 | Jun 4 | 2Ch 13-16 | Jn 14 | 217 | Aug 4 | Ps73-74 | Rom 5 |
| 157 | Jun 5 | 2Ch 17-19 | Jn 15 | 218 | Aug 5 | Ps75-77 | Rom 6 |
| 158 | Jun 6 | 2Ch 20-22 | Jn 16:1-15 | 219 | Aug 6 | Ps78 | Rom 7 |
| 159 | Jun 7 | 2Ch 23-25 | Jn 16:16-23 | 220 | Aug 7 | Ps79-81 | Rom 8:1-18 |
| 160 | Jun 8 | 2Ch 26-28 | Jn 17 | 221 | Aug 8 | Ps82-84 | Rom 8:19-29 |
| 161 | Jun 9 | 2Ch 29-31 | Jn 18:1-23 | 222 | Aug 9 | Ps 85-87 | Rom 9 |
| 162 | Jun 10 | 2Ch 32-33 | Jn 18:24-40 | 223 | Aug 10 | Ps88-89 | Rom 10 |
| 163 | Jun 11 | 2Ch 34-36 | Jn 19:1-22 | 224 | Aug 11 | Ps90-92 | Rom 11:1-21 |
| 164 | Jun 12 | Ezra 1-2 | Jn 19:23-42 | 225 | Aug 12 | Ps93-95 | Rom 11:22-36 |
| 165 | Jun 13 | Ezra 3-5 | Jn 20 | 226 | Aug 13 | Ps96-98 | Rom 12 |
| 166 | Jun 14 | Ezra 6-8 | Jn 21 | 227 | Aug 14 | Ps99-102 | Rom 13 |
| 167 | Jun 15 | Ezra 9-10 | Acts 1 | 228 | Aug 15 | Ps103-104 | Rom 14 |
| 168 | Jun 16 | Neh 1-3 | Acts 2:1-13 | 229 | Aug 16 | Ps105-106 | Rom 15:1-20 |
| 169 | Jun 17 | Neh 4-6 | Acts 2:14-47 | 230 | Aug 17 | Ps 107-108 | Rom 15:21-33 |
| 170 | Jun 18 | Neh 7-8 | Acts 3 | 231 | Aug 18 | Ps 109-111 | Rom 16 |
| 171 | Jun 19 | Neh 9-11 | Acts 4:1-22 | 232 | Aug 19 | Ps 112-115 | 1 Cor 1 |
| 172 | Jun 20 | Neh 12-13 | Acts 4:23-37 | 233 | Aug 20 | Ps 116-118 | 1 Cor 2 |
| 173 | Jun 21 | Est 1-3 | Acts 5:1-16 | 234 | Aug 21 | Ps 119:1-48 | 1 Cor 3 |
| 174 | Jun 22 | Est 4-6 | Acts 5:17-42 | 235 | Aug 22 | 119:49-104 | 1 Cor 4 |
| 175 | Jun 23 | Est 7-10 | Acts 6 | 236 | Aug 23 | 119:105-176 | 1 Cor 5 |
| 176 | Jun 24 | Job 1-3 | Acts 7:1-19 | 237 | Aug 24 | Ps 120-123 | 1 Cor 6 |
| 177 | Jun 25 | Job 4-6 | Acts 7:20-43 | 238 | Aug 25 | Ps 124-127 | 1 Cor 7:1-24 |
| 178 | Jun 26 | Job 7-9 | Acts 7:44-60 | 239 | Aug 26 | Ps 128-131 | 1 Cor 7:25-40 |
| 179 | Jun 27 | Job 10-12 | Acts 8:1-25 | 240 | Aug 27 | Ps 132-135 | 1 Cor 8 |
| 180 | Jun 28 | Job 13-15 | Acts 8:26-40 | 241 | Aug 28 | Ps 136-138 | 1 Cor 9 |
| 181 | Jun 29 | Job 16-18 | Acts 9:1-22 | 242 | Aug 29 | Ps 139-141 | 1 Cor 10:1-13 |
| 182 | Jun 30 | Job 19-20 | Acts 9:23-43 | 243 | Aug 30 | Ps 142-144 | 1 Cor 10:14-33 |
| | | | | 244 | Aug 31 | Ps 145-147 | 1 Cor 11:1-15 |

# DAILY BIBLE READING PLAN - I

| Day | Date | AM | PM | Day | Date | AM | PM |
|---|---|---|---|---|---|---|---|
| 245 | Sep 1 | Ps 148-150 | 1 Cor 11:16-34 | 306 | Nov 1 | Jer 31-32 | Titus 2 |
| 246 | Sep 2 | Pr 1-2 | 1 Cor 12 | 307 | Nov 2 | Jer 33-35 | Titus 3 |
| 247 | Sep 3 | Pr 3-4 | 1 Cor 13 | 308 | Nov 3 | Jer 36-37 | Philem |
| 248 | Sep 4 | Pr 5-6 | 1 Cor 14:1-20 | 309 | Nov 4 | Jer 38-39 | Heb 1 |
| 249 | Sep 5 | Pr 7-8 | 1 Cor 14:21-40 | 310 | Nov 5 | Jer 40-42 | Heb 2 |
| 250 | Sep 6 | Pr 9-10 | 1 Cor 15:1-32 | 311 | Nov 6 | Jer 43-45 | Heb 3 |
| 251 | Sep 7 | Pr 11-12 | 1 Cor 15:33-58 | 312 | Nov 7 | Jer 46-48 | Heb 4 |
| 252 | Sep 8 | Pr 13-14 | 1 Cor 16 | 313 | Nov 8 | Jer 49-50 | Heb 5 |
| 253 | Sep 9 | Pr 15-16 | 2 Cor 1 | 314 | Nov 9 | Jer 51-52 | Heb 6 |
| 254 | Sep 10 | Pr 17-18 | 2 Cor 2 | 315 | Nov 10 | Lam 1-2 | Heb 7 |
| 255 | Sep 11 | Pr 19-20 | 2 Cor 3 | 316 | Nov 11 | Lam 3-5 | Heb 8 |
| 256 | Sep 12 | Pr 21-22 | 2 Cor 4 | 317 | Nov 12 | Eze 1-3 | Heb 9 |
| 257 | Sep 13 | Pr 23-24 | 2 Cor 5 | 318 | Nov 13 | Eze 4-6 | Heb 10:1-23 |
| 258 | Sep 14 | Pr 25-27 | 2 Cor 6 | 319 | Nov 14 | Eze 7-9 | Heb 10:24-39 |
| 259 | Sep 15 | Pr 28-29 | 2 Cor 7 | 320 | Nov 15 | Eze 10-12 | Heb 11:1-19 |
| 260 | Sep 16 | Pr 30-31 | 2 Cor 8 | 321 | Nov 16 | Eze 13-15 | Heb 11:20-40 |
| 261 | Sep 17 | Ecc 1-3 | 2 Cor 9 | 322 | Nov 17 | Eze 16 | Heb 12 |
| 262 | Sep 18 | Ecc 4-6 | 2 Cor 10 | 323 | Nov 18 | Eze 17-19 | Heb 13 |
| 263 | Sep 19 | Ecc 7-9 | 2 Cor 11:1-15 | 324 | Nov 19 | Eze 20-21 | James 1 |
| 264 | Sep 20 | Ecc 10-12 | 2 Cor 11:16-33 | 325 | Nov 20 | Eze 22-23 | James 2 |
| 265 | Sep 21 | Song 1-3 | 2 Cor 12 | 326 | Nov 21 | Eze 24-26 | James 3 |
| 266 | Sep 22 | Song 4-5 | 2 Cor 13 | 327 | Nov 22 | Eze 27-28 | James 4 |
| 267 | Sep 23 | Song 6-8 | Gal 1 | 328 | Nov 23 | Eze 29-31 | James 5 |
| 268 | Sep 24 | Isa 1-3 | Gal 2 | 329 | Nov 24 | Eze 32-33 | 1 Pet 1 |
| 269 | Sep 25 | Isa 4-6 | Gal 3 | 330 | Nov 25 | Eze 34-35 | 1 Pet 2 |
| 270 | Sep 26 | Isa 7-9 | Gal 4 | 331 | Nov 26 | Eze 36-37 | 1 Pet 3 |
| 271 | Sep 27 | Isa 10-12 | Gal 5 | 332 | Nov 27 | Eze 38-39 | 1 Pet 4 |
| 272 | Sep 28 | Isa 13-15 | Gal 6 | 333 | Nov 28 | Eze 40 | 1 Pet 5 |
| 273 | Sep 29 | Isa 16-18 | Eph 1 | 334 | Nov 29 | Eze 41-42 | 2 Pet 1 |
| 274 | Sep 30 | Isa 19-21 | Eph 2 | 335 | Nov 30 | Eze 43-44 | 2 Pet 2 |
| 275 | Oct 1 | Isa 22-23 | Eph 3 | 336 | Dec 1 | Eze 45-46 | 2 Pet 3 |
| 276 | Oct 2 | Isa 24-26 | Eph 4 | 337 | Dec 2 | Eze 47-48 | 1 John 1 |
| 277 | Oct 3 | Isa 27-28 | Eph 5 | 338 | Dec 3 | Dan 1-2 | 1 John 2 |
| 278 | Oct 4 | Isa 29-30 | Eph 6 | 339 | Dec 4 | Dan 3-4 | 1 John 3 |
| 279 | Oct 5 | Isa 31-33 | Phil 1 | 340 | Dec 5 | Dan 5-6 | 1 John 4 |
| 280 | Oct 6 | Isa 34-36 | Phil 2 | 341 | Dec 6 | Dan 7-8 | 1 John 5 |
| 281 | Oct 7 | Isa 37-38 | Phil 3 | 342 | Dec 7 | Dan 9-10 | 2 John |
| 282 | Oct 8 | Isa 39-40 | Phil 4 | 343 | Dec 8 | Dan 11-12 | 3 John |
| 283 | Oct 9 | Isa 41-42 | Col 1 | 344 | Dec 9 | Hos 1-4 | Jude |
| 284 | Oct 10 | Isa 43-44 | Col 2 | 345 | Dec 10 | Hos 5-8 | Rev 1 |
| 285 | Oct 11 | Isa 45-47 | Col 3 | 346 | Dec 11 | Hos 9-11 | Rev 2 |
| 286 | Oct 12 | Isa 48-49 | Col 4 | 347 | Dec 12 | Hos 12-14 | Rev 3 |
| 287 | Oct 13 | Isa 50-52 | 1 Thess 1 | 348 | Dec 13 | Joel 1-3 | Rev 4 |
| 288 | Oct 14 | Isa 53-55 | 1 Thess 2 | 349 | Dec 14 | Amos 1-3 | Rev 5 |
| 289 | Oct 15 | Isa 56-58 | 1 Thess 3 | 350 | Dec 15 | Amos 4-6 | Rev 6 |
| 290 | Oct 16 | Isa 59-61 | 1 Thess 4 | 351 | Dec 16 | Amos 7-9 | Rev 7 |
| 291 | Oct 17 | Isa 62-64 | 1 Thess 5 | 352 | Dec 17 | Obad | Rev 8 |
| 292 | Oct 18 | Isa 65-66 | 2 Thess 1 | 353 | Dec 18 | Jonah | Rev 9 |
| 293 | Oct 19 | Jer 1-2 | 2 Thess 2 | 354 | Dec 19 | Mic 1-3 | Rev 10 |
| 294 | Oct 20 | Jer 3-4 | 2 Thess 3 | 355 | Dec 20 | Mic 4-5 | Rev 11 |
| 295 | Oct 21 | Jer 5-6 | 1 Tim 1 | 356 | Dec 21 | Mic 6-7 | Rev 12 |
| 296 | Oct 22 | Jer 7-8 | 1 Tim 2 | 357 | Dec 22 | Nah | Rev 13 |
| 297 | Oct 23 | Jer 9-10 | 1 Tim 3 | 358 | Dec 23 | Hab | Rev 14 |
| 298 | Oct 24 | Jer 11-13 | 1 Tim 4 | 359 | Dec 24 | Zeph | Rev 15 |
| 299 | Oct 25 | Jer 14-16 | 1 Tim 5 | 360 | Dec 25 | Hag | Rev 16 |
| 300 | Oct 26 | Jer 17-19 | 1 Tim 6 | 361 | Dec 26 | Zech 1-3 | Rev 17 |
| 301 | Oct 27 | Jer 20-22 | 2 Tim 1 | 362 | Dec 27 | Zech 4-6 | Rev 18 |
| 302 | Oct 28 | Jer 23-24 | 2 Tim 2 | 363 | Dec 28 | Zech 7-9 | Rev 19 |
| 303 | Oct 29 | Jer 25-26 | 2 Tim 3 | 364 | Dec 29 | Zech 10-12 | Rev 20 |
| 304 | Oct 30 | Jer 27-28 | 2 Tim 4 | 365 | Dec 30 | Zech 13-14 | Rev 21 |
| 305 | Oct 31 | Jer 29-30 | Titus 1 | 366 | Dec 31 | Mal | Rev 22 |

# Daily Bible Reading Plan - II

| | | | | | |
|---|---|---|---|---|---|
| Jan 1 | Gen 1-3 | Feb 20 | Lev 13-14 | Apr 10 | 1Sa 4-7 |
| Jan 2 | Gen 4:1–6:8 | Feb 21 | Lev 15-17 | Apr 11 | 1Sa 8-10 |
| Jan 3 | Gen 6:9–9:29 | Feb 22 | Lev 18-20 | Apr 12 | 1Sa 11-13 |
| Jan 4 | Gen 10-11 | Feb 23 | Lev 21-23 | Apr 13 | 1Sa 14-15 |
| Jan 5 | Gen 12-14 | Feb 24 | Lev 24-25 | Apr 14 | 1Sa 16-17 |
| Jan 6 | Gen 15-17 | Feb 25 | Lev 26-27 | Apr 15 | 1Sa 18-19; Ps 59 |
| Jan 7 | Gen 18-19 | Feb 26 | Nu 1-2 | Apr 16 | 1Sa 20-21; |
| Jan 8 | Gen 20-22 | Feb 27 | Nu 3-4 | | Ps 56; 34 |
| Jan 9 | Gen 23-24 | Feb 28 | Nu 5-6 | Apr 17 | 1Sa 22-23; |
| Jan 10 | Gen 25-26 | | | | 1Ch 12:8-18; |
| Jan 11 | Gen 27-28 | Mar 1 | Nu 7 | | Ps 52; 54; 63; 144 |
| Jan 12 | Gen 29-30 | Mar 2 | Nu 8-10 | Apr 18 | 1Sa 24; Ps 57; |
| Jan 13 | Gen 31-32 | Mar 3 | Nu 11-13 | | 1Sa 25 |
| Jan 14 | Gen 33-35 | Mar 4 | Nu 14-15 | Apr 19 | 1Sa 26-29; |
| Jan 15 | Gen 36-37 | Mar 5 | Nu 16-18 | | 1Ch 12:1-7; 19-22 |
| Jan 16 | Gen 38-40 | Mar 6 | Nu 19-21 | Apr 20 | 1Sa 30-31; 1Ch 10; |
| Jan 17 | Gen 41-42 | Mar 7 | Nu 22-24 | | 2Sa 1 |
| Jan 18 | Gen 43-45 | Mar 8 | Nu 25-26 | Apr 21 | 2Sa 2-4 |
| Jan 19 | Gen 46-47 | Mar 9 | Nu 27-29 | Apr 22 | 2Sa 5:1-6:11; |
| Jan 20 | Gen 48-50 | Mar 10 | Nu 30-31 | | 1Ch 11:1-9; 12:23- |
| Jan 21 | Job 1-3 | Mar 11 | Nu 32-33 | | 14:17 |
| Jan 22 | Job 4-7 | Mar 12 | Nu 34-36 | Apr 23 | 2Sa 22; Ps 18 |
| Jan 23 | Job 8-11 | Mar 13 | Dt 1-2 | Apr 24 | 1Ch 15-16; |
| Jan 24 | Job 12-15 | Mar 14 | Dt 3-4 | | 2Sa 6:12-23; Ps 96 |
| Jan 25 | Job 16-19 | Mar 15 | Dt 5-7 | Apr 25 | Ps 105; 2Sa 7; |
| Jan 26 | Job 20-22 | Mar 16 | Dt 8-10 | | 1Ch 17 |
| Jan 27 | Job 23-28 | Mar 17 | Dt 11-13 | Apr 26 | 2Sa 8-10; |
| Jan 28 | Job 29-31 | Mar 18 | Dt 14-17 | | 1Ch 18-19; Ps 60 |
| Jan 29 | Job 32-34 | Mar 19 | Dt 18-21 | Apr 27 | 2Sa 11-12; |
| Jan 30 | Job 35-37 | Mar 20 | Dt 22-25 | | 1Ch 20:1-3; Ps 51 |
| Jan 31 | Job 38-42 | Mar 21 | Dt 26-28 | Apr 28 | 2Sa 13-14 |
| | | Mar 22 | Dt 29:1–31:29 | Apr 29 | 2Sa 15-17 |
| Feb 1 | Ex 1-4 | Mar 23 | Dt 31:30–34:12 | Apr 30 | Ps 3; 2Sa 18-19 |
| Feb 2 | Ex 5-8 | Mar 24 | Jos 1-4 | | |
| Feb 3 | Ex 9-11 | Mar 25 | Jos 5-8 | May 1 | 2Sa 20-21; 23:8-23; |
| Feb 4 | Ex 12-13 | Mar 26 | Jos 9-11 | | 1Ch 20:4-8;11:10-25 |
| Feb 5 | Ex 14-15 | Mar 27 | Jos 12-14 | May 2 | 2Sa 23:24–24:25; |
| Feb 6 | Ex 16-18 | Mar 28 | Jos 15-17 | | 1Ch 11:26-47; |
| Feb 7 | Ex 19-21 | Mar 29 | Jos 18-19 | | 21:1-30 |
| Feb 8 | Ex 22-24 | Mar 30 | Jos 20-22 | May 3 | 1Ch 22-24 |
| Feb 9 | Ex 25-27 | Mar 31 | Jos 23–Jdg 1 | May 4 | Ps 30; 1Ch 25-26 |
| Feb 10 | Ex 28-29 | | | May 5 | 1Ch 27-29 |
| Feb 11 | Ex 30-31 | Apr 1 | Jdg 2-5 | May 6 | Ps 5-7; 10; 11; 13; |
| Feb 12 | Ex 32-34 | Apr 2 | Jdg 6-8 | | 17 |
| Feb 13 | Ex 35-36 | Apr 3 | Jdg 9 | May 7 | Ps 23; 26; 28; 31; |
| Feb 14 | Ex 37-38 | Apr 4 | Jdg 10-12 | | 35 |
| Feb 15 | Ex 39-40 | Apr 5 | Jdg 13-16 | May 8 | Ps 41; 43; 46; 55; |
| Feb 16 | Lev 1:1-5:13 | Apr 6 | Jdg 17-19 | | 61; 62; 64 |
| Feb 17 | Lev 5:14-7:38 | Apr 7 | Jdg 20-21 | May 9 | Ps 69-71; 77 |
| Feb 18 | Lev 8-10 | Apr 8 | Ruth | May 10 | Ps 83; 86; 88; 91; |
| Feb 19 | Lev 11-12 | Apr 9 | 1Sa 1-3 | | 95 |

# Daily Bible Reading Plan - II

| | | | | | |
|---|---|---|---|---|---|
| May 11 | Ps 108; 109; 120; 121; 140; 143; 144 | Jun 12 | Pr 28-29 | Jul 16 | Isa 31-35 |
| May 12 | Ps 1; 14; 15; 36; 37; 39 | Jun 13 | Pr 30-31; Ps 127 | Jul 17 | 2Ki 18:1-8; 2Ch 29-31 |
| May 13 | Ps 40; 49; 50; 73 | Jun 14 | Song of Songs | Jul 18 | 2Ki 17; 18:9-37; 2Ch 32:1-19; Isa 36 |
| May 14 | Ps 76; 82; 84; 90; 92; 112; 115 | Jun 15 | 1Ki 11:1-40; Ecc 1-2 | Jul 19 | 2Ki 19; 2Ch 32:20-23; Isa 37 |
| May 15 | Ps 8; 9; 16; 19; 21; 24; 29 | Jun 16 | Ecc 3-7 | Jul 20 | 2Ki 20; 2Ch 32:24-33; Isa 38-39 |
| May 16 | Ps 33; 65-68 | Jun 17 | Ecc 8-12; 1Ki 11:41-43; 2Ch 9:29-31 | Jul 21 | 2Ki 21:1-18; 2Ch 33:1-20; Is 40 |
| May 17 | Ps 75; 93; 94; 97-100 | | | Jul 22 | Isa 41-43 |
| May 18 | Ps 103; 104; 113; 114; 117 | Jun 18 | 1Ki 12; 2Ch 10:1–11:17 | Jul 23 | Isa 44-47 |
| May 19 | Ps 119:1-88 | Jun 19 | 1Ki 13-14; 2Ch 11:18–12:16 | Jul 24 | Isa 48-51 |
| May 20 | Ps 119:89-176 | Jun 20 | 1Ki 15:1-24; 2Ch 13-16 | Jul 25 | Isa 52-57 |
| May 21 | Ps 122; 124; 133-136 | Jun 21 | 1Ki 15:25–16:34; 2Ch 17; 1Ki 17 | Jul 26 | Isa 58-62 |
| May 22 | Ps 138; 139; 145; 148; 150 | Jun 22 | 1Ki 18-19 | Jul 27 | Isa 63-66 |
| May 23 | Ps 4; 12; 20; 25; 32; 38 | Jun 23 | 1Ki 20-21 | Jul 28 | 2Ki 21:19-26; 2Ch 33:21-34:7; Zephaniah |
| May 24 | Ps 42; 53; 58; 81; 101; 111; 130; 131; 141; 146 | Jun 24 | 1Ki 22:1-40; 2Ch 18 | Jul 29 | Jer 1-3 |
| | | Jun 25 | 1Ki 22:41-53; 2Ki 1; 2Ch 19:1–21:3 | Jul 30 | Jer 4-6 |
| May 25 | Ps 2; 22; 27 | Jun 26 | 2Ki 2-4 | Jul 31 | Jer 7-9 |
| May 26 | Ps 45; 47; 48; 87; 110 | Jun 27 | 2Ki 5-7 | | |
| May 27 | 1Ki 1:1–2:12; 2Sa 23:1-7 | Jun 28 | 2Ki 8-9; 2Ch 21:4–22:9 | Aug 1 | Jer 10-13 |
| | | | | Aug 2 | Jer 14-16 |
| May 28 | 1Ki 2:13–3:28; 2Ch 1:1-13 | Jun 29 | 2Ki 10-11; 2Ch 22:10–23:21 | Aug 3 | Jer 17-20 |
| May 29 | 1Ki 5-6; 2Ch 2-3 | Jun 30 | Joel | Aug 4 | 2Ki 22:1–23:28; 2Ch 34:9–35:19 |
| May 30 | 1Ki 7; 2Ch 4 | | | Aug 5 | Nahum; 2Ki 23:29-37; 2Ch 35:20–36:5; Jer 22:10-17 |
| May 31 | 1Ki 8; 2Ch 5:1-7:10 | Jul 1 | 2Ki 12-13; 2Ch 24 | | |
| | | Jul 2 | 2Ki 14; 2Ch 25; Jonah | | |
| Jun 1 | 1Ki 9:1–10:13; 2Ch 7:11–9:12 | Jul 3 | Hosea 1-7 | Aug 6 | Jer 26; Habakkuk |
| Jun 2 | 1Ki 4; 10:14-29; 2Ch 1:14-17; 9:13-28; Ps 72 | Jul 4 | Hosea 8-14 | Aug 7 | Jer 46; 47; 2Ki 24:1-4 + 7; 2Ch 36:6-7; Jer 25; 35 |
| | | Jul 5 | 2Ki 15:1-7; 2Ch 26; Amos 1-4 | | |
| Jun 3 | Pr 1-3 | Jul 6 | Amos 5-9; 2Ki 15:8-18 | Aug 8 | Jer 36; 45; 48 |
| Jun 4 | Pr 4-6 | | | Aug 9 | Jer 49:1-33; Dan 1-2 |
| Jun 5 | Pr 7-9 | Jul 7 | Isa 1-4 | | |
| Jun 6 | Pr 10-12 | Jul 8 | 2Ki 15:19-38; 2Ch 27; Isa 5-6 | Aug 10 | Jer 22:18-30; 2Ki 24:5-20; 2Ch 36:8-12; Jer 37:1-2; 52:1-3; 24; 29 |
| Jun 7 | Pr 13-15 | Jul 9 | Micah | | |
| Jun 8 | Pr 16-18 | Jul 10 | 2Ki 16; 2Ch 28; Isa 7-8 | | |
| Jun 9 | Pr 19-21 | Jul 11 | Isa 9-12 | Aug 11 | Jer 27; 28; 23 |
| Jun 10 | Pr 22-24 | Jul 12 | Isa 13-16 | Aug 12 | Jer 50-51 |
| Jun 11 | Pr 25-27 | Jul 13 | Isa 17-22 | Aug 13 | Jer 49:34-39; 34; Eze 1-3 |
| | | Jul 14 | Isa 23-27 | Aug 14 | Eze 4-7 |
| | | Jul 15 | Isa 28-30 | | |

# Daily Bible Reading Plan - II

| | | | | | |
|---|---|---|---|---|---|
| Aug 15 | Eze 8-11 | Sep 16 | Esth 1-4 | | Mt 13:54-58; 9:35- |
| Aug 16 | Eze 12-14 | Sep 17 | Esth 5-10 | | 11:1; 14:1-12; |
| Aug 17 | Eze 15-17 | Sep 18 | Ezr 7-8 | | Lk 9:1-10 |
| Aug 18 | Eze 18-20 | Sep 19 | Ezr 9-10 | Oct 16 | Mt 14:13-36; |
| Aug 19 | Eze 21-23 | Sep 20 | Neh 1-5 | | Mk 6:31-56; |
| Aug 20 | 2Ki 25:1; | Sep 21 | Neh 6-7 | | Lk 9:11-17; |
| | 2Ch 36:13; | Sep 22 | Neh 8-10 | | Jn 6:1-21 |
| | Jer 39:1; 52:4; | Sep 23 | Neh 11-13 | Oct 17 | Jn 6:22-7:1; |
| | Eze 24; | Sep 24 | Malachi | | Mt 15:1-20; |
| | Jer 21:1-22:9; 32 | Sep 25 | 1Ch 1-2 | | Mk 7:1-23 |
| Aug 21 | Jer 30; 31; 33 | Sep 26 | 1Ch 3-5 | Oct 18 | Mt 15:21–16:20; |
| Aug 22 | Eze 25; 29:1-16; | Sep 27 | 1Ch 6 | | Mk 7:24–8:30; |
| | 30; 31 | Sep 28 | 1Ch 7:1-8:27 | | Lk 9:18-21 |
| Aug 23 | Eze 26-28 | Sep 29 | 1Ch 8:28–9:44 | Oct 19 | Mt 16:21–17:27; |
| Aug 24 | Jer 37:3-39:10; | Sep 30 | Jn 1:1-18; Mk 1:1; | | Mk 8:31–9:32; |
| | 52:5-30; 2Ki 25:2-21; | | Lk 1:1-4; 3:23-38; | | Lk 9:22-45 |
| | 2Ch 36:17-21 | | Mt 1:1-17 | Oct 20 | Mt 18; 8:19-22; |
| Aug 25 | 2Ki 25:22; | | | | Mk 9:33-50; |
| | Jer 39:11–40:6; | Oct 1 | Lk 1:5-80 | | Lk 9:46-62; |
| | Lam 1-3 | Oct 2 | Mt 1:18–2:23; Lk 2 | | Jn 7:2-10 |
| Aug 26 | Lam 4-5; Obadiah | Oct 3 | Mt 3:1-4:11; | Oct 21 | Jn 7:11–8:59 |
| Aug 27 | Jer 40:7–43:30; | | Mk 1:2-13; | Oct 22 | Lk 10:1–11:36 |
| | 2Ki 25:23-26 | | Lk 3:1-23a; 4:1-13; | Oct 23 | Lk 11:37–13:21 |
| Aug 28 | Eze 33:21–36:38 | | Jn 1:19-34 | Oct 24 | Jn 9-10 |
| Aug 29 | Eze 37-39 | Oct 4 | Jn 1:35–3:36 | Oct 25 | Lk 13:22–15:32 |
| Aug 30 | Eze 32:1–33:20; | Oct 5 | Jn 4; Mt 4:12-17; | Oct 26 | Lk 16:1–17:10; |
| | Dan 3 | | Mk 1:14-15; | | Jn 11:1-54 |
| Aug 31 | Eze 40-42 | | Lk 4:14-30 | Oct 27 | Lk 17:11–18:17; |
| | | Oct 6 | Mk 1:16-45; | | Mt 19:1-15; |
| Sep 1 | Eze 43-45 | | Mt 4:18-25; 8:2-4+ | | Mk 10:1-16 |
| Sep 2 | Eze 46-48 | | 14-17; Lk 4:31–5:16 | Oct 28 | Mt 19:16–20:28; |
| Sep 3 | Eze 29:17-21; | Oct 7 | Mt 9:1-17; | | Mk 10:17-45; |
| | Dan 4; Jer 52:31-34; | | Mk 2:1-22; | | Lk 18:18-34 |
| | 2Ki 25:27-30; Ps 44 | | Lk 5:17-39 | Oct 29 | Mt 20:29-34; 26:6-13; |
| Sep 4 | Ps 74; 79; 80; 89 | Oct 8 | Jn 5; Mt 12:1-21; | | Mk 10:46-52; 14:3-9; |
| Sep 5 | Ps 85; 102; 106; | | Mk 2:23–3:12; | | Lk 18:35–19:28; |
| | 123; 137 | | Lk 6:1-11 | | Jn 11:55–12:11 |
| Sep 6 | Dan 7-8; 5 | Oct 9 | Mt 5; Mk 3:13-19; | Oct 30 | Mt 21:1-22; |
| Sep 7 | Dan 9; 6 | | Lk 6:12-36 | | Mk 11:1-26; |
| Sep 8 | 2Ch 36:22-23; | Oct 10 | Mt 6-7; Lk 6:37-49 | | Lk 19:29-48; |
| | Ezr 1:1–4:5 | Oct 11 | Lk 7; Mt 8:1+ 5-13; | | Jn 12:12-50 |
| Sep 9 | Dan 10-12 | | 11:2-30 | Oct 31 | Mt 21:23–22:14; |
| Sep 10 | Ezr 4:6–6:13; | Oct 12 | Mt 12:22-50; | | Mk 11:27–12:12; |
| | Haggai | | Mk 3:20-35; | | Lk 20:1-19 |
| Sep 11 | Zech 1-6 | | Lk 8:1-21 | | |
| Sep 12 | Zech 7-8; | Oct 13 | Mk 4:1-34; | Nov 1 | Mt 22:15-46; |
| | Ezr 6:14-22; Ps 78 | | Mt 13:1-53 | | Mk 12:13-37; |
| Sep 13 | Ps 107; 116; 118 | Oct 14 | Mk 4:35–5:43; | | Lk 20:20-44 |
| Sep 14 | Ps 125; 126; 128; | | Mt 8:18+23-34; | Nov 2 | Mt 23:1-39; |
| | 129; 132; 147; 149 | | 9:18-34; Lk 8:22-56 | | Mk 12:38-44; |
| Sep 15 | Zech 9-14 | Oct 15 | Mk 6:1-30; | | Lk 20:45–21:4 |

# Daily Bible Reading Plan - II

| | | | |
|---|---|---|---|
| Nov 3 | Mt 24:1-31;<br>Mk 13:1-27;<br>Lk 21:5-27 | Nov 28<br>Nov 29<br>Nov 30 | 1Cor 9-11<br>1Cor 12-14<br>1Cor 15-16 |
| Nov 4 | Mt 24:32–26:5+<br>14-16; Mk 13:28-<br>14:2, 10–11;<br>Lk 21:28-22:6 | Dec 1<br><br>Dec 2 | Acts 19:23–20:1;<br>2Cor 1-4<br>2Cor 5-9 |
| Nov 5 | Mt 26:17-29;<br>Mk 14:12-25;<br>Lk 22:7-38; Jn 13 | Dec 3<br>Dec 4<br>Dec 5 | 2Cor 10-13<br>Rom 1-3<br>Rom 4-6 |
| Nov 6 | Jn 14-16 | Dec 6 | Rom 7-8 |
| Nov 7 | Jn 17:1–18:1;<br>Mt 26:30-46;<br>Mk 14:26-42;<br>Lk 22:39-46 | Dec 7<br>Dec 8<br>Dec 9 | Rom 9-11<br>Rom 12-15<br>Rom 16;<br>Acts 20:2-21:16 |
| Nov 8 | Mt 26:47-75;<br>Mk 14:43-72;<br>Lk 22:47-65;<br>Jn 18:2-27 | Dec 10<br>Dec 11<br>Dec 12<br>Dec 13 | Acts 21:17–23:35<br>Acts 24-26<br>Acts 27-28<br>Eph 1-3 |
| Nov 9 | Mt 27:1-26;<br>Mk 15:1-15;<br>Lk 22:66–23:25;<br>Jn 18:28–19:16 | Dec 14<br>Dec 15<br>Dec 16<br>Dec 17 | Eph 4-6<br>Colossians<br>Philippians<br>Philemon;<br>1Tim 1-3 |
| Nov 10 | Mt 27:27-56;<br>Mk 15:16-41;<br>Lk 23:26-49;<br>Jn 19:17-30 | Dec 18<br>Dec 19<br>Dec 20 | 1Tim 4-6; Titus<br>2 Timothy<br>1 Peter |
| Nov 11 | Mt 27:57–28:8;<br>Mk 15:42–16:8;<br>Lk 23:50–24:12;<br>Jn 19:31–20:10 | Dec 21<br>Dec 22<br>Dec 23<br>Dec 24 | Jude; 2 Peter<br>Heb 1:1-5:10<br>Heb 5:11–9:28<br>Heb 10-11 |
| Nov 12 | Mt 28:9-20;<br>Mk 16:9-20;<br>Lk 24:13-53;<br>Jn 20:11–21:25 | Dec 25<br><br>Dec 26<br>Dec 27 | Heb 12-13;<br>2 John; 3 John<br>1 John<br>Rev 1-3 |
| Nov 13 | Acts 1-2 | Dec 28 | Rev 4-9 |
| Nov 14 | Acts 3-5 | Dec 29 | Rev 10-14 |
| Nov 15 | Acts 6:1–8:1 | Dec 30 | Rev 15-18 |
| Nov 16 | Acts 8:2–9:43 | Dec 31 | Rev 19-22 |
| Nov 17 | Acts 10-11 | | |
| Nov 18 | Acts 12-13 | | |
| Nov 19 | Acts 14-15 | | |
| Nov 20 | Gal 1-3 | | |
| Nov 21 | Gal 4-6 | | |
| Nov 22 | James | | |
| Nov 23 | Ac 16:1–18:11 | | |
| Nov 24 | 1 Thessalonians | | |
| Nov 25 | 2 Thessalonians;<br>Acts 18:12-19:22 | | |
| Nov 26 | 1Cor 1-4 | | |
| Nov 27 | 1Cor 5-8 | | |

# Scripture Index

# Scripture Index

# Scripture Index

# Scripture Index

# Scripture Index

# Scripture Index

# Scripture Index

# Scripture Index

# Topical Index

# Topical Index

# Topical Index

gold 389
golden calf 167, 263
Goliath 237-239
goodness 85, 86, 171, 281, 329, 355-357
goodness of God 86, 281, 329, 355-357
grace 15, 22, 72, 76, 170, 171, 173, 175, 271, 361, 374
greatness 326

## H

Habakkuk 288
Hagar 22
Haggai 294, 296
Ham 17
Haman 305, 306
hand of God 354
Hannah 71, 227-229
hardness 94, 95, 97, 276
hate 26, 126, 155
healing 106, 124, 221, 317, 319, 327, 347, 348, 351, 353
heart 4, 44, 74, 133, 236
heaven 2, 5, 40, 73, 157, 359, 366, 372
hell 126, 155, 156, 378, 393, 394
Herod 389
Hezekiah 277, 279, 280, 285
Hiram 258
holiness 62, 67, 71, 114, 138, 174, 276, 359
Holy Spirit 1, 40, 42, 63, 177, 179, 181, 236, 247, 310, 312, 313, 315, 320, 326, 344, 346, 365, 366, 379, 385, 391, 395
holy war 118, 201, 206, 207, 210, 211, 235
homosexuality 137
honor 125, 140, 182
hope 61, 69, 72, 77, 81
Hosea 275
Hoshea 278, 279
humility 256, 367
husbands 182, 185-187
hypocrites 158-160, 162, 327

## I

idolatry 150, 167, 169, 208, 209, 215, 233, 261, 263, 267-269, 271, 277, 278, 284, 291, 292, 391
idols 70, 121, 122
image of God 8, 126, 369, 378
immorality 169, 200
integrity 31, 36
intercession 168
intermarriage 261

interpretation 292
Isaac 22-24, 27, 28, 52, 53, 376
Isaiah 276, 280
Ishmael 22
Israel in the desert 188-191, 193-195, 199, 200

## J

Jacob 25-28, 49, 52, 53
Jael 211
James 107, 316, 323, 338
Japheth 17
jealousy 26, 27, 240, 241
Jeremiah 283-285
Jericho, battle of 205, 206
Jeroboam 262, 263
Jeshua (Joshua) 294, 296
Jesse 236
Jesus as High Priest 44, 148, 374, 387
Jesus as King 386
Jesus as Lord 58
Jesus as Savior 61, 72
Jesus as Shepherd 222, 223, 244, 308
Jesus as the King of Israel 105, 111, 308, 335, 389
Jesus as the Lamb 5, 56, 73, 103, 114
Jesus as the Messiah 110, 322, 383, 384
Jesus as the Prophet 105, 321
Jesus as the Rock 169, 380
Jesus as the Servant of the LORD 308
Jesus as the Son of David 105-107, 310, 387
Jesus as the Son of God 103, 111, 154, 181, 195, 309, 311-313, 315, 318, 323, 324, 326, 336, 340, 351, 383, 384, 386
Jesus as the Son of Man 9, 104, 110, 195, 309, 317, 322, 333, 340, 392
Jesus as the Word 1, 67, 173
Jesus says "I am" 42, 220-226
Jethro 52
Jezebel 267, 268
Joab 245, 246
Job 29-31, 35-38, 176
Joel 273, 346
John the Baptist 103, 104, 160, 312, 325
John, the apostle 107, 108, 316, 323, 338, 347, 348, 392
Jonah 251, 270-272
Jonathan 240-242
Joseph 26-28, 49, 310, 311, 388
Joshua 191, 203-206, 208, 209, 294, 296

# Topical Index

# Topical Index

# Topical Index

# Israel In Old Testament Times

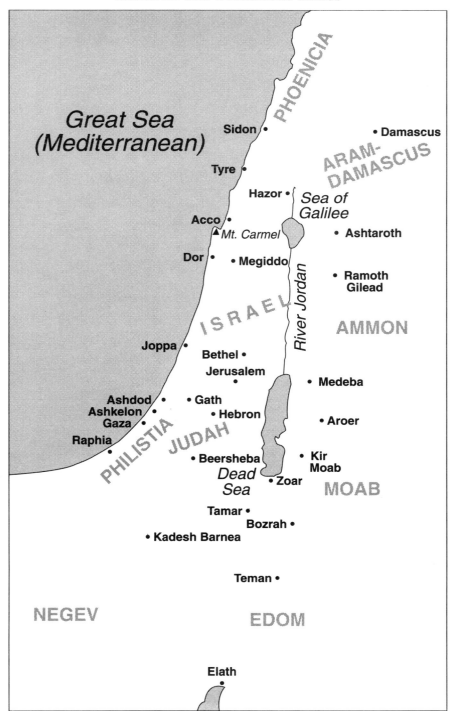

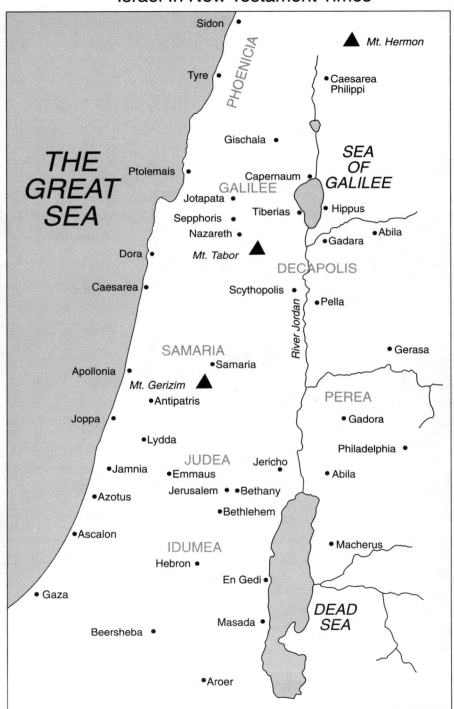

# Israel In New Testament Times

# The Assyrian Empire

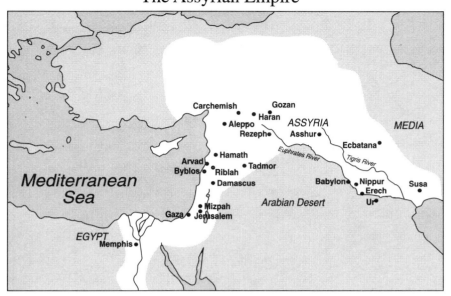

# Babylonian & Persian Empires

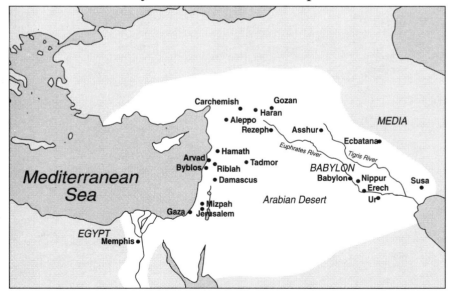

# The Roman Empire

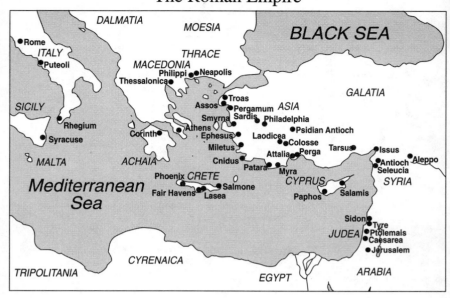

# Lands of the Bible Today